PHILOSOPHY AND THE STUDY OF EDUCATION

Combining contributions from international academics and practitioners, this new text develops students' ability to *philosophise* as well as *learn about* philosophy and education. It considers issues concerned with the interface between education and wider society but goes beyond this to explore education and philosophy at a micro level: the teacher–learner relationship. It challenges and empowers students to use philosophy as a tool within education, as a set of theories to understand education and as a potential means to develop solutions to problems as they occur within practice.

Assuming no pre-existing philosophical background, *Philosophy and the Study of Education* explores complex topics including:

- encouraging young people to criticise and challenge all authority;
- the limits of a religious-based education;
- the desire for 'alternative facts' or 'truths';
- the second-class status of vocational pursuits;
- the inherent struggle in the teacher–student relationship;
- the relationship between emotion, morality and autonomy in teaching.

Including discussion questions and further recommended reading, this thought-providing book will support and inspire all those on Education Studies, Childhood Studies and Youth Studies courses in developing a critical perspective and understanding the true value of philosophy within education.

Tom Feldges is a lecturer at the University Centre North Lindsey and a research associate at the Institute for Applied Ethics at the University of Hull, UK. He is a member of the executive board of the British Education Studies Association (BESA), as well as a member of the editorial and review board for the journal *Educational Futures*.

The Routledge Education Studies Series

Series Editor: Stephen Ward, Bath Spa University, UK

The **Routledge Education Studies Series** aims to support advanced-level study on Education Studies and related degrees by offering in-depth introductions from which students can begin to extend their research and writing in years 2 and 3 of their course. Titles in the series cover a range of classic and up-and-coming topics, developing understanding of key issues through detailed discussion and consideration of conflicting ideas and supporting evidence. With an emphasis on developing critical thinking, allowing students to think for themselves and beyond their own experiences, the titles in the series offer historical, global and comparative perspectives on core issues in education.

For a full list of titles in this series, please visit www.routledge.com/The-Routledge-Education-Studies-Series/book-series/RESS

Inclusive Education
Edited by Zeta Brown

Gender, Education and Work
Christine Eden

International and Comparative Education
Brendan Bartram

Contemporary Issues in Childhood
Zeta Brown and Stephan Ward

Psychology and the Study of Education
Edited by Cathal Ó Siochrú

Philosophy and the Study of Education
Edited by Tom Feldges

PHILOSOPHY AND THE STUDY OF EDUCATION

New Perspectives on a
Complex Relationship

Edited by
Tom Feldges

LONDON AND NEW YORK

First published 2019
by Routledge
2 Park Square, Milton Park, Abingdon, Oxon, OX14 4RN

and by Routledge
52 Vanderbilt Avenue, New York, NY 10017

Routledge is an imprint of the Taylor & Francis Group, an informa business

© 2019 selection and editorial matter, Tom Feldges; individual chapters, the contributors

The right of Tom Feldges to be identified as the author of the editorial material, and of the authors for their individual chapters, has been asserted in accordance with sections 77 and 78 of the Copyright, Designs and Patents Act 1988.

All rights reserved. No part of this book may be reprinted or reproduced or utilised in any form or by any electronic, mechanical, or other means, now known or hereafter invented, including photocopying and recording, or in any information storage or retrieval system, without permission in writing from the publishers.

Trademark notice: Product or corporate names may be trademarks or registered trademarks and are used only for identification and explanation without intent to infringe.

British Library Cataloguing-in-Publication Data
A catalogue record for this book is available from the British Library

Library of Congress Cataloging-in-Publication Data
A catalog record has been requested for this book

ISBN: 978-1-138-58375-7 (hbk)
ISBN: 978-1-138-58376-4 (pbk)
ISBN: 978-0-429-50653-6 (ebk)

Typeset in News Gothic
by Newgen Publishing UK
Printed by CPI Group (UK) Ltd, Croydon CR0 4YY

Karl R.
always true to himself, generous and loving
but often misunderstood.

Contents

	List of contributors	*ix*
	Series editor's preface	*xiii*
	List of abbreviations	*xv*
1	Introduction: philosophy and education TOM FELDGES	1
2	Socrates for teachers DENNIS HAYES	13
3	Philosophy with Children and self-determination in education ARIE KIZEL	28
4	Philosophy in Islam and its limit on teaching reason in humanities NUR SURAYYAH MADHUBALA ABDULLAH	41
5	Children's epistemic rights and hermeneutical marginalisation in schools LISA MCNULTY AND LUCY HENNING	54
6	Consciousness, physicalism and vocational education TERRY HYLAND	65
7	Emotion and effective learning ALEXANDROS TILLAS	80
8	The social, the natural and the educational KOICHIRO MISAWA	91
9	The teacher–student relationship: an existential approach ALISON M. BRADY	104

viii *Contents*

10 Educational phenomenology: is there a need and space for such a pursuit? 118
SONIA PIECZENKO

11 Making sense of it all? A concluding attempt 130
TOM FELDGES

Index *144*

Contributors

The editor

Tom Feldges has lectured for the past ten years on a variety of programmes and modules. He is currently working at the University Centre in North Lindsey and his formal training in psychology, sociology and philosophy of the mind and his PhD in phenomenological philosophy allow him to cover a wide range of educationally important aspects regarding the transformative relationship between learner and instructor. He has edited a book focusing on the subject and the social and published several papers on the interplay between psychological explanations of the human mind and its limitations when trying to account for the richness of human experience. His interest is the phenomenology of education, one that leaves behind the limitations of the cognitive-scientific approach and incorporates the felt experience of embodied human life with direct implications upon teaching and research practice as it happens within the teaching environment.

The contributors

Alison M. Brady is a PhD candidate and Teaching Fellow at the UCL Institute of Education. She is also the administrator for the London Branch of the Philosophy of Education Society of Great Britain (PESGB). Her research, partly funded by PESGB, involves questions around the nature of teaching, which she is considering in relation to existentialism, and in particular, the thought of Jean-Paul Sartre. Her recent publications include 'The regime of self-evaluation: self-conception for teachers and schools' (2016, *British Journal of Education Studies* 64(4): 523–541) and her work with Kyoto University on the International Frontiers in Education and Research project, which includes two publications: 'Exile and inclusion: excerpts from Albert Camus' "Exile and the Kingdom"' (2017) and 'Entering the void: representation and experience in the work of Yves Klein' (2018).

Dennis Hayes is Professor of Education at the University of Derby and Director of the influential campaign group Academics For Academic Freedom (AFAF). He describes himself as a philosopher manqué and continues to write on philosophically related issues such as critical thinking (in his paper 'Is everyone a Socrates now? A critical look at critical thinking', 2015) and how the modern university can become the 'Socratic university' (in *Beyond McDonaldization: Visions of Higher Education*, 2017). His latest book is *The 'Limits' of Academic Freedom* (2017). In the

x *Contributors*

educational world he is well-known for his controversial co-authored book *The Dangerous Rise of Therapeutic Education* (2008), which has been described as 'one of the most important books to have been written in at least the last twenty years in that crucial area where philosophy, policy and practice coincide'.

Lucy Henning is a lecturer in Primary Education (English) at Roehampton University. She has a PhD from Kings College, London. Her study took a 'literacy as a social practices' perspective to investigate young children's encounters with schooled literacy in a London primary school. In addition to her academic activities, Dr Henning has extensive professional experience of literacy in schooling having been a primary class teacher, school literacy lead and consultant on literacy for the Primary National Strategies.

Terry Hyland has 40 years' experience of teaching in schools, further, adult and higher education. He retired as Professor of Education and Training at the University of Bolton, UK, in 2009 and now spends his time on academic research and writing, research student supervision, teaching mindfulness and philosophy courses, and PhD external examining at UK universities. He was appointed Honorary Visiting Professor at the University of Huddersfield, UK in 2006 and is attached to the university's Centre for Research in Post-Compulsory Education. Dr Hyland has written more than 180 articles, 20 book chapters, and six books on a diverse range of topics within philosophy of education and professional Education Studies. He is currently Lecturer in Philosophy at the Free University of Ireland in Dublin, and his most recent book is *Mindfulness and Learning: Celebrating the Affective Dimension of Education*, published by Springer in 2011.

Arie Kizel is President of the International Council of Philosophical Inquiry with Children (ICPIC) and head of the Development of Educational Systems MA programme at the department of learning, instruction and teacher education at the faculty of education, University of Haifa, Israel. His research areas are: philosophy of education, philosophy with (and for) children, research of curriculum and textbooks and study of social groups' narrative. He was the head of the Israeli-German commission for textbooks research (2010–2015). Among his publications are the books *Subservient History: A Critical Analysis of History Curricula and Textbooks in Israel, 1948–2006* (Hebrew), *The New Mizrahi Narrative in Israel* (Hebrew) and dozens of articles on philosophy of education, Philosophy with Children and textbooks and curricula.

Nur Surayyah Madhubala Abdullah is a senior lecturer in Moral Education (Pedagogy) at the Department of Language and Humanities Education in the Faculty of Educational Studies, Universiti Putra Malaysia. Her research interests include moral education, pluralism and personhood. She authored a book on *A Crisis of Common Humanity: Moral and Citizenship Education in Malaysia* (2015). In 2016 she was appointed lead consultant by UNESCO Bangkok for their research Educating for Sustainable Futures through Integration of Values in School-Based and Community-Based Programs Targeting Young People: Study of Cambodia, Laos PDR, and the Philippines. She was also country consultant for Malaysia on UNESCO Mahatma Gandhi Institute of Education, New Delhi's research project, Current State of Education For Peace and, Sustainable Development and Global Citizenship in Asia and the Pacific (2016–2017).

Lisa McNulty is an Honorary Research Fellow in the Education Department at the University of Roehampton, and an Accredited Practitioner with the Philosophy Foundation, an educational charity providing philosophy in schools. Prior to this she taught philosophy, including philosophy of education, at Regents University London, where she also worked in the Department of Academic Practice. She has a PhD from the University of Kent. Prior to her PhD, she taught English as a foreign language at Anuban Dan Chang, a primary school in Thailand. She has published in the *Journal of Philosophy of Education* and the *Sage Encyclopaedia of Educational Theory and Philosophy*, and contributed to the Philosophy Shop, a multi-award-winning anthology of philosophy for children.

Koichiro Misawa is an Associate Professor in the Faculty of Education at Gunma University in Japan. His scholarly interests centre on the relation between nature and normativity and, relatedly, on the social nature of the mind, knowledge and human beings, as well as their links to issues in the philosophy of education. His most recent publications include 'Education as the cultivation of second nature: two senses of the given' (*Educational Theory*, 63, 2013), 'Nature, nurture, second nature: broadening the horizons of the philosophy of education' (*Educational Philosophy and Theory*, 46, 2014), 'Animality and rationality in human beings: towards enriching contemporary educational studies' (*Cosmos and History*, 10, 2014), 'Rethinking the "social" in educational research: on what underlies scheme-content dualism' (*Ethics and Education*, 11, 2016), 'No need to worry: multiple profiles of philosophy of education in, and in relation to, the world of education and the world of philosophy' (*Philosophical Inquiry in Education*, 23, 2016) and 'Humans, animals and the world we inhabit: on and beyond the symposium Second Nature, *Bildung*, and McDowell – David Bakhurst's *The Formation of Reason*' (*Journal of Philosophy of Education*, 51, 2017).

Sonia Pieczenko is an experienced lecturer, teaching for years on Health and Social Care-related programmes. She has obtained an MA in the Philosophy of Psychiatry with a dissertation, using Husserl's phenomenology to make sense out of hallucinatory experiences. Pieczenko has worked on a number of education-related research projects and has published on these issues. She is currently editing a book on the relation between mental health and education.

Alexandros Tillas works primarily in the philosophy of psychology and cognitive science and has authored several articles addressing such topics as observational learning and education, concept learning, perception and selective attention, the relation between language and thinking, and the neural underpinnings of endogenous thoughts. Currently he is working on emotion regulation and effective learning. Furthermore, he has published on clustering, rational processing and intuitions, and has offered a novel construal of Gibson's traditional notion of affordances, while arguing against dual-processes theories. Dr Tillas has also worked on social agency, communication and the role of emotion in thinking and learning. His PhD thesis has been a defence of concept empiricism against nativism and he situates his work in the scientifically informed tradition of philosophy. He has developed an interdisciplinary research project that investigates the nature of intuitions and the extent to which standing unconscious knowledge contributes to higher cognitive processes like reasoning and decision-making. Tillas is currently a postdoctoral researcher at Düsseldorf University in the Mathematical Modelling and Ontology of (representational) frames (in the human mind) project, while also teaching Cognitive and Experimental Psychology at Panteion xii *Contributors*

University in Athens and Ancient Philosophy at the Hellenic Open University. He has previously held a postdoctoral position in a project focusing on Grounding Cognition.

Series editor

Stephen Ward is Emeritus Professor of Education, Bath Spa University, formerly Dean of the School of Education and subject leader for Education Studies. A founder member of the British Education Studies Association, he has published on the primary curriculum, primary music teaching and Education Studies. His research interests are education policy and university knowledge.

Series editor's preface

Education Studies has become a popular and exciting undergraduate subject in some 50 universities in the UK. It began in the early 2000s mainly in the post-1992 universities which had been centres of teacher training but, gaining academic credibility, the subject is being taken up by post-1992 and Russell Group institutions. In 2004 Routledge published one of the first texts for undergraduates, *Education Studies: A Student's Guide* (Ward, 2004), now in its third edition. It comprises a series of chapters introducing key topics in Education Studies and has contributed to the development of the subject.

Education Studies is concerned with understanding how people develop and learn throughout their lives, the nature of knowledge and critical engagement with ways of knowing. It demands an intellectually rigorous analysis of educational processes and their cultural, social, political and historical contexts. In a time of rapid change across the planet, education is about how we both make and manage such change. So Education Studies includes perspectives on international education, economic relationships, globalisation, ecological issues and human rights. It also deals with beliefs, values and principles in education and the way that they change over time.

It is important to understand that Education Studies is not teacher training or teacher education. Its theoretical framework in psychology, philosophy, sociology, and history is derived from teacher education, and undergraduates in the subject may well go on to become teachers after a PGCE or school-based training. However, Education Studies should be regarded as a subject with a variety of career outcomes, or indeed none: it can be taken as the academic and critical study of education in itself. At the same time, while the theoretical elements of teacher training are continually reduced in PGCE courses and school-based training, undergraduate Education Studies provides a critical analysis for future teachers who, in a rapidly changing world, need so much more than training to deliver a government-defined curriculum.

Since its inception in the late 1990s there has been continuing discussion about the roles of the so-called 'contributory disciplines' in Education Studies. Some have argued that psychology, sociology, philosophy, history even economics, should form its theoretical basis. Others urge that Education Studies should be seen as a 'discipline' in itself, that the other disciplines should be less prominent and make the study of education too difficult and complex. This book is based on the former assumption that, for a rigorous analysis of education, a grounding in the disciplines is essential: students should have an understanding of the nature of each of the disciplines, be aware of the theoretical issues in the subject and familiar with its publications in education. Intended for second- and third-year undergraduates and Master's students, this book is the sixth in the Routledge

xiv   *Series editor's preface*

Education Studies series which builds on the introductory guide and looks in depth at philosophy in education. It is the second in sequence of books on the five disciplines: *Psychology and the Study of Education* (Ó Siochrú, 2018) is in print, to be followed by publications on sociology, economics and history.

Philosophy has a long and sometimes controversial history in education and teacher training, but this has often been superficial in nature, with a lack of understanding of the true nature of the subject. This book engages the reader in the task of philosophising about education, dispelling popular myths and bringing us up to date with what philosophy can offer the study of education.

Stephen Ward
Bath Spa University

Note

The academic network for tutors and students in Education Studies is the British Education Studies Association (BESA). It has an annual conference that share academic practice and research in Education Studies and to which students are welcome. There are two e-journals, one designated for students and early researchers: www.educationstudies.org.uk.

References

Ó Siochrú, C. (2018) *Psychology and the Study of Education*. London: Routledge.
Ward, S. (2004) *Education Studies: A Student's Guide*. London: Routledge.

Abbreviations

DfE	Department for Education
DfES	Department for Education and Skills
ENS	educational neuroscience
HEFCE	Higher Education Funding Council for England
RICE	religious Islamic cultural environments
UNICEF	United Nations Children's Fund
VET	vocational education and training

1 Introduction
Philosophy and education

Tom Feldges

Introduction

As the title reveals, this book is about philosophy and the study of education. However, instead of a comprehensive story about what philosophers had to say about education over the past 2,500 years, the book invites the readers to engage with philosophical thought about education for themselves. That might sound rather too ambitious a project. At the end of the day, what would the average student who enrolled on one of the many educational programmes have to say that could possibly ever match the importance of what the great philosophers had to say about education? It is exactly this sort of question that poses a real danger of putting a premature and unwarranted end to any aspiring educationalist's attempt to engage in philosophising about education. That would be a shame as philosophy is too valuable a tool merely to be treated as a stock of knowledge that every student of education has to learn and reiterate. Philosophy is much more a way of thinking and a way of engaging with the world and with our place within this world. It provides a set of tools that allows us to think more clearly about the problems we want to engage with. In that respect philosophy can be done by everyone and education provides a good number of problems, well worthy of a philosophising approach. Nevertheless, a word of caution is needed here: this is not to say that anyone who says something presumably 'deep' about education is actually contributing to the field of the philosophy of education. But it equally does not mean that philosophical thought about education could only count if it came from one of the usually recognised great philosophers of education.

This is where an important distinction appears: a) we could learn about the ideas of the great philosophers regarding educational matters, or b) we could try to develop an individual ability to engage in philosophical thought about education. It is our own choice regarding how we want to engage with the pairing of philosophy and education.

An initial thought about philosophy and education

The engagement with the philosophy of education is not only a list of historic facts to be learned in the form of an intellectual history. Philosophy of education should be an active engagement with current and future problems in a philosophical way. This nevertheless needs to be done alongside one's awareness of what has been said or written by the great philosophers.

---

2 Tom Feldges

It is this distinction between a descriptive engagement with the philosophy of education and our own experience of engaging in philosophical thought that the first section of this introduction aims to develop. Yet, while making this demarcation between describing what kind of philosophies of education are available and our own experience of engaging with philosophical thought about education, another important differentiation becomes apparent. This is:

a) the mere provision of some description of an object or situation; and
b) our own individual experience of encountering this object or matter of fact.

While the first section of this introduction will develop the *doing philosophy* aspect further, the second section focuses upon this second differentiation between scientific descriptions and individual experience.

Unpacking the problem

It is probably the time now to make clear that, in getting more clarity about the subject matter of this book – philosophy and education – we are already philosophising. We have revealed the *learning about* and the *doing* approaches to philosophy and we have, in a second step, revealed a further distinction between descriptive and experiential accounts. This is what philosophers call 'unpacking an issue or problem', i.e., developing some clarity about what sort of potential dimensions a problem has. Every kind of philosophical engagement should start with such a conceptual clarification.

Learning about philosophy vs. doing philosophy

Undoubtedly it is possible to provide a narrative capturing all the worthwhile educational-related philosophical thought that has survived over time and is still available to us. These narratives, as a written or spoken account of what has been achieved before, provide a good first approach to the philosophy of education. They enable us to know what has been thought and what has been argued before and thus save us from having to start from scratch. These descriptive accounts regarding the intellectual history of the philosophy of education allow us, as Sir Isaac Newton is reported to have said, to stand on the shoulders of the giants who lived before us. Approaching the philosophy of education in this way provides us with the ability to utilise our philosophical predecessors' knowledge and insight. This gives us a vantage point from which to see further while utilising existing insight to apply it to current problems. Nevertheless, in doing so, we have left the field of merely *learning about philosophy* and we have started to *do philosophy*.

The philosophy of education is a difficult area to engage with. This is not necessarily because the topic is especially complex or complicated. It is more that there is a certain *fuzziness* in the concept of the 'philosophy of education'. There is some debate around the question of who is supposed to be qualified to do this sort of philosophy. Should it be left to trained and qualified philosophers only, or rather be a field for trained and qualified educationalists, or should one be trained in both subjects, or does one not need any formal training at all?

> For a discussion of these questions and a good overview on the philosophy of education it is worth to have a look at Philips and Siegel (2013). (See the recommended reading suggestions at the end of this chapter.)

However, we leave this question of the academic division out of our focus, while remaining with the earlier statement about the *fuzziness* of the 'philosophy of education'. This fuzziness is often the reason why rather fruitless debates are carried out in the most controversial manner. Quite often it appears as if the participants in these debates have no shared definition of the concepts that should form the basis of their ensuing debate. To make this point a little bit clearer, it is probably best to explain it with recourse to the concept of 'education' itself.

- 'Education' can be understood as an attempt to transfer knowledge and skills from an instructor to a learner on a merely individual basis. The learner gains knowledge or skills if the teacher has been successful in establishing such a transformative relationship. Hence, education, and with that the philosophy of education, could concern itself with the transformative relationship between both of them.
- 'Education' could equally be understood as the sum total of a society's efforts to engender knowledge and skills in its children and young people. Hence, education as an institutionalised effort, taking place in schools, workplaces and universities, aiming to secure the 'social continuity of life' (Dewey, 1942 [1916]: 3).

It is possible to ignore the individual aspect of the knowledge transfer and leave it to psychological experimentation and theorising and/or educational practice. Within this section we focus upon the social aspect of education and we thus remain – currently –oblivious to all the recent developments as they are currently discussed in the philosophy of the mind; therefore we need to come back to this individual focus. Nevertheless, there are more questions for us. If education is about the transfer of knowledge and skill, then the need arises to define what exactly would or should qualify as knowledge or as a desirable skill in the first place. And if education is about preparing young people to lead successful lives in their societies, then it is equally necessary to develop a clear differentiation between education, enculturation and indoctrination.

In order to develop our distinction between *learning about philosophy* and *doing philosophy*, it is probably best to examine Dewey's notion of the *social continuity of life*. Utilising Dewey as an example here is appropriate because he is a widely recognised philosopher of education. His 1916 book *Democracy and Education* is a standard work of educational philosophy. Undoubtedly, anyone wanting to study education seriously should have read it or at least be familiar with its main claims; hence one should have learned about Dewey's philosophy of education.

When Dewey (1942 [1916]: 3) developed his educational philosophy he did so against the background of the 'social continuity of life': he made the point that, although societies are formed by individuals who are born and eventually bound to die, 'the life of the group goes on'. The title of Dewey's book, *Democracy and Education*, is testament to the fact that he saw this group or society as a democratic one. When looking at the institution of 'education' within a society, it is important to understand that education does not just happen. Education comes at a cost to any society, and to justify the allocation of societal resources in the form of time or money towards educational efforts, education itself has to offer some return to society. Institutionalised education, on a societal plane, is thus a goal-orientated endeavour: it serves a social function to bring about a benefit to the society that engages in such efforts. Education contributes to something that society wants to achieve or wants the learners to be able to contribute to this society. On realising this, the first step towards a philosophising engagement with Dewey's educational philosophy has successfully been made. We are no longer the passive recipients, taking Dewey's writing at face value, but we gained the ability to start developing our own thoughts in relation to Dewey by beginning to think, with him and/or against him about current issues.

Against this conceptualisation of educational practice as a goal-orientated, functional process, Dewey (1942 [1916]) claims that education should aim to bring about the development of autonomous individuals. These individuals should be able to think for themselves and to engage critically in debates to challenge existing rules and regulations of society. Hence, and in relation to Dewey's idea of democratic societies, education should serve democratic societies by educating the young to develop into engaged, democratic citizens. The function of Dewey's education is thus the safeguarding of a society's democratic continuation by initiating the young to democratic values.

On a more general level

It is important to realise that these functions, supposed to serve a specific goal, are processes guided by the end that they aim to achieve. Philosophers call these 'teleological' processes and they are to be accounted for by their intended purpose, rather than by their cause.

However, care is needed here. On encountering the notion of 'inherent purposes', as in Dewey's conceptualisation of education, it is necessary to critically question who defined or set this specific goal and with what sort of justifications. It is not good enough, just because Dewey's claims about democracy and our feelings are the same, to assume that everything is fine and no critical engagement would be required or even possible. An example will help to make this clearer.

History has shown that totalitarian regimes often utilise education for other purposes than educating a critical and autonomous individual. In many of these societies the individual is given only a limited critical-intellectual space to think and reason. Education is often reduced to the transmission of a specific worldview or the doctrines of such societies. Education is turned into a system-stabilising indoctrination of learners to serve the society they were born into. But is that really so fundamentally different from what happens in democratic societies? When it comes to the functional nature of education as a social endeavour that aims to achieve a goal, then both educational processes – Dewey's 'pure' education and the indoctrination of totalitarian regimes – are working along the same lines. Both forms of education strive to achieve *something* for their surrounding society, i.e., to yield a stabilising effect to maintain a society's continuation. However, following our line of thought, this *something* manifests itself as the opposing ends of a spectrum that reaches from Dewey's presumably legitimate educational efforts at one end towards the supposedly sinister totalitarian educational indoctrination on the other. Nevertheless, the functional mechanisms striving towards this society-maintaining *something* are the same: they are functional processes.

Introduction 5

The functional similarity of societal educational efforts opens up the puzzle of having to decide where to draw the line between legitimate educational efforts and illegitimate indoctrination. In both cases we have functional processes that are only different in terms of the positive value usually attached to one goal, and the negative value commonly attached to the other. This is not good news, because these arbitrary value judgements emerge in relation to the surrounding culture which makes such judgements. Hence, democratic societies will appreciate the critical engagement of its citizens in an open communicative exchange in which the better argument prevails; whereas totalitarian societies will rate positively their citizens' conformity to enable the flourishing of their society. But who is to say which one of these purposes holds moral superiority and should thus be endorsed? Even more so, it must remain questionable as to whether it could be possible to draw a clear dividing line between these opposing standpoints. That is, to answer to the question at which point one is about to leave one of these goals behind, striving too far towards the opposite. This is important as, in the absence of the necessary clarity, one cannot form a definite idea of which educational practice belongs to which sort of value. So how could one ever be sure that the learners are not already being indoctrinated while teaching them to become critical thinkers? The question of what constitutes suitable knowledge and desirable skill in any society is thus a genuinely philosophical one. To highlight this point, consider the issue of 'environmental awareness' as an example here. The question of a school/university-facilitated awareness of the problems with environmental and ecological issues exemplifies the problem of having to decide what sort of knowledge should be passed on to the learners and what should be left out of the curriculum. Whatever the answer to this question is, it will invariably reflect our own values. One might opt for an education that encourages resource-preserving restraint for the sake of future human beings. Alternatively, one could perceive such an environmental agenda as nothing but a misguided attempt to indoctrinate the young to undermine society by teaching them to refuse consumption and thus threaten our current wellbeing. We will have to pick this specific issue up again in the concluding part of this book, but for now it should already be evident that these current problems and questions allow a critical engagement with existing philosophies of education. Our example focused upon Dewey's *Democracy and Education* and it revealed that education serves a function and that its function is defined by its purpose. However, these purposes are culturally situated, and the justification of educational aims turns out to be invariably dependent upon the cultural context.

> Education is always driven by underlying societal/cultural values and these values are so entrenched in every aspect of everyday life that they are normally not even recognised.

Philosophy is an attempt to develop the conceptual clarity to be able to engage with such fundamental questioning. This is not to say that Dewey's aim for a self-sustaining, democratic society is a bad one, but when Dewey proclaimed that education should strive to foster, stabilise and develop democracy, he did this more than a hundred years ago. The background for his claims was a period known as Modernity, a time that had overcome totalitarian regimes of the past. In line with the idea of the Enlightenment that had celebrated reason and the force of the better argument as the building-blocks for a more just and democratic society, Dewey presented his educational philosophy to contribute to this.

6 Tom Feldges

However, more than a century later, it is a valid question to ask how much of all this still holds true for the current educational reality. The force of the better argument appears all too often to be weakened by an onslaught of 'fake news' and populism, whereby citizens are told what they *want* to hear instead of what they *need* to hear, however uncomfortable the latter may be. These recent movements come with the inherent danger of hollowing out democracy: while citizens still have the right to vote, but are kept ill-informed about their choices and their looming consequences. Some of the following chapters will elaborate on these issues further (see especially Chapters 3, 4 and 5), but it is at this juncture that one may even be tempted to critically challenge the very idea of the sort of democracy that provided the drive for Dewey's educational philosophy a century ago. Nevertheless, if there is reason to doubt some of the underlying assumptions that Dewey's concept of democracy entailed, it would be an interesting project to discover what sort of implications that has for his overall account. Of course, this is something that cannot be achieved in this introduction. However, what *is* achieved here is to reveal the fundamental difference between merely learning about Dewey's educational philosophy on one hand and genuine attempts to engage with him and against him to make his philosophy bear fruit in relation to current questions in education.

This line of philosophical engagement may be experienced as shocking, uncomfortable or alternatively quite welcome. At the end of the day, we are challenging the tacit aspects of our social life, the ones that many of us hold most dear. However, whatever the individual experience of following up these lines of enquiry may have been, it is to be hoped that this experience of a philosophical discussion of the philosophy of Dewey and others may shed new light on his work. It should equally offer a multitude of new ways to think about educationally relevant issues. It should enable us to make Dewey's philosophy go further than Dewey and others could have envisaged in their own time. Everyone who has engaged in such an active questioning of existing philosophies should be able to learn something about educational philosophy and that on a much deeper level than merely *learning about* Dewey's philosophy could have ever reached. However, this first section should also have contributed to a substantially altered understanding of educational philosophy and its use-value for the currently living.

A summary

The distinction between learning about philosophy and doing philosophy is gradual rather than clear-cut. It is therefore warranted to state: While learning about the philosophy of education, we gain the ability to put it to work, to apply it to current problems. In doing so, we gain a better and deeper learning of these philosophies and the ability to apply them in an attempt to make sense out of current problems.

Nevertheless, there is still some unfinished business. The individual level of the knowledge transfer and the notion of individual experience in the context of learning was only briefly mentioned here and that aspect will be the focus of the next section.

Experience and description

The previous section engaged with the transfer of philosophical knowledge and/or skills as content-orientated learning in the form of providing a historic description of the philosophy of education. As opposed to this practice, the point was developed that the actual experience of *doing philosophy* can open up a completely different dimension to philosophy and reveal its practical use-value when, as in the example case, the suitability of curriculum content and development is assessed. This fundamental difference between the availability of a description of someone's philosophy or one's own experiential access via active philosophising is at the core of this section. Nevertheless, it is probably better to draw a wider picture first.

While discussing education in the previous section, the direct relationship between instructor and learner was mentioned. It became apparent that everything that is supposed to go on in this transfer relationship is always, and by necessity, woven into the wider fabric of the culture and society in which this instructive relationship unfolds. However, education is in essence the instructive relationship between two people, the learner and the instructor, and that despite the always-present, tacitly or explicitly demanding or even limiting socio-cultural horizon. This even holds if the learner is surrounded by other learners in a classroom or a lecture theatre, or even in the case of electronically mediated teaching methods. *Something has to go on* between learner and instructor and it is to be expected that the better that *something* is, the more successful and probably even the more enjoyable this instructive encounter will be for both parties. It thus seems fair to claim that the instructive relationship between two people is at the heart of what education is about. Nevertheless, thoughts about the relationship between learner and instructor are often left out of the focus of the current philosophy of education. It is this obvious loss of a pronounced focus upon this personal interaction that provides the motive for this section. However, it is not a mere attempt to provide a (scientific?) description of this interaction that this section is about, but it is much more the question of how the two interlocutors experience this interaction.

Of course, every practitioner, even with little experience, knows that the experiential aspect of teaching is exactly that what makes teaching enjoyable or, at times, frustrating. Finishing a day's work in school or university with the genuine feeling that one has done something good to enrich a learner's understanding is probably what makes most teachers come back day after day. While equally the frustration that comes from less satisfactory encounters often enough provide a reason to be critical, become cynical or even leave the profession. It thus appears that the experiences associated with teaching are of key importance. These individually held attitudes, opinions and beliefs along with the situated emergence of feelings, of emotions and affects are an integral part of the educational reality in everyday educational practice. Nevertheless, the academic subject of Education Studies aims to free itself from the particular situation of the classroom encounter. Education Studies tries to cat-egorise practical *particular* experience to be able to develop a *general* understanding. It aims to pro-vide a theoretical space for ideas to resonate and to be thus sorted into an overall frame of reference whereby it becomes possible to theorise about education. This is where Education Studies draws on a wide variety of already-existing knowledge from neighbouring academic disciplines to link this with the input derived from the practice of educational day-to-day work and from the educational tradition.

Education Studies

Education is a practice stretching back, probably as long as humans exist. However, the academic discipline of Education Studies is a rather more recent phenomenon. As with other academic disciplines, such as criminology, Education Studies utilises the already-existing knowledge and sometimes even the theories as they were developed in other disciplines.

8   *Tom Feldges*

When it comes to theorising about individual development, behaviour and capability, education draws from the rich body of knowledge and theory that was established by the academic discipline of psychology. If, however, the educational focus is directed upon the social field in which education takes place, the academic discipline of sociology provides a plethora of theoretical approaches to make sense of educational efforts on the level of society.

However, and this is where the *doing philosophy* comes in again, if one takes the academic subject of Educational Studies as:

a) a reflective level for the contemplation about educational practice; and
b) a rigorous effort to achieve a categorisation of educational practice in an attempt to make sense of this practice by connecting it towards an explanatory framework of relevant theories and existing research;

then it seems to follow that

c) any such educationally motivated contemplation and categorisation can only ever be as good as the theories that are used for this contemplation and categorisation.

The absence of an education-focused contextualisation of the direct encounter between learner and instructor is something that is quite prevalent in most of the currently available textbooks on the philosophy of education.

Educational theory and practice

The link between *practice* and *theory* is a genuine philosophical problem as it is important to establish a valid link between the *particular* of everyday practice and empirical research on one side and the *general* of theories. This meaningful categorisation is something that Education Studies has to achieve in an attempt to formulate an independent and comprehensive educational theory.

Nevertheless, when it comes to this direct relationship one can find some helpful sociological theory as for example Bourdieu (1993) and his notion of the *field* in which the educational, social interaction can be contextualised. Psychology, on the other hand, provides a plethora of theory aiming to make sense of specific aspects of human interaction. In that respect one could be tempted to assume that more or less every angle of the instructive relationship is somehow covered by already-existing research and theory, and that the task of the academic discipline of education would be one of sorting these theories into an education-relevant context.

Especially in relation to the educational use of psychological research and theory, one has to bear in mind that the currently dominant paradigm of psychology favours a cognitive or even a neuroscientific approach to account for the human mind.

However, there are challenges to these predominant approaches within psychology itself (e.g., Wallace *et al.*, 2007), but also from the sub-discipline of the philosophy of the mind (e.g., Gilbert and Lennon, 2005). The charges focus around the fact that mere scientific descriptions of the instructive encounter cannot reach the actual core of this interpersonal relationship. Hence, the philosophically motivated criticism suggests the utilisation of experience-based (phenomenological) approaches to account for the mind, while the psychologically motivated challenges, among other suggestions, work from the assumption that the mind is always an embodied one. In essence, then, most of these critical interjections maintain that the currently predominant focus upon functional, cognitive processes of the mind and/or their underlying (biological) structures cannot provide a comprehensive explanation of human action as being directed by human experience. This introduction does not leave enough space to develop the implications in full detail. However, if there is indeed a lack of explanatory reach in current psychological theorising, especially when it comes to human experiences and embodiment, then it seems that the academic discipline of education cannot make use of these cognitive-psychological theories in an uncritical way. And if, as it was claimed earlier, the direct encounter between learner and instructor is indeed at the very heart of what education is about, then it looks as if a wider view upon these experiential and embodied alternatives to account for educational practice is needed. That is exactly what this book encourages its readers to do. It is an invitation to start to *do philosophy* while having a critical eye upon the contemporary challenges to the current cognitive-psychological contextualisation of educational theory. It also tries to develop an appetite to engage with different theories that promise to go beyond a mere scientific description of the educational, interpersonal encounter.

How to read and utilise this book and what to expect from it

To achieve its aim and to provide a wide range of perspectives, this book brings together contributions from a number of educationalists and/or philosophers. It caters for a broad range of different approaches to relevant issues and allows contributors at various stages of their academic careers to offer their view. It is also hoped that recent and relevant developments in the philosophy of education will find a suitable way to influence future generations of educationalists.

Each of the chapters reflects its author's view, and not all of them agree with each other. It is therefore not necessary to read the chapters in the order in which they are presented. However, the collection follows three thematic focal points around which the contributions are grouped. This should ensure that relevant philosophical problems find a wide and differentiated discussion from a variety of points of view. The reader is free to decide upon which aspects to focus on, but in an attempt to incite the reader's own engagement with the topic there are signposts towards further reading and questions to provide some challenging and inspiring *food for (philosophical) thought*, and hopefully for the reader's appetite to engage in further philosophising about educational issues. Chapters are grouped around three overarching topics.

I. Reason and knowledge

Chapter 2 – Socrates for teachers

Dennis Hayes goes back to Socrates to develop his argument for the superiority of clear and logical reasoning, un-influenced by any relativistic fashion of the times. In that respect, Hayes is able to provide an interesting view upon the actual nature of Socratic questioning which, as he argues, has been changed to become nothing but a means to make students adopt mainstream views instead of being truly critical.

10 Tom Feldges

Chapter 3 – Philosophy with Children and self-determination in education

Arie Kizel proposes, with recourse to Mathew Lipman, an educational, transformational engagement with students to form a critical, true seedbed for democracy in the form of a philosophical laboratory. Within these communities of inquiry, students are encouraged to engage in creative practices, to look for 'meaning' and to create concepts relevant to their own environment and their background. Kizel challenges the Socratic emphasis on a 'truth-related' search for information favoured by Hayes in the previous chapter, and rather has the students experience the quest for 'meaning-orientated' information that matters to their lives and futures. Following Lipman, Kizel argues that Philosophy with Children could thus bring about a truly democratic education.

Chapter 4 – Philosophy in Islam and its limit on teaching reason in humanities

Nur Surayyah Madhubala Abdullah presents her argument about the limitation that religious belief could have on correct reasoning practices. Based on her own teaching experiences in Malaysia, she makes the case that students from a strong religious background find it difficult to endorse argumentative lines of reasoning if these logical pursuits conflict with their faith. The argument is made in relation to the Muslim faith, and her point is that these faith-intrinsic limits stand in the way of the students flourishing. However, it has to be kept in mind, that any strong religious belief in general – as opposed to empirical knowing – appears to have the inevitable tendency to limit reason, because if everything would be known, or could be knowable, then faith would no longer be required.

Chapter 5 – Children's epistemic rights and hermeneutical marginalisation in schools

Lisa McNulty and Lucy Henning provide an insightful argument about the concept of epistemic injustice. This proceeds from the claim in the previous chapter. McNulty and Henning critique the immanent limitation for schooled children to engage with a world that that is 'pre-described' and 'contextualised' by well-meaning adults. They argue that the children's localised attempts to make sense of their learning experiences must lead to an already limiting social norm of knowledge acquisition within their peer-group. Both authors offer an interesting set of tools to avoid injustice in terms of the children's right to knowledge.

II. The mind and body and the social

Chapter 6 – Consciousness, physicalism and vocational education

Terry Hyland takes the division between academic and vocational studies as his starting point. He argues, like many others, for the importance of reducing the stigma of vocational studies and recognising them as worthwhile in their own right. However, Hyland approaches this problem not by historical or sociological reasoning but with recourse to the to the philosophy of the mind. By arguing for a specific form of mind–body relation (non-reductive monism) Hyland is able to reveal the Cartesian division between the mental and the physical as wrong-headed and argues for an embodied approach to the mind. In that respect, and along with an increasing usage of electronic media to extend our mind via the operations executed by our body, Hyland hopes to overcome the current ascription of a lesser value to vocational as opposed to academic studies.

Chapter 7 – Emotions and effective learning

Alexandros Tillas utilises the psychological concept of 'flow' as a pre-cognitive immersion into a task and its completion. He brings this concept in a fruitful relation to a philosophical explanation of emotions as provided by Prinz. This allows him to suggest that valenced emotional states can be induced and thus educationally utilised via task-design that induce this flow, which leads to a high-performance task completion.

Chapter 8 – The social, the natural and the educational

Koichiro Misawa draws on McDowell's argument that education is essential for human beings that are both social and natural beings. Misawa also draws on Rorty and Davidson to argue against the well-established content-scheme divide that has formed the basis of association psychology ever since Locke and Hume. While the notion of 'truth' (see Chapter 2) thus becomes less fixed than the ancient Greeks would want to have it, Misawa argues the case for education to take hold by transforming a natural being into a social one.

III. Experiences and scientific accounts

Chapter 9 – The student–teacher relationship: an existential approach

Alison Brady focuses upon the 'lived experience' of the teacher–student relationship. She couches her investigation into a wider debate around the marketisation of education within a neoliberal environment to develop a notion of 'freedom'. With a historical detour via progressivist and liberal educational approaches, Brady suggests an existential framework to redefine the notion of freedom and to make it bear fruit for the educational pursuit. By unpacking Sartre's concept of 'freedom', Brady is able to frame freedom of both the teacher and the student in an existentialist way as a relation that is neither fixed by authority, nor by predefined roles (such as consumer), but one that is characterised by the constant struggle for recognition on both sides.

Chapter 10 – Educational phenomenology: is there a need and space for such a pursuit?

Sonia Pieczenko outlines the established limitations of cognitive science and cognitive-neuroscientific approaches for educational purposes. She then introduces phenomenology as a first-person-centred investigation regarding the experiences associated with the intentional relation between an experiencing subject and objects. With recourse to Husserl, Pieczenko develops the difference between mental content and lived experience in an educational setting to argue for the importance of the inclusion of these experiences into educational research along a phenomenological methodology.

Chapter 11 – Making sense of it all? A concluding attempt

The concluding chapter draws the main strands of the previous chapters together. The nature of knowledge as situated in time and space is discussed, alongside the limits of pure reason. Such a conception leaves room to move away from a mind-dominated perception of human being, towards one where mind and body are both essential parts of our human being and of being humane.

12   *Tom Feldges*

However, such a call for embodied and individual perspectives suggests the need to reconsider the current use of sociological and psychological theories for the educational relationship between teacher and learner.

Recommended reading

For a good overview on the philosophy of education, it is worth having a look at the Phillips and Siegel (2013) entry concerning the *Philosophy of Education* in the online available Stanford Encyclopaedia of Philosophy at: https://plato.stanford.edu/entries/education-philosophy/.

References

Bourdieu, P. (1993) *The Field of Cultural Production*. Cambridge: Polity Press.
Dewey, J. (1942 [1916]) *Democracy and Education*. New York: Macmillan.
Gilbert, P. and Lennon, K. (2005) *The World, the Flesh and the Subject*. Edinburgh: Edinburgh University Press.
Wallace, B., Ross, A., Davies, J. and Anderson, T. (2007) *The Mind, the Body and the World: Psychology after Cognitivism?* Charlottesville, VA: Imprint.

2 Socrates for teachers

Dennis Hayes

Introduction

'Socratic questioning' is popular with many teachers. But Socratic questioning is more than simply asking questions. The teaching of Socrates embodied the highest form of morality. In his way of living and in his way of dying, Socrates stands as a beacon of morality through the ages. He was put to death by the Athenian democracy for corrupting youth and denying the gods the city believed in. A modern formulation of this charge would be to condemn him for encouraging young people to criticise everything and to challenge all authority. To understand the ethical nature of Socratic thought requires familiarity with the purpose of his arguments. The failure of many educationalists to understand his works reduces their teaching to exercises in cynicism or conformism. 'Reject your current assumptions and beliefs and adopt the correct ones' is what contemporary 'Socratic questioning' amounts to. It is an expression of the conforming attitude and not an expression of the critical spirit.

In the *Phaedo*, Socrates argues that no greater misfortune can befall someone than to lose the love of argument. The state of 'misology', or hatred of argument, is the state of education today. This chapter offers an explanation of how an understanding of the philosophy of Socrates can restore the spirit of criticism in the twenty-first century. It introduces Plato's Socrates and his philosophy. The nearest we can get to authentic Socratic thought is in Plato's earlier dialogues, where he presents the views of his tutor in powerful dramatic form. Socrates embodies in his life, and death, a commitment to freedom of speech that was not shared by the *polis* of Athens (or by most people today). Sections of Plato's dramatic dialogues are presented at length to illustrate his life, his commitment to argument and to examining all beliefs however strongly held. Socrates embodies the critical spirit and the understanding that freedom of speech was the only way to knowledge.

To convince anyone of the power of Socrates' thinking and his moral example cannot be achieved through any introduction. The success of this chapter will be decided by those who go on to read the dialogues. If you stop here and pick up and read any of the Socratic dialogues, the *Apology*, the *Crito*, the *Phaedo*, the *Protagoras*, the *Meno* or the *Theaetetus* then you will know the man without any intermediary other than Plato. The lesson of this chapter is 'always study the original texts'. (Stephanus numbers are used to refer to Plato's works throughout – see References.)

14 *Dennis Hayes*

Any teacher today should be proud if the charges levelled at Socrates, during his trial, of 'corrupting youth' and 'not believing in the gods the city believes in' were levelled against them by a latter-day Meletus. In a more modern formulation, the charges would be that the teacher encouraged students to criticise everything and this corruption of youth included criticising the most cherished and strongly held beliefs in society. An immediate caveat is necessary, as the idea of 'criticism' and even 'Socratic criticism' has been inverted. Many educationalists and teachers are happy to get their students to criticise their assumptions or the wrong views of others in society, but only in order to get them to adopt what are currently deemed to be the 'correct' views. This is criticism as conformism and more likely to lead to an award from those who promote belief in contemporary 'gods' rather than their being made to drink from the deadly hemlock cup, which was Socrates' reward for criticism (Hayes, 2014, 2015).

The importance of Socrates

The Scottish-Australian realist philosopher John Anderson claimed that '[t]he manner of his life, and still more the manner of his death, have made Socrates an outstanding figure in the history of European thought and morals' (Anderson, 1980 [1931]: 64). Today, this comment needs explanation, as Socrates' philosophy has been reduced to a pedagogic commonplace about 'questioning', bearing no resemblance to his thinking or his ethics.

Socrates' death is consistent with this manner of living and of his thought and that consistency is an aspect of his greatness. Socrates, aged 70, was condemned to death in 399 bce by a religious court, as there was a political amnesty at the time and he could not be tried in a political court. He cleverly refutes the charges in his speech in defence of himself, the *Apology*. But the Athenians who constituted his jury were convinced that he was subverting Athenian democracy and his moral greatness does not rest simply on being an innocent killed on spurious charges. Socratic thinking and a Socratic education put both tradition and contemporary or modern and progressive orthodoxies to the test of criticism. They were an intellectual challenge to the uncritical acceptance of the values of Athenian democracy (*Apology* 39c–39d). In this sense Socrates was guilty, but not as charged.

A modern-day Socrates would challenge all of the received opinions of teachers and educationalists. These include the belief that education is about working for 'social justice' and the safeguarding obsession that makes 'safety' the overriding value in education and wider society. 'Criticise, criticise, criticise' is the lesson of Socrates' teaching. That lesson has to be learned again in very different and difficult circumstances. The current culture of education is dominated by therapeutic self-expression rather than philosophical argument (see Ecclestone and Hayes, 2008). A good example of how therapeutic self-expression has replaced argument is the plea for 'safe spaces' in universities. This is essentially a space in which ideas can be expressed without challenge and where no ideas held to be 'offensive' will be heard. It is the opposite of the philosophy of Socrates.

In ancient Athens there was a culture of debate dominated by the Sophists who taught young people how to argue solely to win, but not for any moral purpose. Socrates, claims Protagoras, a leading Sophist, was very influential and rich (*Meno* 91a–93a). Despite his criticisms of the Sophists, Socrates was caricatured as a Sophist in Aristophanes' comic play *The Clouds*, where he appears as the head of a school for wastrels called 'The Thinkery'. The play caricatures Sophistic argumentation, which must have been familiar to the audiences who came to see the play.

In contemporary culture, argument can rarely be made comic, with rare exceptions such as the tutorial scene in Nathan Hill's novel *The Nix* where informal fallacies are parodied (Hill, 2017) or in some of comedian Jonathan Pie's YouTube videos. The reason why comedy about argumentation is almost impossible is that we have lost the art of argument. Consider any lecture, seminar or conference. When discussion happens it is curtailed and the comments are random exercises in the expression of feelings and personal experiences. There is no focused attention to the subject or the argument. In universities (and the media) discussion is dominated by what a generation ago any fresher would have recognised as a logical fallacy, *argumentum ad hominem*, an attack on the person rather than their arguments. A well-known legal joke illustrates this fallacy. An instructing solicitor instructs his barrister: 'No case: abuse the plaintiff's barrister!'

Arguments are no longer addressed. Instead the sex, age, colour or other personal feature of the speaker is the sole focus of discussion or the reason why they are not allowed to discuss a topic. It is not just the extreme censors who engage in this: for example, those who shout that 'You can't discuss abortion unless you have a womb!' It is a commonplace to hear 'Speaking as an X, Y or Z' or to have comments about the make-up of a discussion panel: 'Why is there no X, Y or Z on the panel?' More generally, in a therapeutic culture, criticising someone's arguments is taken personally as a criticism of them. This is not just the natural response to having deeply held beliefs challenged. Our beliefs are part of what we are as a person and those who Socrates debated did not always respond positively to criticism. But if we are to grow intellectually and as individuals, we must have our beliefs challenged. In a therapeutic culture, the new and fashionable assumption is that we must never be made to feel uncomfortable. Argument makes people uncomfortable, whereas openness and non-judgementalism keeps them feeling safe (Hayes and Mieschbuehler, 2015).

A study of Socrates' philosophy as expressed in the early dialogues of Plato is an antidote to the contemporary antipathy to argument in our therapeutic culture.

Questions for discussion

From your own experience of conferences, seminars and panel discussions – or think of this at the next ones you attend – how much time is allocated to discussion, and do participants argue or do they merely relate personal experiences?

The death of Socrates: his method and morality

Many introductions to Socrates' thought bypass the dialogues, and merely give summaries of his thinking and reduce his 'method' to a formula. This does his thought an injustice, for it is in the dialogues that his thinking and his 'method' are most clear. Many of the early 'eristic' or argumentative dialogues in which Plato represented Socrates' thought were written to be performed at competitions and festivals and most last two or three hours. Some are shorter. The *Crito* could be performed in 40 minutes and the *Apology* in an hour and 40 minutes. A later work, the *Republic*, if read aloud as an audio book, would take some 12 hours. It is of a different form after Book I, which is essentially an eristic dialogue on the topic of 'What is justice?' often labelled Plato's 'Thrasymachus' after Socrates' opponent, or interlocutor, in that dialogue. As well as topics like 'What is justice?' being set as a challenge for works to be performed at Greek festivals and games

16   *Dennis Hayes*

for prizes, these dialogues were later learned by heart and their arguments rehearsed by Plato's students in the *Academy* where they held eristic moots (Ryle, 1966).

Plato's dialogues are masterpieces of literature, their 'method' is polite (and public) conversation and 'the way in which Plato makes Socrates talk to young men is the model of what such talk should be' (Fox, 1945: 73). This is not the case when Socrates deals with 'conceited or overbearing people [who] boast and bluster' (Fox, 1945: 73), such as Thrasymachus in the Republic or Anytus in the *Meno*. The *Apology* contains few uses of the elenchus – a form of argument associated with Socrates, but those that do appear are bitter and far from 'polite conversation'. In this first of three extracts from the dialogues, Socrates refutes the charge of corrupting youth levelled at his by one of his three accusers, Meletus (*Apology* 24b–26b):

Soc. Come hither, Meletus, and let me ask a question of you. You think a great deal about the improvement of youth?

Mel. Yes, I do.

Soc. Tell the judges, then, who is their improver; for you must know, as you have taken the pains to discover their corrupter, and are citing and accusing me before them. Speak, then, and tell the judges who their improver is. Observe, Meletus, that you are silent, and have nothing to say. But is not this rather disgraceful, and a very considerable proof of what I was saying, that you have no interest in the matter? Speak up, friend, and tell us who their improver is.

Mel. The laws.

Soc. But that, my good sir, is not my meaning. I want to know who the person is, who, in the first place, knows the laws.

Mel. The judges, Socrates, who are present in court.

Soc. What do you mean to say, Meletus, that they are able to instruct and improve youth?

Mel. Certainly they are.

Soc. What, all of them, or some only and not others?

Mal. All of them.

Soc. By the goddess Hera, that is good news! There are plenty of improvers, then. And what do you say of the audience, – do they improve them?

Mel. Yes, they do.

Soc. And the senators?

Mel. Yes, the senators improve them.

Soc. But perhaps the members of the citizen assembly corrupt them? – or do they too improve them?

Mel. They improve them.

Soc. Then every Athenian improves and elevates them; all with the exception of myself; and I alone am their corrupter? Is that what you affirm?

Mel. That is what I stoutly affirm.

Soc. I am very unfortunate if that is true. But suppose I ask you a question: Would you say that this also holds true in the case of horses? Does one man do them harm and all the world good? Is not the exact opposite of this true? One man is able to do them good, or at least not many;- the trainer of horses, that is to say, does them good, and others who have to do with them rather injure them? Is not that true, Meletus, of horses, or any other animals? Yes, certainly. Whether you and Anytus say yes or no, that is no matter. Happy indeed would be the condition of youth if they had one corrupter only, and all the rest of the world were their improvers. And you, Meletus, have sufficiently shown that you never had a thought about the young: your carelessness is seen in your not caring about matters spoken of in this very indictment.

And now, Meletus, I must ask you another question: Which is better, to live among bad citizens, or among good ones? Answer, friend, I say; for that is a question which may be easily answered. Do not the good do their neighbours good, and the bad do them evil?

Mel. Certainly.

Soc. And is there anyone who would rather be injured than benefited by those who live with him? Answer, my good friend; the law requires you to answer – does anyone like to be injured?

Mel. Certainly not.

Soc. And when you accuse me of corrupting and deteriorating the youth, do you allege that I corrupt them intentionally or unintentionally?

Mel. Intentionally, I say.

Soc. But you have just admitted that the good do their neighbours good, and the evil do them evil. Now is that a truth which your superior wisdom has recognised thus early in life, and am I, at my age, in such darkness and ignorance as not to know that if a man with whom I have to live is corrupted by me, I am very likely to be harmed by him, and yet I corrupt him, and intentionally, too; – that is what you are saying, and of that you will never persuade me or any other human being. But either I do not corrupt them, or I corrupt them unintentionally, so that on either view of the case you lie. If my offence is unintentional, the law has no cognizance of unintentional offences: you ought to have taken me privately, and warned and admonished me; for if I had been better advised, I should have left off doing what I only did unintentionally – no doubt I should; whereas you hated to converse with me or teach me, but you indicted me in this court, which is a place not of instruction, but of punishment.

I have shown, Athenians, as I was saying, that Meletus has no care at all, great or small, about the matter.

The dismissive and contemptuous tone reflects Plato's continuing anger at what happened to Socrates. His ultimate literary revenge will be in the *Republic* where he makes philosopher kings the rulers of the state. In the *Apology* he restricts himself to lectures by Socrates on his life and thought as lessons for the Athenians:

> If... I tell you that to let no day pass without discussing goodness and all the other subjects about which you hear me talking and examining both myself and others is really the best thing that a man can do, and that life without this kind of examination is not worth living, you will be even less inclined to believe me.
>
> (*Apology* 38a; Plato, 1993: 63)

Taking an expression from other translations out of context we often hear that Socrates said that 'the unexamined life is not worth living'. This leads to therapeutic or navel-gazing interpretations rather than the challenge of criticising yourself and others on a daily basis. The jury did not think Socrates was engaging in some helpful form of reflection; they condemned him to death. After the guilty verdict and the penalty of death, Socrates is vitriolic about what the jury has done and the consequences for Athens:

18   *Dennis Hayes*

> You have brought about my death in the belief that through it you will be delivered from submitting the conduct of your lives to criticism: but I say the result will be just the opposite. You will have more critics, whom up to now I have restrained without your knowing it; and being younger they will be harsher to you and will cause you more annoyance.
>
> (*Apology* 39c–39d; Plato, 1993: 64–5)

Socrates does not compromise or plead for his life. The state may have lost the 'gadfly' (*Apology* 30d–30e) that kept the state intellectually and morally alive, but a swarm would follow. In part Socrates is indifferent to death because it may be that death produces the 'unimaginable happiness' (*Apology* 41c) of spending eternity seeking out the wise and famous and 'examining and searching people's minds, to find out who is really wise among them, and who only thinks that he is' (*Apology* 41b). Eternity to Socrates was like being at the best university forever.

Robin Waterfield explains Socrates' decision to accept his punishment because he was 'obliged to respect its laws: by accident of having been born and having grown up in democratic Athens, he had, as someone who was committed to the rule of law, taken on this obligation' (Waterfield, 2009: 180). As a true Athenian citizen he could not do otherwise. As Socrates explains in the *Crito*, he could easily go into exile but could never engage in the life worth living again. How could he argue with those he meets in exile and examine them about morality and the good life when he had betrayed his own belief that 'the really important thing is not to live, but to live well' (*Crito* 48b)?

Socrates' role as a gadfly is not to be understood as a mere irritant on the state. His arguments were not 'eristic' in the modern sense of argument for argument's sake. Socratic criticism had a moral purpose. That purpose was the pursuit of knowledge through the removal of all false claims to knowledge. The Oracle of Apollo at Delphi had declared that no one was wiser than Socrates but he claimed that he himself knew nothing. In response, Socrates went interviewing one person after another and in the end decided that it was best for him to be as he was (*Apology* 20e–22e). For Socrates the search for knowledge was a moral search because 'Wisdom and knowledge were… either identical with moral goodness or its necessary conditions' (Waterfield, 2009: 176). Knowledge is not an end to anything, it is a value in itself. It is not something we seek for other instrumental purposes. Education is also a value in this sense. It is not 'for' anything. There may be contingent consequences such as contentment or unhappiness as a result of having knowledge or an education, but these are not why we seek either.

Many people talk of the 'Socratic method', but there is a debate among classicists as to whether Socrates had a method or whether he responded in different ways to the various characters who were his interlocutors in the dialogues (Scott, 2002; Waterfield, 2002). The 'method' usually associated with the Socrates of the early eristic dialogues of Plato – the Socrates we are concerned with here – is the 'method' that centres on the 'elenchus'. We must remember that Socrates never claimed to have a method and the elenchus is said to have been used by others, including Protagoras. Schematically, the 'Socratic method' is often represented as consisting of four stages leading to action based on the outcome of the inquiry. The first is a 'wonder' involving a question usually of the form 'What is x?' ('What is justice?' *Republic*, Book I). The second involves the simple statement of a possible answer 'X is Y' ('Justice is the advantage of the stronger'). The third stage is the actual elenchus or refutation in which a counter-example to the hypothesis is given and the conclusion is that Socrates' interlocutor does not know what he claims to know. This process

Socrates for teachers   19

can be repeated with the interlocutor, or interlocutors, offering new hypotheses (see Boghossian, 2012). This can lead to clarity and the recognition by the interlocutor that he held a false belief, or to a state of 'aporia' in which the interlocutor no longer knows what to think and must think for himself and, when he can, say once again what he thinks he knows. For Socrates, 'knowledge' means saying what you think you know to others.

Just as there are disputes about what Socrates' 'method' is, there are disputes about the purpose of the elenchus. It can be seen as abusive and hurtful, which is how it would seem to students today if they were suddenly exposed to the elenchus by a skilful practitioner. But the elenchus must not be equated with bad teaching in the facile way some commentators do when they claim the elenchus is no more than teachers showing off their superior knowledge (Boghossian, 2012). Another and popular interpretation of the elenchus is to sees it as a therapeutic approach to philosophy and to teaching. Armies of online psychologists and consultants take this view. A few philosophers have also attempted to defend a more nuanced interpretation of the elenchus as therapeutic (Higgins, 1994; Kerdeman, 1994). These interpretations constitute an interesting development of the contemporary understanding of Socrates' 'method'. The idea that the 'elenchus' is offensive and abusive or that the 'elenchus' is therapy merely reflect the therapy culture of today, just as those in the past who saw the Socratic method as spiritual reflected the view of an age dominated by faith (see Cornford, 1988 [1932]).

The best way of understanding the aporetic force of Socrates' philosophy and its importance in dispelling fashionable beliefs is to consider his 'exquisite argument' that refutes relativism.

Questions for discussion

If students learned by heart and performed the dialogues today, would that be an antidote to a therapeutic interpretation of the Socratic 'method'?

The refutation of relativism

A famous example of the more conversational but philosophically profound use of the elenchus is the 'table turning', 'recoil' or 'exquisite argument' in the *Theaetetus* (169d–171c). The argument has had over two thousand years of interpretation and criticism and the debate as to whether it is a valid refutation of relativism about truth is as heated as it ever was (see Burnyeat, 1990; Chappell, 2006; Erginel, 2009; Keeling, 2015). This extract given here is taken out of the context of earlier discussions in the dialogue that are often seen to be important to its interpretation, but it can also be taken to be a new argument.

Soc.   How then, Protagoras, would you have us treat the argument? Shall we say that the opinions of men are always true, or sometimes true and sometimes false? In either case, the result is the same, and their opinions are not always true, but sometimes true and sometimes false. For tell me, Theodorus, do you suppose that you yourself, or any other follower of Protagoras, would contend that no one deems another ignorant or mistaken in his opinion?

Theod. The thing is incredible, Socrates.

20   *Dennis Hayes*

Soc.   And yet that absurdity is necessarily involved in the thesis which declares man to be the measure of all things.

Theod. How so?

Soc.   Why, suppose that you determine in your own mind something to be true, and declare your opinion to me; let us assume, as he argues, that this is true to you. Now, if so, you must either say that the rest of us are not the judges of this opinion or judgment of yours, or that we judge you always to have a true opinion: But are there not thousands upon thousands who, whenever you form a judgment, take up arms against you and are of an opposite judgment and opinion, deeming that you judge falsely?

Theod. Yes, indeed, Socrates, thousands and tens of thousands, as Homer says, who give me a world of trouble.

Soc.   Well, but are we to assert that what you think is true to you and false to the ten thousand others?

Theod. No other inference seems to be possible.

Soc.   And how about Protagoras himself? If neither he nor the multitude thought, as indeed they do not think, that man is the measure of all things, must it not follow that the truth of which Protagoras wrote would be true to no one? But if you suppose that he himself thought this, and that the multitude does not agree with him, you must begin by allowing that in whatever proportion the many are more than one, in that proportion his truth is more untrue than true.

Theod. That would follow if the truth is supposed to vary with individual opinion.

Soc.   And the best of the joke is, that he acknowledges the truth of their opinion who believe his own opinion to be false; for he admits that the opinions of all men are true.

Theod. Certainly.

Soc.   And does he not allow that his own opinion is false, if he admits that the opinion of those who think him false is true?

Theod. Of course.

Soc.   Whereas the other side do not admit that they speak falsely?

Theod. They do not.

Soc.   And he, as may be inferred from his writings, agrees that this opinion is also true.

Theod. Clearly.

Soc.   Then all mankind, beginning with Protagoras, will contend, or rather, I should say that he will allow, when he concedes that his adversary has a true opinion – Protagoras, I say, will himself allow that neither a dog nor any ordinary man is the measure of anything which he has not learned-am I not right?

Theod. Yes.

Soc.   And the truth of Protagoras being doubted by all, will be true neither to himself to anyone else?

Theod. I think, Socrates, that we are running my old friend too hard.

What Jowett here translates as 'the best of this joke' in his argument is better translated as 'this exquisite feature' (Levett 171a in Burnyeat, 1990), hence the label the 'exquisite argument'.

The argument here is often taken to mean that Protagoras' relativism is refuted through self-contradiction. He believes that what the many judge to be true is true, although he believes the opposite of what they believe to be true. Therefore, he holds his own 'truth' to be true but also false. This re-statement makes the passage equivalent to many 'quick' refutations of relativism used by many with some knowledge of philosophy and some eminent philosophers of education (Hayes and Mieschbuehler, 2015). Suppose someone says 'There is no such thing as truth' and we ask 'Is that true?' If it is 'true' then the statement is self-contradictory. The reply often comes 'But it is true for me!' This is a misleading way of saying 'I believe that there is no such thing as truth', which is a subjective statement and not a truth claim. A more contemporary version of relativism is the statement 'Everything is a matter of opinion', to which the above responses can be made *mutatis mutandis*. Colleagues and students have argued that this approach to what is often called 'subjectivism' rather than 'relativism' is crude, and the subjectivist can merely accept that there is just one statement – or any other statement that attempts to put subjectivism in truth claiming terms – that sits outside of many subjectivities where truths are 'true for me'. But this is to play with the concept of truth as no account of this other subjective 'truth' can be given. It is a step into incoherence.

The 'exquisite argument' has had many interpretations, as it seems to be a flawed and weak argument compared with others in the *Theaetetus*. These centre on the lack of relativising quantifiers on Protagoras' arguments. The qualification 'true for x' is missing when it is there in previous arguments and demanded by Protagoras' theory. It seems to some that the argument is not 'exquisite' but a blip, a failing in Plato's otherwise careful reasoning (see the discussion in Chappell, 2006 and Erginel, 2009). One recent and interesting argument by Evan Keeling suggests that those who are the measure of truth do not inhabit discrete 'private worlds' but are the city-state, 'the polis' (Keeling, 2015). Plato's aim is to attack the relativism of the city-state. It is further revenge for the death of Socrates.

That the 'exquisite argument' is philosophically challenging is not an accident. Erginel believes that Plato deliberately made it aporetic. We have to do the thinking. He concludes, as many of the classicists and philosophers do after discussing many interpretations and reinterpretations, that the self-refutation argument works:

> We must conclude, therefore, that Plato's self-refutation argument against Protagoras is as successful as any self-refutation argument can be. The importance of this achievement can hardly be overstated, since the argument applies equally to most, if not all, contemporary versions of relativism about truth. Plato reveals the inescapable absurdity of the relativist's position, though he does not make it easy for the reader to see how exactly he is doing this.
>
> (Erginel, 2009: 65)

The aporetic 'exquisite argument' is worth studying as the attempt to understand it will foster the critical spirit and may lead more students and teachers to challenge the relativism that is rife in education. It is the basis of the obsession with 'subjectivities', 'experiences', 'perspectives' and 'viewpoints' that thoughtlessly undermine the search for truth in educational thought and research.

Relativism today

Relativism takes many forms, but all forms of relativism are subject to the challenge made in the 'exquisite' argument. Take fashionable 'cultural relativism' as an example. Cultural relativists see the views of any group or culture as being 'true for them'. But these groups or cultures do not hold the same things to be true. If cultural relativists hold that the truths of all groups or cultures are

22 Dennis Hayes

'true for them', they are in the same position of Protagoras and face self-contradiction or a slide into incoherence.

All such claims to 'truth' are made in 'truth talk' which is universal and not particular to a group or a culture. The pull of relativism in education often expresses itself in a concern with people's 'perspectives' and 'interpretations'. What this means is that 'belief' is allowed to masquerade as truth and seeks to avoid subjecting these 'perspectives' or 'interpretations' to the test of reason through debate. Too many educators take refuge in relativism because it is an intellectually lazy option (Hayes and Mieschbuehler, 2015).

Questions for discussion

Does Socrates' refutation of relativism work? The best way of answering this question is to get into arguments. When a student or lecturer makes a statement like 'Everything is a matter of opinion' or 'There is no such thing as (absolute) truth', respond with the quick refutation of relativism – ask 'Is that true?' and start a discussion that is as Socratic as you can make it.

The importance of public debate

Socrates was known for arguing with anyone in the agora of Athens or anywhere. He never wrote anything down because he believed philosophy must be a discussion or dialogue between people. Philosophy could only be public. In the *Protagoras*, the importance of public debate is made through a falling-out between Socrates and Protagoras about how to conduct a philosophical debate (*Protagoras* 334c–335c):

> When he had given this answer, the company cheered him. And I said: Protagoras, I have a wretched memory, and when any one makes a long speech to me I never remember what he is talking about. As then, if I had been deaf, and you were going to converse with me, you would have had to raise your voice; so now, having such a bad memory, I will ask you to cut your answers shorter, if you would take me with you.
>
> What do you mean? he said: how am I to shorten my answers? shall I make them too short?
>
> Certainly not, I said.
>
> But short enough?
>
> Yes, I said.
>
> Shall I answer what appears to me to be short enough, or what appears to you to be short enough?
>
> I have heard, I said, that you can speak and teach others to speak about the same things at such length that words never seemed to fail, or with such brevity that no one could use fewer of them. Please therefore, if you talk with me, to adopt the latter or more compendious method.
>
> Socrates, he replied, many a battle of words have I fought, and if I had followed the method of disputation which my adversaries desired, as you want me to do, I should have been no better than another, and the name of Protagoras would have been nowhere.
>
> I saw that he was not satisfied with his previous answers, and that he would not play the part of answerer any more if he could help; and I considered that there was no call upon me to

continue the conversation; so I said: Protagoras, I do not wish to force the conversation upon you if you had rather not, but when you are willing to argue with me in such a way that I can follow you, then I will argue with you. Now you, as is said of you by others and as you say of yourself, are able to have discussions in shorter forms of speech as well as in longer, for you are a master of wisdom; but I cannot manage these long speeches: I only wish that I could. You, on the other hand, who are capable of either, ought to speak shorter as I beg you, and then we might converse. But I see that you are disinclined, and as I have an engagement which will prevent my staying to hear you at greater length (for I have to be in another place), I will depart; although I should have liked to have heard you.

Socrates claimed that he didn't teach. This is not a paradoxical statement. It has to been seen in the context of the 'teachers' of his day, the Sophists. The Sophists sold their 'knowledge' to individuals for a fee. They were not interested in showing people how to think for themselves. Reading the passage above, it is easy to recall teachers, lecturers and some students that have gone on at great length, closing down the possibility of criticism and revealing their intellectual indifference to who is listening to them.

What happens in the subsequent part of the dialogue is that those present discuss how to persuade Socrates to stay but also discuss what debate is for (*Protagoras* 335d–338e). Socrates himself makes a distinction between 'public speaking' and 'companionable talk' (*Protagoras* 336b). He considers Protagoras to be an orator and asks him to change his style. Callias asks Socrates to stay and says that a conversation between the two would 'be doing us all a kindness' (*Protagoras* 335d). Prodicus makes a plea that Protagoras and Socrates are reconciled (*Protagoras* 337a–337c):

That, Critias, seems to me to be well said, for those who are present at such discussions ought to be impartial hearers of both the speakers; remembering, however, that impartiality is not the same as equality, for both sides should be impartially heard, and yet an equal meed [reward] should not be assigned to both of them; but to the wiser a higher meed should be given, and a lower to the less wise. And I as well as Critias would beg you, Protagoras and Socrates, to grant our request, which is, that you will argue with one another and not wrangle; for friends argue with friends out of goodwill, but only adversaries and enemies wrangle. And then our meeting will be delightful; for in this way you, who are the speakers, will be most likely to win esteem, and not praise only, among us who are your audience; for esteem is a sincere conviction of the hearers' souls, but praise is often an insincere expression of men uttering falsehoods contrary to their conviction. And thus we who are the hearers will be gratified and not pleased; for gratification is of the mind when receiving wisdom and knowledge, but pleasure is of the body when eating or experiencing some other bodily delight. Thus spoke Prodicus, and many of the company applauded his words.

The proposal for an arbiter for the discussion is also rejected, for no one could be superior to Protagoras in intellect and judgement. It is agreed to reverse the roles and for Protagoras rather than Socrates to ask questions, so that Socrates can show him how to answer. After making this proposal Socrates concludes 'And this will require no special arbiter – all of you shall be arbiters' (*Protagoras* 338e). The conclusion is important in confirming that philosophy is a collective and public endeavour.

24 *Dennis Hayes*

In an important paper, Jonathan Cohen reads this section of the *Protagoras* as an insight into the interconnections between philosophy, education and politics (Cohen, 1998). The title of his paper makes the point more forcefully: 'Philosophy is education is politics'. From the discussion we have seen that philosophy should be undertaken in a friendly way between kinsmen and must be conducted impartially. Rules for the practice of philosophy must be those that benefit the community not an individual. Philosophy is politics. Philosophy is also educational. By replacing Protagoras with Socrates, a new method of philosophising is being suggested for Athens, a philosophy based on criticism rather than having the wise deliver what they supposedly know. Cohen interprets this as being 'like John Dewey's vision of collaborative education' (Cohen, 1998: 5). This is to take the discussion out of historical context. Today the views of Dewey are dominant in educational thought and a Socratic critical spirit today might challenge them as ultimately putting education instrumentally as the service of the state.

This entertaining and insightful episode in the *Protagoras* has three lessons for philosophy, education and politics today. First, they are public activities; second, they are critical activities; and third, they are democratic activities involving as many people as possible. For teachers the lessons are: conduct all discussions and debates in public, together, rather than in small group activities; discussions and debates must be critical in the Socratic sense of questioning what is said to be known by the wise, and they must be open to all. Socrates taught anyone in the agora and did not think that some individuals could not learn.

The current state of misology

In the 1990s the sociologist Christopher Lasch wrote an important essay on 'The lost art of argument', in which he articulated a Socratic view of education as outlined in the discussion of the *Protagoras* above:

> If we insist on argument as the essence of education, we will defend democracy not as the most efficient but as the most educational form of government, one that extends the circle of debate as widely as possible and thus forces all citizens to articulate their views, to put their views at risk, and to cultivate the virtues of eloquence, clarity of thought and expression, and sound judgement.
>
> (Lasch, 1996: 171)

More than two decades later, the art of argument, along with the freedom of speech on which argument is founded, are under greater threat (Hayes, 2017). The fear of being offensive and the censorious consequences of speaking out undermine our confidence in 'subjecting our own ideas about the world to the test of public controversy' (Lasch, 1996: 162). Socrates describes our current dangerous state in the *Phaedo* (89c–89e):

Soc. But first let us take care that we avoid a danger.
Ph.   And what is that? I said.
Soc. The danger of becoming misologists, he replied, which is one of the very worst things that can happen to us. For as there are misanthropists or haters of men, there are also misologists or haters of ideas, and both spring from the same cause, which is ignorance of the world.

Misanthropy arises from the too great confidence of inexperience; you trust a man and think him altogether true and good and faithful, and then in a little while he turns out to be false and knavish; and then another and another, and when this has happened several times to a man, especially within the circle of his most trusted friends, as he deems them, and he has often quarrelled with them, he at last hates all men, and believes that no one has any good in him at all. I dare say that you must have observed this.

The Tredennick and Tarrant translation reads more forcefully: 'No greater misfortune can happen to anyone than that of developing a dislike for argument' (*Phaedo* 89d; Plato, 1993: 151). In a time when the greatest misfortune has befallen society, one of the remedies we have, because of the writings of Plato, is to go back to ancient Athens and meet and learn the art of argument from Socrates and revive the critical spirit.

Conclusion: are you a modern Socrates?

Anyone who seriously and knowledgably claims to be a 'Socratic' thinker today choses debate as their 'method' and, through debate, criticism. It means that no opinion is sacred whether expounded by Ofsted, government, political parties, trade unions, head teachers and so-called 'experts' in every subject from mental health and emotional wellbeing to drinking, diet, sex and relationships. That much many people may be comfortable with. People may be less comfortable with criticism of the assumptions on which their own thought is supposedly founded. The Socratic philosophy of criticism must also be put to the test of criticism. A quick response to the criticism of criticism is that the question 'why criticise?' is itself a critical question. There is circularity in asking for any justification of criticism. The true criticism of criticism is censorship or worse. The opponents of criticism require servitude to their opinions and some weak or fearful individuals may acquiesce. They choose servitude. This is an immoral and dehumanising choice. It is philosophy as criticism alone that can save us from intellectual slavery to the opinions of others.

Summary

This chapter provided an introduction to the philosophy of Socrates (470–399 bce) to show that a study of his life and thought, more than that of any other philosopher, can restore the critical spirit needed to challenge the intellectual malaises of the twenty-first century, in particular, to:

- confront the contemporary avoidance of argument;
- provide arguments to refute the relativism that is rife in education and elsewhere; and
- encourage public debate in philosophy, education and politics.

Recommended reading

Substantial extracts from the eristic dialogues have been given in this chapter as a taster of Socratic thought and argument. It is best to read (or better still to listen to an audio book or watch an online theatre performance of) the original works before wading into commentaries. A start could be made

26   *Dennis Hayes*

with the Penguin compilation, *The Last Days of Socrates*, which contains the *Euthyphro*, *Apology*, *Crito* and *Phaedo* along with an introduction and a detailed commentary by Harold Tarrant. The *Meno* is the next dialogue to read or listen to for good examples of the use of elenchus leading to aporia. Its theme is 'Can virtue be taught?'

For a short introduction Francis Cornford's *Before and After Socrates*, first published in 1932, sets Socratic thinking in its historical context.

'Socrates as educator', by John Anderson, written in 1931, remains the best account of the educational philosophy of Socrates, while Roy Harris' 'Freedom of speech and philosophy of education', published in the *British Journal of Educational Studies* in 2009, usefully compares the attitudes of Socrates, Plato and Aristotle to freedom of speech.

References

The conventional way of referring to Plato's works is to use the Stephanus pagination. These are the page numbers in the complete works translated in 1578 by Joannes Serranus (Jean de Serres) and published in Geneva by Henricus Stephanus (Henri Estienne). This method allows easy reference to a variety of translations but unfortunately not to those reproduced online.

For ease of access, the translations of Plato's dialogues in the longer selections are those of Benjamin Jowett. They are out of copyright and are freely available online. To facilitate cross-referencing to other translations, the Stephanus numbers have been added.

Anderson, J. (1980 [1931]) Socrates as educator. In J. Anderson, *Education and Inquiry*. Oxford: Basil Blackwell.

Boghossian, P. (2012) Socratic pedagogy: perplexity, humiliation, shame and a broken egg. *Educational Philosophy and Theory* **44**(7): 710–720.

Burnyeat, M. (1990) *The Theaetetus of Plato* (with a translation by M. J. Levett). Indianapolis, IN and Cambridge: Hackett Publishing Company.

Chappell, T. D. J. (2006) Reading the περιτροπή: "Theaetetus" 170c–171c. *Phronesis* **51**(2): 109–139.

Cohen, J. (1998) Philosophy is education is politics: a somewhat aggressive reading of Protagoras 334d–338e. A paper presented at *Ancient Philosophy*, the Twentieth World Congress of Philosophy, Boston, Massachusetts, USA 10–15 August. Available at: www.bu.edu/wcp/Papers/Anci/AnciCohe.htm (Accessed 7 June 2018).

Cornford, F, M. (1988 [1932]) *Before and After Socrates*. Cambridge: Cambridge University Press.

Ecclestone, K. and Hayes, D. (2008) *The Dangerous Rise of Therapeutic Education*. London and New York: Routledge.

Erginel, M. M. (2009) Relativism and self-refutation in the Theaetetus. *Oxford Studies in Ancient Philosophy* **37** Winter: 1–45 (1–68 online). Available at: www.academia.edu/177920/Relativism_and_Self-Refutation_in_the_Theaetetus (Accessed 23 May 2018).

Fox, A. (1945) *Plato for Pleasure*. London: John Westhouse.

Hayes, D. (2014) Let's stop trying to teach students critical thinking. *The Conversation*. 8 August 2014. https://theconversation.com/lets-stop-trying-to-teach-students-critical-thinking-30321 (Accessed 23 May 2018).

Hayes, D. (2015) Is everyone a Socrates now? A critical look at critical thinking. In A. O'Grady and V. Cottle (eds.), *Exploring Education at Postgraduate Level*. London: Routledge.

Hayes, D. (2017) Freedom of speech in a therapeutic age. In A. Pablé, (ed.), *Critical Humanist Perspectives: The Integrational Turn in Philosophy of Language and Communication*. London and New York: Routledge.

Hayes, D. and Mieschbuehler, R. (2015) The refuge of relativism. In A. O'Grady and V. Cottle (eds.), *Exploring Education at Postgraduate Level*. London: Routledge.

Higgins, C. (1994) Socrates' effect/Meno's affect: Socratic Elenchus as kathartic therapy. *Philosophy of Education Society Yearbook 1994*. Available at: https://web.archive.org/web/20060423035015/http://www.ed.uiuc.edu:80/EPS/PES-Yearbook/94_docs/HIGGINS.HTM (Accessed 7 June 2018).

Hill, N. (2017) *The Nix*. London: Picador.

Keeling, E. (2015) Truth for a person and truth for a *polis*: a note on Theaetetus 171a1-6. *Ancient Philosophy* **35**(1): 63–73.

Kerdeman, D. (1994) Platonic dialogue and the communicative virtues: a reconsideration. *Philosophy of Education Society Yearbook 1994*. Available at: https://web.archive.org/web/20060830191357/http://www.ed.uiuc.edu/eps/PES-Yearbook/94_docs/KERDEMAN.HTM (Accessed 23 June 2018).

Lasch, C. (1996) The lost art of argument. In C. Lasch, *The Revolt of the Elites and the Betrayal of Democracy*. New York and London: W.W. Norton & Company.

Plato (1993) *The Last Days of Socrates*. Translated by H. Tredennick and H. Tarrant. Harmondsworth: Penguin.

Ryle, G. (1966) *Plato's Progress*. Cambridge: Cambridge University Press.

Scott, G. A. (ed.) (2002) *Does Socrates Have a Method? Rethinking the Elenchus in Plato's Dialogues and Beyond*. University Park, PA: The Pennsylvania State University Press.

Waterfield, R. (2002) Review of G. A. Scott (Ed.) Does Socrates Have a Method? Rethinking the Elenchus in Plato's Dialogues and Beyond. *Bryn Mawr Classical Review*, 5 June 2002. Available at: http://bmcr.brynmawr.edu/2002/2002-07-05.html (Accessed on 7 June 2018).

Waterfield, R. (2009) *Why Socrates Died: Dispelling the Myths*. London: Faber and Faber.

3 Philosophy with Children and self-determination in education

Arie Kizel

Introduction

The chapter will discuss and analyse the connection between self-determination and the community of philosophical inquiry as part of an educational programme known as Philosophy with Children. The main focus will be children's ability to express themselves by a critical, creative and caring thinking in those communities in schools. The chapter is divided into four sections: the first explores the perception of meaning given by the community of philosophical inquiry. The second explores the perception of meaning as expressed widely in the writings of Matthew Lipman, the founding father of Philosophy for Children (P4C). The third section links community of inquiry as a practical laboratory, social activism and self-determination. The last section concerns the concept of meaning in communities of inquiry and self-determination. The chapter points out the difference between a lesson providing knowledge and a community of philosophical inquiry in schools that encourages high-level thinking and claims that early educational exposure to what philosophy offers can cultivate a more self-actualising and caring individual.

Meaning in community of philosophical inquiry

Philosophy for Children, and in particular its development across the globe over the past 40 years as Philosophy *with* Children, is a platform that facilitates self-determined learning and thus also critical, caring and creative thinking combining philosophical with socio-economic sensitivity. Being a meta-approach and field practice, Philosophy with Children exists both within and without educational institutions, thus not being confined to a specific time or place such as a school. As a way of life and educational method, Philosophy with Children differs from philosophy as taught in schools and academia. While the teaching of philosophy is becoming increasingly common in schools (especially secondary schools), within the history of philosophy and philosophical thought Philosophy with (and for) Children has established itself as a model for cultivating human beings who ask existential questions about themselves, their world, and their surroundings from an early age (Kohan, 2014). In contrast to the academic study of philosophy, in which students are passively exposed to philosophical ideas, Philosophy with Children seeks to create a place and space for active engagement in philosophical thought that promotes broad, critical thinking skills in its young practitioners. Rather than focusing on acquaintance with philosophy as a field of knowledge to be mastered (Mohr Lone, 2012a), it revolves around questions relating to the pupil's existence in the

Philosophy and self-determination 29

world. It thus develops young people's philosophical sensitivity (Mohr Lone, 2012b; Kizel, 2015a), presenting questions to them as a living, breathing, vigorous space that fosters creativity, caring, and concern (Wartenberg, 2009).

As Lipman *et al.* (1980) observe, Philosophy with Children is based on the idea that students ask questions that can be extraordinarily sweeping in scope and grandeur: 'What happens to people when they die?' 'Am I really *me* on the Internet?' They thus raise issues of enormous metaphysical importance (Lipman *et al.*, 1980: 29). This ability indicates that children 'begin with a thirst for holistic explanations, and it is patronising to say the least not to try to help them develop concepts equal in generality to the questions they ask' (Lipman *et al.*, 1980: 29). For many years the director of the Institute for the Advancement of Philosophy for Children at Montclair College, New Jersey, Matthew Lipman posits that children begin to develop philosophically when they begin to ask 'why' (Lipman *et al.*, 1980: 29). Building on Charles Peirce's ideas regarding the scientific community of inquiry, Lipman proposed the concept of 'a community of philosophic inquiry':

> We can now speak of 'converting the classroom into a community of inquiry' in which students listen to one another with respect, build on one another's ideas, challenge one another to supply reasons for otherwise unsupported opinions, assist each other in drawing inferences from what has been said, and seek to identify one another's assumptions.
>
> (Lipman, 1991: 20)

In the framework of an approach adopted in schools worldwide – middle as well as secondary schools – that has been extensively empirically documented, children sit in a circle and read or watch a text (clip, drawing, etc.) that prompts them to ask questions. Deciding in a democratic fashion which of the questions they will discuss, they listen to one another, creatively develop their thoughts, and gain experience of a space marked by empathy and trust.

Philosophic communities of inquiry are frequently run by the children or adolescents themselves, without adult intervention or necessary ties to an educational institution. Taking place in a school environment, as part of a youth movement, or private initiatives, they provide a framework within which students can think and talk about problematic issues with support from adults and their peers. In this way, Lipman argued, classes may be transformed into communities of inquiry whose members listen respectfully to one another, construct ideas together, challenge one another, and above all look for and discover their fundamental values and tenets.

As Haynes and Murris (2012: 4) observe, 'the Community of Inquiry pedagogy is not about a return to child-centredness: neither teacher nor pupil is at the centre. The search for better understanding and justified beliefs through collaborative reasoning and dialogue are at the centre'. Gareth Matthews (1994) notes that parents and teachers are often so overwhelmed by the burden of nurturing, instructing, reassuring and inspiring children that they fail to appreciate the fresh philosophical perspective children can offer. Children's philosophical discussions have thus added a dimension to Bruner's (1987) view of constructivism as 'worldmaking' and narratives as 'lifemaking'.

The children who participate in communities of inquiry are likely to find themselves in a narrative-philosophical situation that presupposes a worldview and subjective interpretation that shun unequivocality and objectivism. On the level of understanding, a person understands herself through narrative. On the level of concern, she – the 'self' – seeks to realise her identity and fundamental truth and that of the group as part of her certainty. Existing in uncertainty and pondering whether it has internalised something external in the correct manner that then becomes a solid part of its identity, the 'self' reverberates as narrative. Alternatively, it is the object of an external manipulation that internalises, determines and establishes a truth – despite its group's narrated (if on occasion imaginary) events of the past – that contains patently incorrect elements the 'self' cannot filter and regulate as part of the construction of identity. A Philosophy with Children community of inquiry, in contrast, encourages children to develop a philosophical sensitivity that entails awareness of abstract questions related to human existence (Kizel, 2015b). Hereby, it allows insight into significant philosophical aspects of various situations and their analysis.

In contrast with the competitive atmosphere and rivalry frequently promoted (even if only tacitly) in schools today, communities of inquiry encourage cooperation and collaboration in order to support self-determined and shared learning. The diminishing of the competitive element in classrooms in and of itself further promotes the establishment of communities of inquiry characterised by inclusion, partnership and cooperation (Sharp, 1988). These traits enable the openness necessary for the emergence of – and sometimes solutions to – philosophical ideas. By delimiting the space in which students are allowed to voice certain ideas, adults tend to ensure that these remain banal, serving their surroundings and adult needs, wishes and goals.

In his day, Lipman argued that Philosophy with Children should be thought of as the philosophy of science, the philosophy of religion and the philosophy of history. This goaded Gareth Matthews, who had initially cast doubt on children's capacity to philosophise, to begin working with children. His involvement promptly led Matthews (1994) to discover that the latter were not only curious but also capable of asking profound philosophical questions. Numerous studies conducted in recent years across the globe have confirmed and proven time and again that children possess the ability to engage in inventive thinking, their questions and work in philosophic communities of inquiry developing their creative and caring thinking skills (García-Moriyón et al., 2002; Cam, 2013; Gorard et al., 2015). Rather than impinging on their learning achievements in diverse fields of knowledge, these in fact hone their faculties.

In my view, based on researches, Philosophy with Children (PwC) differs itself from a lesson providing knowledge in six dimensions. PwC communities of inquiry:

1. aim to propose places of learning from a place of questions rather than a corpus of answers at its centre;
2. facilitate a form of learning that resists the educational hierarchy that boasts of omniscience;
3. place the coordinator as a participant in the learning process rather than as a 'judge';
4. set learning in the (real) present against learning for the (unknown) future;
5. legitimise improvisation as a way of learning in place of predetermined content;
6. regard learning as liberating the learner from disciplinary boundaries.

All six dimensions view Philosophy with Children as a pedagogy of searching at whose centre lies the pursuit of meaning that facilitates personal development – and thus self-direction and capability. This stands in stark contrast to the pedagogy of fear (Kizel, 2016a) that makes perpetual demands on the learner, induces apprehension about taking risks, reduces her competence and creates the constant need for an omniscient 'guide' that is so prevalent within traditional learning settings.

Matthew Lipman's writings on 'meaning'

Matthew Lipman in both his early and later writings argues that methods such as 'critical thinking' fail to enable children to understand in their own unique way the richness and complexity of the world in which they live and to exemplify their own perspective, especially with regard to the change they think should happen. In contrast, philosophical reflection possesses an innately activist dimension:

> If philosophy is seen to represent the natural fulfilment and culmination of childhood curiosity and wonder, of childhood speculation about the nature of things, and of childhood concern for truth about reality, then nothing could be more in keeping with children's own intellectual dispositions than philosophical activities.
>
> (Lipman and Sharp, 1978: 7)

Let us address first the philosophical community of inquiry Lipman discusses in his writings. According to him, this seeks to inculcate two simultaneous positions: 'affirmative' and 'critical'. The first perceives, elucidates and affirms the 'existing situation' and social status quo; the second challenges present reality. If you like, we may say that the first plays 'inside', the second – frequently at the same time – wanting to be 'offside', 'other' or 'alternative'. By definition this 'game' is characterised not only by a complex dialectic but also by a pedagogic and social activism based on Kohan's 'dissatisfaction' factor (2014: 7) or Lipman and Sharp's 'distrust' principle (1978: 8).

A systematic and in-depth reading of Lipman's works indicates that his thought is informed by the belief that the philosophical community of inquiry can serve to help build (young) individuals' sense of self- and community-construct, enabling them to identify the problems and deficiencies of the society in which they live, and propose solutions to them. Philosophy is thus a motivating force not only for (self) action but also for (social and environmental) activism, helping to transform personal competency into social activism. It actively searches through questions and finds by gaining answers, both these circles being driven by a teleological form of thinking that constitutes the platform from which change can be implemented. As Lipman (1997a:4) states: 'Our contemporary conception of education as inquiry combines both of these aims. Its emphasis is on the process as well as on the product.'

Lipman's paradigm here is the pedagogy of looking for meaning – not merely in abstract but also in practical terms. I suggest that this may be called 'meaning-making as an action' or 'the action of meaning-making'. Within the school framework, this initially takes the form of the legitimising of questions, encouraging students to become active in preparing for their future lives: 'Meanings show themselves so intricately involved in our lives that a philosophical analysis of qualitative experience can hardly avoid dealing with them' (Lipman, 1956: 41). This space in which students are exposed to valuable experiences is one of the most important goals of the educational process:

> Once it is acknowledged that, as far as children themselves are concerned, no educational plan will be worthy of the name unless it results in meaningful school and after-school experiences, we can feel some confidence in having arrived at one of the significant criteria for the evaluation of an educational design.
>
> (Lipman et al., 1980: 8)

32   *Arie Kizel*

Lipman thus views philosophical activity as a form of training for action, the school serving as a dialogical space within which students can experience paradigmatic thought change. At the basis of his philosophy lies the belief that the best way to improve education as part of the betterment of society at large would be to create philosophical communities of inquiry in the classroom that would constitute a model for a democratic and pluralistic society. Determining that the first step towards accomplishing this goal was to address the classroom text and learning materials, he began writing a philosophical textbook 'that would allow both teachers and children to engage simultaneously and openly in inquiry at the same time in the classroom' (Lipman, 2008: 109). When he published his first philosophical novel for children in 1967, however, he promptly realised that it could not easily be integrated into the school curriculum without an accompanying pedagogy – P4C. Analysing the existing curriculum, he proposed a pilot project 'whose ostensible aim was to determine the feasibility of teaching reasoning to fifth-grade children', carried out at the Rand School, Montclair, New Jersey during the 1970–1971 academic year (Lipman, 1973: 17).

Following a meeting with two groups of 20 elementary-school students, he understood that the active element of young people's activity is predicated on the pursuit of meaning – in this case, learning. Youngsters could be not only passive learners relying on answers to the questions their teachers asked them but also self-motivated to ask questions of their own. Lipman's conclusions from his initial experiments highlighted the centrality of the fact that school learning in its current pedagogic environment is stagnant. He thus decided that philosophy could and should enhance the development and construction of a dialectic relationship with the present situation: the cultivation of criticism and opposition to 'reality'. He writes,

> I am now convinced that philosophy can and should be a part of the entire length of a child's education. In a sense this is a kind of tautology, because it is abundantly clear that children hunger for meaning and get turned off from education when it ceases to be meaningful to them.
>
> (Lipman, 1973: 27)

Throughout his writings, Lipman attaches importance to training activist learners by involving all their literacy capabilities. One of these circles of meaning pertains to understanding texts and drawing meaning from words and art. In order to gain this skill, students must be equipped linguistically and literarily – i.e., to gain mastery of those channels that enable them to make valuable and profound use of texts whose significance may only become apparent as they grow older. He not only declared conversation to be the 'minimal condition for civility' (Lipman, 1988a: 49) but also encouraged a multi-element communal process moving from question to dialogue, from doubt to looking for common answers, from answers to personal and group activity in general in deed and action.

A multi-year philosophical community of inquiry operating in an educational institution, he believed, could provide a framework for the gaining of these skills, turning them into 'second nature' and transforming students into inquirers into their surroundings and thus being capable of engaging in critical and creative thinking about them. It would also foster in them a multidimensional care and concern for their environment and its ecology. Such students would not only be agents but also participants in society – not just employed but also responsible citizens: 'Even if philosophy does not provide ultimate meanings, it conveys to the child that the quest is feasible and worthwhile' (Lipman and Sharp, 1978: 8).

He then proceeded to posit that 'it is, thus, by doing philosophical inquiry generally that children prepare themselves to do ethical inquiry, and by doing ethical inquiry with regard to instrumental and procedural consideration they prepare themselves to give serious attention to substantive values' (Lipman, 1997a: 3). He makes an essential differentiation between truth-related information and meaning-oriented philosophy – one of the formative constituents of meaning being relevancy and one of its central goals action.

This view opposes the Socratic and Platonic ethos of pursuit of the truth and doing philosophy as the highest educational goal, perceiving experience in a Deweyan sense and attributing importance to it from, not only in intellectual terms, but also practical ones: the betterment of human life: 'above all a community of inquiry involves questioning, more narrowly a quest for truth, more broadly a quest for meaning' (Lipman, 2003a: 95).

Philosophical laboratory/community of inquiry, social activism and self-determination

What elements promote activism in children in the philosophical laboratory/community of inquiry? In a 2003 interview, Lipman identified two, working in conjunction with one another. The first he calls the 'social goal' (i.e., democracy), maintaining that we must use philosophy as a tool to train students to become members of a democratic society as part of the striving to bring democracy to the whole world. The second is the 'personal goal', wherein philosophy encourages children to think for themselves: 'we could use thinking that is well disciplined, logical, creative, caring for other and for oneself' (Lipman, 2003b). The active philosophical laboratory thus functions as a space for training in Deleuze and Guattari's (1994) sense of 'doing philosophy'. As Gale notes:

> for Deleuze... creating concepts and the active process of conceptualisation is also a practice of *becoming* which not only involves using ideas and concepts in practices of meaning-making but also acknowledging their inevitable connection with affects and percepts in the complexities of relational space.
>
> (Gale, 2015: 71–72, emphasis in original)

Being active, philosophy is always a creative practice. Applying Deleuzean philosophy and thinking, students can learn to be actively involved in the creation of concepts, participating with others in the processes and practices of conceptualisation. This stimulates them to exercise agency and make their own experience real: 'By promoting a form of agency of this kind, learners are encouraged to be involved in *meaning-making* rather than being constrained to conform to pedagogical practices which involve *teaching meaning*' (Gale, 2015: 71, emphasis in original). The goal of prompting activism via the asking of questions and engaging in discussion to develop thinking skills is to enable children to find meaning in their lives. Thereby children gain both a sense of purpose and a sense of direction, the latter representing the ability to identify aims and targets including those that may later be subject to change: 'once the child can perceive what the basic direction of his or her own life is, then that becomes the basic criterion against which he measures the choices he makes in particular situations' (Lipman,1980: 178). In both instances, 'the point is that students must be encouraged to become reasonable for their own good (i.e., as a step toward their own autonomy),

34   *Arie Kizel*

and not just for our good (i.e., because the growing rationalization of society requires it)' (Lipman, 1988b: 10).

The activities of philosophical communities of inquiry occur in two parallel dimensions – time and space. Communal spaces now allow for the anticipation of future social spaces, thus being oriented towards both short- and long-term thinking habits and activism. As Lipman notes,

> either way philosophical inquiry is student-centred, and it is the thinking of each student that is dramatised, as well as the thinking of each collective group. The philosophical admonition to 'Know Thyself' is not to be taken lightly, nor is the Socratic warning that 'the unexamined life is not worth living'. It is the life of each and every philosophy student that must be examined and understood. Each student's mind becomes 'a theatre within a theatre, a drama within a drama'.
>
> (Lipman, 1997b: 77)

In order to encourage activism, philosophical communities of inquiry must feel relevant. The group-collective process thus seeks to avoid closed information, focusing rather on questioning and openness, as though in a years-long race during which the building blocks of development are put into place to ensure that children grow into future citizens. Relevance is essential because

> knowledge and life are not alien to one another, and talking about understanding of the world, and the problems that one faces in one's personal life, is really important to education. It is essential to education that we show the relevance of that education to the world and to the subjects that study the world.
>
> (Lipman and Sharp, 1992: 45)

Studying the world begins inside the classroom. In the initial primary-philosophical circle, students learn to recognise and develop their own views and those of their peers: 'The meaning to children of their own experience may be, in part, its exclusiveness – the realisation that what is impossible for others is indeed possible for them, and them alone' (Lipman, 1980: 294). The encounter with otherness within the philosophical community of inquiry is paramount, forming an essential tool for the cultivation of the ability to influence others by acknowledging their influence upon us: 'the discussion promotes children's awareness of one another's personalities, interests, values, beliefs and biases' (Lipman, 1973: 12). Within this circle, young students are not only listened to but also engage in discussion with others, thereby developing the openness and flexibility that is vital for espousing the activism necessary to implement change. In this way, P4C can be expected to flourish in a heterogeneous space where learners speak out of a variety of lifestyles and experiences, where different beliefs as to what is important are explicit, and where a plurality of thinking styles exists.

The philosophical laboratory/community of inquiry also allows its members to experience the boundaries of their capabilities, helping them to understand not only what is possible but also what is impossible and to ask questions about the space I suggest calling 'impossible' or 'difficult and limited'. Such a view of problems enables them to realise their limitations and to develop cognitive and social skills (such as empathy and listening) that aid them with interacting with people from different backgrounds. The coalitions of influence and strategies that develop in philosophical communities of inquiry can form the pattern for other coalitions beyond the school walls. In this way, the democratic experience is not only a learning goal but also forms the basis for meaning and action:

An exercise can have a logical function and at the same time it can simulate social practices that play an important role in social experience. In this connection, games represent exercises that sharpen student thinking about their daily lives... [being] helpful in distinguishing between intended and unintended meanings.

(Lipman, 1997b: 75)

In the first circle of influence that is the community of inquiry, 'children must be allowed to experience what it is like to exist in a context of mutual respect, of disciplined dialogue, of cooperative inquiry, free of arbitrariness and manipulation' (Lipman, 1988a: 47). In the second, 'without the possibilities of ideal conditions, or at least of improvement, things wouldn't have their present meanings for us... So a case could be made for meanings as the contrast between the actual and the possible' (Lipman, 1980: 11, 294). Philosophical communities of inquiry thus afford the opportunity for the development of ethical, dialogical students with the potential to be activists characterised by '1) Respect for other point of view; 2) patience with other deliberators; 3) dedication to rationality; 4) intellectual creativity in the formulation of new hypotheses' (Lipman, 2003a: 115).

How do youngsters develop an activist awareness in the philosophical laboratory/community of inquiry? Social indifference begins to be replaced by personal awareness in stages, beginning with the asking of questions relevant to the students' experiences and social contexts, in particular when the members of the laboratory/community come from different backgrounds and sectors. This heterogeneity heightens awareness and acceptance of diverse identities (Kizel, 2016b). Philosophical practice thus prompts awareness not only as an intellectual activity but also as a call to social learning:

it is, thus, by doing philosophical inquiry generally that children prepare themselves to do ethical inquiry, and by doing ethical inquiry with regard to instrumental and procedural consideration [that] they prepare themselves to give serious attention to substantive values.

(Lipman, 1997a: 3)

Social learning necessarily takes place within a context:

An individual has relationships with his work, home, ideals, activities, his past, with the country he lives in, and with humanity in general... Meanings consist precisely in the relationships things have to one another... To understand what something means to us is to grasp the relationships in which it stands to us and to everything else to which it is related.

(Lipman, 1980: 350)

Already in his early writings with Ann Margaret Sharp, Lipman notes how important the social framework is to young learners, positing that it enables them to engage in activist thinking by putting their thinking into 'some kind of context which will make their thoughts more meaningful to them, for the more comprehensive the setting of an idea is, the richer will that idea be in meaning' (Lipman and Sharp, 1975: 20). He thus argues that contexts are the source of meaning: 'one way in which we discover meaning is to discover connections... As long as one does not know the context of an episode, it may seem meaningless' (Lipman and Sharp, 1975: 67). Activist thought therefore includes at least six elements: '1) discovering alternatives; 2) discovering impartiality...

36   Arie Kizel

discovering consistency; 3) discovering the feasibility of giving reasons for beliefs; 4) discovering comprehensiveness; 5) discovering situations; 6) discovering part-whole relationships' (Lipman et al., 1980: 68).

Combing meaning in communities of inquiry and self-determination

The concept of self-determined learning, which posits that students are capable of guiding their own learning, contrasts sharply with the classical view of learning that revolves around a 'knowledge elevator' that leads the 'unknowing' by way of the 'knower' to 'knowledge' – i.e., 'culture,' the 'world at large,' or 'success'. The traditional approach placing little trust in the learner either as a person or as a knower/one capable of knowing, the school has established itself as a central institution over the centuries, reinforcing student dependence upon its structure and its teaching staff. As Ricci and Pritscher observe, it is thus 'little wonder that classroomed children lack confidence in themselves' (2015: 4).

The self-determined approach, in contrast, expands upon the role of human agency in the learning process. Thus, the learner is seen as, 'the major agent in their own learning, which occurs as a result of personal experiences' (Hase and Kenyon, 2007: 112). This approach assumes that what the student 'chooses to learn is worthwhile and that she should listen deeply to her mind, body, spirit and emotions as guides to her willed curriculum' (Ricci and Pritscher, 2015: 4). In this way, the student needs to be flexible, able to shift as learning occurs, and forge new paths, new questions, and new contexts. During this process, the emphasis is put on developing capability, self-reflection, and meta-cognition, or an understanding of one's own learning process, double-loop learning, and non-linear learning and teaching processes (Blaschke, 2012).

Rejecting the view that the teacher (and he or she alone) should direct the learner, it argues that 'schooling today is more for grades and degrees than for developing curious, self-directing, lovers of learning' (Ricci and Pritscher, 2015: 4). It thus sets out to help learners develop the capacity for self-direction, supporting transformational learning and promoting 'emancipatory learning and social action' (Merriam, 2001: 9). As learning occurs along a self-directed path, the learner's perspective changes as she matures and reflects on her life-experiences, self-perception, beliefs, and lifestyle (Mezirow, 1997). According to Brandt (2013: 111) 'the students' self-determined studies lead to transformational experiences; this benefits individual learners and ultimately society'. Today's learners are faced with an environment that is different from that experienced by previous generations. The pace of change is rapid, particularly within the workforce. Employers want and need employees who are innovators, complex problem-solvers, and good communicators, and who are able to apply what they learn to real-life scenarios (Hart Research Associates, 2013). Graduates need to be productive at the start of employment, and they must adapt quickly to new and disruptive innovations, continuously acquiring new skills. 'The complexities of the workforce in the Twenty-first century require that employees have a wide range of cognitive and meta-cognitive skills, such as creativity, self-directedness, innovativeness, and knowledge of how they learn' (Blaschke, 2014: 1). According to Gerstein (2014) today's learners need to be *inter alia* agile and adaptable, to have good oral and written communication skills, to be able to collaborate across networks, to be curious and imaginative, to have critical thinking and problem-solving skills, to have empathy and a sense of global stewardship. Given the vast amount of information available on the internet, learners need to be able to separate the wheat from the chaff by being able to check data with reputable

Philosophy and self-determination   37

sources, to analyse and synthesise information, to recognise a good argument, and to differentiate between correlational and causal relationships.

The mapping outlined above largely sums up Matthew Lipman's educational thought that led him to propose an alternative philosophy critical of existing educational principles. In his view, this distorted school system suffers from four central flaws: 1) it introduces a negative charisma into the child; 2) it instils in her a gratuitous belief in her intellectual impotence; 3) it promotes in her a distrust of all her intellectual powers other than those required to cope with problems formulated and assigned to her by others; 4) sooner or later, the intransigencies of the educational system beat or batter out of the child the lively curiosity that seems to be an essential part of her natural impulse (Lipman,1973: 7). Philosophy with Children is thus designed to provide students with an opportunity to embark on a search for meaning that is largely guided by self-determined learning and thinking, a pursuit I call the 'pedagogy of searching'. In his formative volume, Lipman asserts:

> Children frequently complain that their courses lack relevant, interest, and meaning... Since many children actually drop out of school and many others are physically present but would like to drop out, this allegation that school is meaningless has to be taken seriously.... The child's claim can be seen as a demand for meaning, the parents' as a demand for rationality. The existing educational process can only be disappointment to both.
>
> (Lipman, 1980: 4, 11)

The search for meaning in education is not merely a way to gain the students' trust but also a way to impact their lives: 'If children find the education they are being given meaningless, they will come to distrust it... The children need to be motivated – not to think, but to think in ways that increase the measure of meaning in their lives' (Lipman, 1973: 9). Constructing meaning is a complex task, including an inner, immediate, inherent element in the framework of which 'Children don't like being told, when they ask what something means, or why they have to do something, "wait, you'll see". They want meaning now. They want meaning to be intrinsic, not extrinsic' (Lipman, 1973:21).

In his *Thinking in Education*, Lipman elaborates on the notion of the philosophic community of inquiry as social model, arguing that 'The community of inquiry wants to build a system of thought' (2003a: 103). The moves it makes are dialectical, calling for a search for a broader social significance: 'Above all a community of inquiry involves questioning, more narrowly a quest for truth, more broadly a quest for meaning' (Lipman, 2003a: 95). The self-determined learning process that constructs meaning thus contains an enigmatic element within the thinking of children. This leads to seven cognitive stages whereby the meanings that arise from experience can be enriched – drawing inferences, identifying relationships, distinguishing, connecting, evaluating, defining and questioning (Lipman, 1988b: 100).

Philosophy helps children integrate formal and informal logic in order to open up before them the possibility of finding meaning. Two primary cognitive moves aid in this task: evaluation of their own reasoning and assessment of the evidence on which their judgement must be based. Philosophy with Children, Lipman thus argues, 'gives sets of interconnected ideas to show them their own thinking need not remain fragmentary'. Preserving children's natural inclination to find meaning must be a guiding principle of the educational process: 'We have to learn how to establish the conditions and opportunities that will enable children, with their natural curiosity and appetite for meaning' (Lipman, 1988a: 13). Philosophy and meaning are closely and integrally related, philosophy clarifying meaning, uncovering assumptions and presuppositions, analysing concepts, assessing the validity of reasoning processes, and investigating the implication of ideas and their consequences in human life.

This 'pedagogy of searching' is the antithesis of the 'pedagogy of fear' (Kizel, 2016a) prevalent within the school system in many respects. It touches on the concept of childhood, the child, the rationale for children's education and practices relating to the pedagogy of upbringing. It fuels the view that the child constitutes a potential educational – generally psychological – problem that must be diagnosed, defended, assisted and, of course, aided and abetted. I suggest that pedagogy motivated by fear prevents young students – as well as teachers – from dealing with the great existential questions that relate to the essence of human beings. In my opinion, it thus pathologises children and childhood, stunting the active and vital educational growth of young people and making them passive and dependent upon external disciplinary sources. Under the guise of a living, breathing educational system that seeks progress, it inculcates fear and apprehension of a conscious and alert life guided by an educational space that enables the philosophical life that is so necessary for the young person. It is thus no wonder that Martin Seligman, the founder of Positive Psychology, posits that modern psychology has been co-opted by the disease model. We've become too preoccupied with repairing damage when our focus should be on building strength and resilience, especially in children. In its over-enthusiastic adoption of the model of 'repairing damage,' the pedagogy of fear views students as in constant need of 'correction'.

Conclusion

Philosophy with Children offers a space for addressing existential questions, some dealing with urgent social issues. Philosophic communities of inquiry can be framed in six dimensions that enable and encourage self-determined learning within and outside schools. Philosophy with Children is based on a pedagogy of searching, in particular the search for meaning espoused by Matthew Lipman. Shaking free of the pedagogy of fear and recognising children's questions demands a fundamental conceptual change within education. Adults frequently view the move to replace the existential certainty they claim within the existing education system with existential questions as subversive. It demands a return to starting points and a willingness to provide children with a free and safe educational space in which they can sound out fertile preliminary questions about themselves, their lives, their environment and, most of all, the changing world they discover with their innate forms of originality. It thus calls for an abandonment of adult colonisation in favour of childlike immaturity and an acknowledgment of an innocence that promotes a philosophic sensitivity imbued with hope that the questions asked will facilitate and sanction discovery and growth.

Summary

- Philosophy with Children is a platform (philosophy and practice) that facilitates self-determined learning and thus also critical, caring and creative thinking.
- Dialogical learner-researchers can move out of the philosophical laboratory of a community of philosophical inquiry into the field of social activism, engaging in a critical and creative examination of society and seeking to change it.

- Based on Matthew Lipman's proposal that communities of philosophical inquiry can serve as a model of social activism in the present, it presents the community of philosophical inquiry as a model for social activism in the future.
- Philosophy with Children has six dimensions that contrast with classic classroom disciplinary learning, advocating a 'pedagogy of searching' to replace the 'pedagogy of fear' that dominates traditional learning systems.

Questions for discussion

1. What is the advantage of a philosophical community of inquiry to encourage critical thinking?
2. What skills does a facilitator in a philosophical community need in order to prevent the encounter from becoming a regular lesson?
3. How can a philosophical community encourage activism among its members?

Recommended reading

Kizel, A. (2016). Philosophy with children as an educational platform for self-determined learning. *Cogent Education* **3**(1): 1244026, https://doi.org/10.1080/2331186X.2016.1244026
Matthews, G. (1984). *Dialogues with Children*. Cambridge, MA: Harvard University Press.
The website of the International Council of Philosophical Enquiry with Children at: www.icpic.org

References

Blaschke, L. M. (2012) Heutagogy and lifelong learning: a review of heutagogical practice and self-determined learning. *International Review of Research in Open and Distance Learning* **13**(1): 56–71.
Blaschke, L. M. (2014) Moving students forward in the PAH continuum: maximizing the power of the social web. In L. M. Blaschke, C. Kenyon and S. Hase (eds.), *Experiences in Self-Determined Learning*. United States: Amazon.com Publishing.
Brandt, B. (2013) The learner's perspective. In S. Haseand and C. Kenyon (eds.), *Self-Determined Learning: Heutagogy in Action*. London: Bloomsbury Academic.
Bruner, J. (1987). Life as narrative. *Social Research* **54**(1): 11–32.
Cam, P. (2013) *Philosophy for Children: Values Education and the Inquiring Society*. Australia: Philosophy of Education Society of Australia.
Deleuze, G. and Guattari, F. (1994) *What is Philosophy?* London: Verso.
Gale, K. (2015) Deleuze: the pedagogic potential of always creating concepts. In J. Haynes, K. Gale and M. Parker (eds.), *Philosophy and Education: An Introduction to Key Questions and Themes* (pp. 69–79). New York: Routledge.
García-Moriyón, F., Rebollo, I. and Colom, R. (2002) *Evaluating Philosophy for Children: A Meta-Analysis*. Madrid: Facultad de Formación del Profesorado, Universidad Autónoma de Madrid.
Gerstein, J. (2014) The other 21st century skills. [Blog post.] Available at: http://usergeneratededucation.wordpress.com/2013/05/22/the-other-21st-century-skills/ (Accessed 26 March 2018).
Gorard, S., Siddiqui, N. and Huat, B. (2015) *Philosophy for Children Evaluation Report and Executive Summary*. Durham: Durham University.
Hase, S. and Kenyon, C. (2007) Heutagogy: a child of complexity theory. *Complicity: An International Journal of Complexity and Education* **4**(1): 111–119.
Hart Research Associates (2013) It takes more than a major: Employer priorities for college learning and student success. *Association of American Colleges and Universities (AACU)* **99**:2. Available at: www.aacu.org/liberaleducation/le-sp13/hartresearchassociates.cfm (Accessed 26 March 2018).
Haynes, J. and Murris, K. (2012) *Picturebooks, Pedagogy and Philosophy*. New York: Routledge.

Kizel, A. (2015a) Philosophy with children, the poverty line, and socio-philosophic sensitivity. *Childhood and Philosophy* **11**(21): 139–162.

Kizel, A. (2015b) 'Life goes on even if there's a gravestone': philosophy with children and adolescents on virtual memorial sites. *Childhood and Philosophy* **10**(20): 421–443.

Kizel, A. (2016a) Pedagogy out of fear of philosophy as a way of pathologizing children. *Journal of Unschooling and Alternative Learning* **10**(20): 28–47.

Kizel, A. (2016b) Enabling identity: the challenge of presenting the silenced voices of repressed groups in philosophic communities of inquiry. *Journal of Philosophy in Schools* **3**(1): 16–39.

Kohan, W. O. (2014) *Philosophy and Childhood: Critical Perspectives and Affirmative Practices.* New York: Palgrave Macmillan.

Lipman, M. (1956) The physical thing in aesthetic experience. *Journal of Aesthetics and Art Criticism* **15**(1): 36–46.

Lipman, M. (1973) *Philosophy for Children.* Montclair, NJ: Institute for the Advancement of Philosophy for Children.

Lipman, M. (1980) *Writing: How and Why.* Montclair, NJ: Institute for the Advancement of Philosophy for Children.

Lipman, M. (1988a) *Philosophy Goes to School.* Philadelphia: Temple University Press.

Lipman, M. (1988b) Critical thinking: what can it be? *Educational Leadership* **46**(1): 38–43.

Lipman, M. (1991) *Thinking in Education.* Cambridge: Cambridge University Press.

Lipman, M. (1997a) In their best interest? *Analytic Teaching* **17**(1): 1–4.

Lipman, M. (1997b) Philosophical discussion plans and exercises. *Analytic Teaching* **16**(2): 64–77.

Lipman, M. (2003a) *Thinking in Education.* New York: Cambridge University Press.

Lipman, M. (2003b) Interview with Matthew Lipman. Available at: www.youtube.com/watch?v=jiGiQIKPxL0 (Accessed 1 March 2018).

Lipman, M. (2008) *A Life Teaching Thinking.* Montclair, NJ: Institute for the Advancement of Philosophy for Children.

Lipman, M. and Sharp, A. M. (1975) *Teaching Children Philosophical Thinking: An Introduction to the Teacher's Manual for Harry Stottlemeier's Discovery.* Montclair, NJ: Institute for the Advancement of Philosophy for Children.

Lipman, M. and Sharp, A. M. (1978) *Growing up with Philosophy.* Philadelphia: Temple University Press.

Lipman, M. and Sharp, A. M. (1992) Interview with Matthew Lipman and Ann Margaret Sharp. *Teaching Thinking and Creativity*, Winter 2004, pp. 42–49.

Lipman, M., Sharp, A. M. and Oscanyan, F. (1980) *Philosophy in the Classroom.* Philadelphia: Temple University Press.

Matthews, G. (1994) *The Philosophy of Childhood.* Cambridge MA: Harvard University Press.

Merriam, S.B. (2001) Andragogy and self-directed learning: pillars of adult learning theory. *New Directions for Adult and Continuing Education* **89**: 3–13.

Mezirow, J. (1997) Transformative learning: theory to practice. *New Directions for Adult and Continuing Education* **74**: 5–12.

Mohr Lone, J. (2012a) *The Philosophical Child.* Lanham: Rowman and Littlefield.

Mohr Lone, J. (2012b) Teaching pre-college philosophy: the cultivation of philosophical sensitivity. In J. Mohr Lone and R. Israrloff (eds.), *Philosophy and Education: Introducing Philosophy to Young People.* Newcastle upon Tyne: Cambridge Scholars Publishing.

Ricci, C. and Pritscher, C.P. (2015) *Holistic Pedagogy: The Self and Quality-Willed Learning.* New York: Springer.

Sharp, A. (1988) What is a community of inquiry? In J. Portelli and W. Hare (eds.), *Philosophy and Education.* Calgary: Detselig Enterprise.

Wartenberg, T.E. (2009) *Big Ideas for Little Kids: Teaching Philosophy Through Children's Literature.* Lanham, MD: Rowman and Littlefield.

4 Philosophy in Islam and its limit on teaching reason in humanities

Nur Surayyah Madhubala Abdullah

Introduction

As teaching is a form of principled moral practice (Carr, 2005), teachers in secular schools in multicultural societies should consider the wellbeing of all students from different backgrounds, including faith, and their needs. This includes students' difficulties in dealing with subjects where the content and its teaching may sit uneasily with aspects of their backgrounds such as culture, religion or ethnicity, and what they ought to learn. Further, teaching in a multicultural classroom is educating with respect for multiple perspectives and the issues that come with this, including ensuring the flourishing of every child (Au *et al.*, 2016).

From an educational perspective then, teachers should focus on the achievement of all students as their role is to improve the lives of their students irrespective of their background. From a philosophical perspective, education should be about the wellbeing of students and what is important for their flourishing as persons (Brighouse, 2005). Hence, it is important for pre-service teachers to consider how their teaching can improve their students' wellbeing given the cultural environment they are situated in. For example, do the elements upon which the environment centres on, such as faith, culture, ethnicity, hinder their flourishing as persons? Against this moral framework, pre-service humanities teachers should consider the fundamental idea of self in the context of the students' environment.

Questions for discussion

Is it important for teachers to consider the needs of all students in their classrooms? Why?

I draw on my experience as a senior lecturer in the field of moral education in a public university in Malaysia, teaching Muslim students from both weak and strong religious Islamic cultural environments (RICE). In my informal observations and discussions with students on moral issues, I find that humanities teachers face a pedagogical difficulty in teaching Muslim students from strong RICE to reason on issues in humanities. There is a limit to how far these students are willing to consider arguments or perspectives that conflict with Islamic religious precepts. They are more likely to reject arguments that counter their religious precepts, even if the argument offers a fair perspective on the issue. These experiences are consistent with Akhtar's (1990) point that a strict Islamic perspective tends to regard reason as undermining religion and should be rejected by Muslims. I argue that, in the context of the teaching of humanities as contributing to the wellbeing of students, this situation is problematic. I suggest that the problem is situated in the philosophy of Islam and its limit to the idea of reason. In order to better address this problem, pre-service teachers need clarity on the tension between Islamic faith and reason within it. This chapter provides this by drawing on Akhtar's description of philosophy in Islam and how reason is viewed within its precepts. I recognise that Akhtar's account may be seen as controversial in its criticisms of Islam, but I find it convincing in its analysis of the situation I found with my students in Malaysia.

The chapter is divided into six sections. The first section sets out the pedagogical concern about teaching humanities to Muslim students. The second section provides a background to the problem, followed by a section describing the nature of humanities and the place of reason in teaching it and the problem with regards to Muslim students' stance on reason. The fourth section offers a perspective on where the problem lies within philosophy in Islam, while the fifth outlines the implication for pre-service teachers in thinking about their pedagogy. The sixth section concludes by noting a challenge for pre-service humanities teachers in teaching Muslim students.

Before the first section, some clarification of the key terms used in the chapter is needed. A 'religious Islamic cultural environment' refers to a Muslim student's personal, familial, societal or institutional and political background that adopts an Islamic perspective on knowledge which emphasises an Islamic ideal of education and its related values (Halstead, 2004; Hussain, 2004). Based on Waghid's (2012) idea of minimal and maximal Islamic education, a strong RICE refers to an environment that strictly endorses an Islamic perspective on education. It is one that initiates Muslim students into the tenets of the faith and emphasises Islamic ideas, including what content in religion and religious education can be questioned and deliberated upon. The problem discussed in this chapter refers exclusively to those Muslim students from a *strong* RICE. 'Secular schools' refers to schools where religion is either excluded from influencing the curriculum or, if included in the development of the curriculum, does not dictate the curriculum of subject matter taught (Arthur, 2017). The teaching of humanities is understood as the development of practical reason in people who can think critically about what affects themselves and others in society and to respond those situations in a manner that maintains their dignity as individuals (Walker, 2009; Nussbaum, 2010).

A pedagogical concern

In this discussion I follow Walker (2009) in arguing that humanities need to teach students to become practical reasoners. However, to educate practical reasoners, teachers have to get students to think critically where 'any reasonable proposition can and should be debated from any reasonable angle' (Bérubé, 2006: 290). While this is the aim, the author's experience of teaching Muslim students to reason in a variety of humanities courses on a humanities teacher education programme found difficulty in getting them really to consider arguments in discussions and debates on issues as to what counts as a reasonable and valid argument. I observed that they fail to give a fair consideration to these arguments in discussion or debates because of how far they are willing to consider the arguments as being right or wrong. For instance, although there are better or more compelling reasons to agree with an issue, Muslim students tend to limit the consideration of acceptable reasons in discussion and debates to only those that their faith denotes as an acceptable reason. Hence, they make decisions primarily based on these reasons, despite perhaps more compelling reasons to the contrary.

Therefore, my main concern is that some Muslim students' wellbeing as persons in a polity may be affected if humanities is not contributing in a substantive manner to their wellbeing. Their inability to make decisions that consider in a deeper sense the interest of themselves and others is affected to a great degree if they do not adequately consider a situation and related matters, including the needs of those involved. Any limitation to what they can consider as reason weakens their consideration of discussion and debates that may be important to what action may be more appropriate to the situation and matter involved. This limitation includes faith-based understanding of reason that limits what they consider as reason and the extent to which they are willing to reason. As humanities teachers, our concern, at least in a minimal sense, should be that the aim of humanities education is ensuring the wellbeing of students as it contributes to the flourishing of themselves and others as persons in a polity.

A review of relevant literature shows that faith-related issues should be considered by pre-service humanities teachers. Research is still lacking into teaching in multicultural classrooms that include Muslim students whose faith plays a strong role in their life and education. Researchers have focused more on issues of culture, race and ethnicity and less on the faith of students and how it affects teaching in secular schools. In addition, discussions about the problem of teaching Muslim students from such an environment are limited in scope. For instance, Rissanen (2014, 2015) points out the lack of studies in multicultural education on religious differences, in particular in the teaching of Muslim students. Despite the 'distinct challenges of dealing with religious differences and the prejudice related to religion' (Rissanen, 2014: 1), and a recognition that religion is a mediator in an individual's educational performance specifically among Muslim students where the salience of religious identity is high, there is still a void in the discussion, particularly about difficulties in teaching Muslim students to reason.

I suggest that the problem is situated in the idea of reason in Islamic faith where religion dominates over reason and revelation is the source of knowledge (Halstead, 2004). However, there is less discussion on this issue, specifically in situating it in Islamic philosophy and the conceptualisation of reason. Before considering this aspect, we need to understand the background to RICE.

Questions for discussion

Why is it important for humanities teachers to consider what and how Muslim students learn specifically in multicultural classrooms?

Education from an Islamic perspective

The situation with Muslim students described in the preceding section is related to the phenomenon of Islamic education and its place in the life of Muslims. With the dramatic growth in the Muslim population around the world, especially in countries where secular education is adopted such as in the United Kingdom, the Muslim population that comes from a religious Islamic cultural environment has increased. This increase has brought about a more prominent presence of Muslim students, be

44   Nur Surayyah Madhubala Abdullah

it through immigration, influx of refugees or existing population, who adopt an Islamic religious perspective on education (Shah, 2018) and have a problem with the philosophy of education and idea of knowledge in secular schools (Halstead, 2004). This has contributed to an increase in demand for Islamic education in those countries, either minimally within secular schools in the form of recognition for Muslim worldview in educational content, or in the provision of faith schools. This demand is fanned partly by concerns among Muslims that the idea of education currently practised is not in line with the requirements of their faith.

Muslims are turning to Islamic education with roots in the idea of knowledge in Islam, and where the pedagogy emphasises the cultivation of an Islamic personality. This move is highlighted in the literature on education for Muslims where the purpose of education as presently practised is questioned as to its support for Muslim ideals, and whether it engenders the values supported by those ideals in their children. This is especially the case in Western countries that adopt a non-Islamic educational environment (McCreery *et al.*, 2007). The concern is situated in the values promoted through neoliberal educational practices in what are considered market-driven practices (Memon, 2011). Therefore, in dealing with the dilemma I describe in this chapter and the pedagogical difficulty it poses for teachers, an explanation of Islamic philosophy of education is given in the next section. The perspective of philosophy within the faith does contribute in a significant sense to the teacher's specific dilemma in teaching humanities to Muslim students (Halstead, 2004).

Questions for discussion

Why is an Islamic idea of education important for some Muslim parents?

Specifically, Muslims from this environment adopt an Islamic perspective on education for various reasons that vary from the need of Muslim youth to keep a cultural identity and a religious identity to protection from racism (Hussain, 2004). However, the explicit reason given by a majority of parents seems to be that 'youth will succumb to the secularist way of life and will leave all that is traditionally valued, i.e., the cultural and religious way of life' (Gilliat, 1994: 223). Beyond all this is the fact that Islamic education is a requirement of the faith, that such a perspective be adopted in the education of all Muslims (Halstead, 2004). This need challenges teachers in secular schools as there is an inherent tension between the Islamic idea of education and secular education that is embedded in the different emphasis both on the idea of a human being and their existence. On the one hand, Islamic education draws upon the notion of a dualistic existence of the human being, both the spiritual and the corporeal (Hussain, 2004). On the other hand, secular education is understood as a 'neutral' or 'non-ideological' approach to public schooling, where the word 'secular' is used as a synonym for an 'objective' approach to education and focuses on the need to 'socialize children into a set of naturalistic political assumptions, affections, and practices' (Arthur, 2017: 15).

Education from an Islamic perspective should contain both human intellect and divine revelation (Hussain, 2004: 318). Based on the Koran, education is to 'nurture and care for the child', to 'impart knowledge' and 'the disciplining of the mind, body and soul' and 'the teaching of good manners, ethics and politeness' (Hussain, 2004: 318). Hence, education in Islam emphasises 'the mind, the body and the soul' (Hussain, 2004: 318–319). It is viewed as 'a tool of society where the idea is

Philosophy in Islam and its limit 45

to create an ethical, moral, spiritual being who is multi-dimensional and who has a direction that is positive and healthy' (Hussain, 2004: 319).

The essence of Islamic education is that 'it comes from a theological understanding of Islam, i.e. a way of life' (Hussain, 2004: 322). Hence, Islamic education is needed because 'Muslim students require an Islamic atmosphere as well as the understanding of a worldview that recognizes the existence of a Creator in all aspects of life' (Hussain, 2004: 322) to ensure that this understanding is upheld. The tension between the two ideas has led to problems for both teachers and students. First, there is a difference in the approach to life in a cosmopolitan society (Niyozov, 2010; Waghid, 2014). 'Muslims differ in their approach to life in western society and how to relate to the non-Muslim majority' (Niyozov, 2010: 25). Second, there is dissatisfaction with public schools (Niyozov, 2010: 25) as to the knowledge taught in these schools, how it is taught and what is to be achieved by schools through education. Third, there are different issues and dilemmas faced by teachers and schools where they are simultaneously grappling with the emergence of multiple religious interpretations in the public arena, competing visions of schools and the purpose of education; how to celebrate religious discourses while promoting students' critical thinking, and autonomy; how to reconcile constructivist views of knowledge and social reality with divinely ordained immutable texts, authorities, and laws (Niyozov, 2010: 25).

Essentially then, Muslims require an Islamic education because many of the mainstream ideas within education as currently practised stand in conflict with the ideals and values that Muslim education is based on. Further, the question in literature on Islamic education is that reform of education should go beyond just preparing Muslim students for the job market (Memon and Qaiser, 2006). Hence, the movement for the Islamisation of education that involves not just making the content of lessons Islamic but also engenders Islamic ideas in all aspects of schooling and hence, education itself (Memon, 2011). The main reason for this perspective can be found in the Islamic philosophy of education.

Although philosophy is accepted as the core of education, the idea and nature of Islamic philosophy of education stands in contrast with ideas as currently practised that are based on a neo-liberal perspective. Islamic philosophy of education is described as holistic in nature (Aminuddin Hassan et al., 2010) and the emphasis is beyond knowledge for knowledge sake. In Islam there is no such thing as knowledge for the sake of knowledge. Knowledge has no value and virtue in and of itself; the actual virtue lies in bringing humankind closer to Allah. The view that knowledge is the path that leads to Allah highlights two things about Islam. First, knowledge in Islam is important for a Muslim's spiritual growth and development. Second, since knowledge is acquired through the active process of going beyond what one already knows, critical thinking is essential for a Muslim to grow intellectually and spiritually. It further suggests that intellectual growth without spiritual development is aimless wandering, and spiritual development without the intellectual component is meaningless.

Islamic education promotes Islamic ideals through the adoption of Islamic values in education so as to preserve Muslim identity through a Muslim educational environment (Ozgur, 2005). Although there are many ideas about the meaning and nature of the Islamisation of education and Islamic education found in the literature, one of the ideas that resonates with the focus of this chapter is that the purpose and focus of the Islamisation of education is about a person of *adab* or manners (Waghid, 2018). This is because the essence of the Islamisation of education is creating a good Muslim. A good Muslim is associated with having *adab*. The cultivation of *adab* requires the Islamisation of knowledge in the system or components of education in a country (Waghid, 2018). In the context of the Islamisation of knowledge, Islamic education is a system of education based on a purely Islamic epistemology. This covers all aspects of education including its fundamentals. It is founded on Islam's perspectives on key ideas including about philosophy. For Muslim students and their parents, this is what should inform the teaching and learning of subjects in a school curriculum, including the humanities.

Therefore, the pedagogical issue for humanities teachers in secular schools in teaching reason among Muslim students can be described based on a consideration within multicultural education and Islamic education respectively. From a multicultural education perspective, all students, irrespective of their backgrounds, 'should have an equal opportunity to learn at school' (Banks, 2007:3). Should they consider the Muslim students' cultural background in thinking about humanities education and its philosophy and accept that there is a limit to what they can consider is good and right? From the perspective of Islamic education, an Islamic concept of education (Halstead, 2004) where the nature of philosophy and education in Islam is different from that in a non-religious Islamic cultural environment, the goals of education may differ from or be in conflict with those of secular education. The goals of education are laid down by revealed religion and therefore have an objective quality; they do not vary according to individual opinion or experience: 'the humanities curriculum should be designed in accordance with the Islamic understanding of the nature of knowledge and the nature of human beings, especially their spiritual nature' (Halstead, 2007: 291). This suggests that teachers should consider the Islamic educational needs of Muslim students in the sense that there may be differences in the understanding of content and how it is valued in their lives based on students' Islamic faith. Based on these two considerations, the issue for teachers is whether the teaching of humanities to Muslim students should have different objectives and student outcomes, including pedagogy, in mind.

In considering this issue, and the implication for humanities teachers, we should note that the fundamental thrust of humanities and humanities subjects in a secular-based education is to teach students to think critically, with the aim of creating 'practical reasoners' (Walker, 2009). If we accept this proposition, in the text that follows I clarify why this is hindered in a significant sense for Muslim students by the place of reason in philosophy in Islam. Before that, I examine the pedagogical concern for the teaching of humanities in the context of Muslim students.

Teaching humanities and the problem among Muslim students

Following Nussbaum's (2010) model, humanities have an ethical role to play in a democracy as mentioned in the preceding section. She describes humanities in a democracy as an area that teaches children to think critically and not follow blindly. It makes them reflect on what is being said and done and to question what should be questioned; humanities stops those in authority from taking away a person's dignity. It provides them with the tools to defend their identity as persons and to sustain it. Humanities can respond to these concerns and develop the knowledge and 'capabilities' of students in ways that foster 'the value of enquiry, the ferment of doubt, a willingness to dialogue, a spirit of criticism, moderation of judgement, philological scruples, and sense of the complexity of things' (Eagleton, 2001: 12).

If we accept this description of humanities, then we can accept that 'the role of humanities is to cultivate the capability for practical reasoning and judgement and for an expanded moral imagination'; it serves 'to develop not only selves, but also attention to others and society' (Walker, 2009: 234). It is the humanities that 'teach people to think deeply and reflectively about the good life, the good society and the idea of the good' (Bérubé, 2006: 295). Humanities provides the space

Philosophy in Islam and its limit 47

for people to consider 'other selves'. This ascribes to the humanities a particular form of 'social utility' (Bérubé, 2003: 23) – not the utility of human capital that says that if education makes one a better economic producer it has succeeded, but a utility that highlights 'our struggles to grasp how things mean as well as what they mean' (Bérubé, 2003: 37). Bérubé explicates further:

> Common to all enterprises of the Humanities... is the recognition that we are in the business of deciphering, or trying to construct and deconstruct meanings that make intelligible to us some aspects of this social world that we sometimes think we know... it is useful only to the extent that humans need to know the meaning of human affairs, past and present.
>
> (Bérubé, 2003: 37)

As valuable as humanities is, it is 'heavily value-laden' (Martin, 2009: 300) – 'a field that bristles with contentious, subjective questions about aesthetics and pleasure, philosophy and governance, morality and justice, to say nothing of divinity and religious belief' (Smith, 2011: 2). As the essence of a humanities class is inquiry, the teaching of humanities requires teachers to get students to consider the content where 'any reasonable proposition can and should be debated from any reasonable angle' (Walker, 2009: 236). It demands a plurality of perspectives, both popular and unpopular, but also that none of these ought to be shielded from robust criticism or obscured by a relativism that claims all views are equal. In a humanities classroom, 'everyone is entitled to his or her opinion, and yet some opinions are more informed by the weight of empirical evidence and the historical record than others' (Walker, 2009: 236). Using Bérubé's example of a professor in the liberal arts and what he should do, it can be said that the humanities teacher's aim is to enable students to discuss and debate matters of a substantive nature through inquiry and to develop attitudes and dispositions that are open to different ideas. The teachers should try and enhance their students' abilities and desires to participate in substantive discussion in and out of school, and to enhance their abilities and desires to compose written arguments about all kinds of complex texts. One example is in the teaching of history:

> History requires us to interrogate all the available evidence, and not just choose the bits that suit us; to search for meaning and narrative in and through this evidence and our own theories; to understand but also evaluate values; to construct provisional yet truthful knowledge which may be reconfigured in the light of new evidence or new conceptualizations (for example feminism, post-structuralism, globalization, post-colonialism, and so on); and, uniquely, enables our understanding of the present through an examination of past events.
>
> (Anderson *et al.*, 2006: 251)

Hence, 'pedagogically, history ought to provoke thinking and demand that students are reflective, critical, honest, analytical and interpretive, cautious, emphatic and dialogic agents in a community of peers' (Walker, 2009: 238).

Questions for discussion

Do you find that the tenets of your beliefs or religion are related to your learning of the humanities? How?

48   *Nur Surayyah Madhubala Abdullah*

The problem for teachers in developing practical reasoners among Muslim students is that these students have come to adopt the idea that religion limits the extent to which one can reason. At this juncture I suggest that this is more than just a pedagogical problem: teachers also face a moral dilemma. They have to choose whether to accept a particularistic version of reason situated within a definition of reason as a consideration of what is an acceptable argument by 'revealed knowledge and spiritual understanding', or to understand reason in a substantive manner, i.e., one that involves a consideration of all reasonable arguments as required in the teaching of humanities.

Drawing on an example from my experience as a lecturer in teaching about the moral issue in abortion to Muslim undergraduate students, I illustrate the dilemma for humanities teachers described in the preceding paragraph. In teaching this issue, I ask all my students – and they are predominantly Muslim students – to consider whether a woman should be allowed to abort her pregnancy by asking them to discuss the moral question of a woman's right to abort the foetus. In asking this question, I encourage them to examine the facts and consider all reasons in deciding whether the woman has a right to choose. As a teacher, I face a dilemma when Muslim students seek only to consider what is a woman's right in Islamic thought about abortion and the related ideas within it, including choice and the idea of termination of life, in deciding whether a woman's action of aborting or not is right or wrong. Although they will examine other ideas, they are not willing to consider them, even if they found them compelling, preferring to choose only to consider what was justifiable in Islam about abortion. Of course, they have the right to choose what they thought was justifiable. However, I question the purposeful act of limiting themselves only to what their religion – Islam – found as an acceptable reason in the context of humanities education.

Philosophy in Islam and the limit to reason

Before going further, reason and personal autonomy are defined as to their meaning within this section. 'Reason' here refers to doing something by virtue of having reasons to do so where the reasons involve the individual and how they come to have such reasons (Smeyers, 2012). This includes persuasion. Personal autonomy means the exercise of choice by a person about what they regard as true or appropriate about some action based on rational reflection and emotional motivation. In exercising choice there is a certain willingness or an expectation that a person will change their views if autonomous judgement seems to require it. Autonomous judgement here does not discount the influence of others on our judgement, based on the idea that the authenticity of a person or his/her identity is very much tied to the people around them. Following Taylor (1994), who a person is – their values, beliefs and those that surround them – influences their attitudes to a certain degree. Thus, both reason and personal autonomy contribute to an individual's choices and both have to be considered when wanting to reveal how individuals choose relevant reasons for themselves. A certain level of autonomy of judgement ultimately lies in our hands because we make decisions based on reasoned judgement. Willingness or expectation has as its underlying presupposition the notion of rights. 'Rights' here refers to the moral imperative that human beings have the natural ability to look into what is truth. In other words, to reason includes a certain measure of emotional motivation such as belief. Rights also include the ability to 'exit', the ability of a person as an individual to make choices that include the option to reverse or change their decision based on a consideration of the same or other reasons. Thus reason does not necessarily lead only to one decision but can change and lead to an alternative decision through our rational reflection: therefore, the idea of expectation.

However, reason from the perspective of Islamic faith serves a particular purpose. In a consideration of reason in modernity, Akhtar (1990) notes that there is a traditional Islamic heretical attitude towards an intelligent and reasoned approach to religious pluralism and secular thought. He points out that 'the sole purpose of human life is the ceaseless worship of Allah' (Akhtar, 1990: 15). The truth at the end of that path is not examined in this perspective; rather what is promoted is to find the path to religious enlightenment. Fundamental to this perspective is that in Islam God is greatest (*Allah-u-akbar*). This is important to appreciate as it forms the backbone of the religion and its perspective on life and how to live, including education. In contrast, Western secularism embodies plausibility, truth and rationality. In Islam, religious pluralism and secular thought are rejected. In fact, the goal of dialogue in Islam is not reason but faith in line with the ultimate Islamic ideal: God is greatest (*Allah-u-akbar*). The traditional Islamic attitude towards an intelligent and reasoned approach to religious pluralism and secular thought is that it is heretical. Despite this, choice is recognised as important and relevant in true faith. '[W]e need to choose a direction, decide for ourselves. Muslims should look upon free choice and personal autonomy not as... a lack of knowledge to what is right' but as 'intellectual honesty' (Akhtar, 1990: 15, 72). However, there is a need to examine the truth at the end of that path. Based on the inherent belief that Islam is the truth, choice should lead true adherents to religion. The purpose of reason is to ensure that faith is pure rather than contrived. Intellectual reasoning in Islam within the realms of faith – specifically as a tool of faith and in cases of 'incompatibility of opinion' (Akhtar, 1990: 105) – becomes a philosophical tool in the service of faith. Modern-world faith and destiny are no longer the prime movers of humans, but choice and decision. 'There is no choice but to choose' (Akhtar, 1990: 20). The presupposition here is that to adopt a received view is in effect to choose our option among others. The problem in the idea of reasoning as a tool of faith is that reason is just a tool used within the boundary of Islamic faith to bring about faith in Islam. In other words, reason is used to serve faith rather than for any other purpose. This is similar to Waghid's (2011) thought in so far as both argue that faith and reason can exist in Islam because the Koran does not reject rational thought (Akhtar, 1990). However, rational thought is viewed as a way of reinforcing faith as truth.

Although Akhtar suggests that reason is a tool that can be used to serve the truth in that it can be a way of determining this truth (Akhtar, 1990: 28), reason is viewed as not differentiating between truth and falsehood but rejecting God. In addition, rational theorising is considered a sign of a lack of faith. The assumption here is that doubt cannot exist when there is faith. In Islam knowledge and faith cannot exist together. Although in the Koran the presupposition is that 'a man can possess knowledge (*'ilm*) while having faith (*iman*)', there is a resistance to this idea. Moreover, God's message is viewed as exclusive to believers although there is a view that it is 'the property of all mankind' (Akhtar, 1990: 32). Based on this view, whoever questions the Koran is not a true believer. Reflection is seen as lowering the integrity of the religion and its believers. This is because religionists argue that only those who submit to the will of God totally can interpret the Koran. Therefore, those who question it must have some ulterior motive for doing so. The trouble here is that the supremacy of religion over reason is paramount. So, although one could argue, like Akhtar, that understanding may be a precondition of faith, faith is certainly not a precondition of understanding. So it is possible for someone to have deep and extensive knowledge about the religion but not necessarily accept it. So reason and understanding are not a threat to religion and faith in it. Despite this, there is something other than knowledge that makes one believe. Akhtar refers to sympathy for the religious ideal. As he argues, reasoning is important for the believer and non-believer in order to discern the truth. Scepticism is not idolatrous (*shirk*) but a sign of a 'believing thinker' (Akhtar, 1990: 29). Reflection is limited and more of a form of 'compassionate coercion' (Akhtar, 1990: 203). The role of independent reason in Islamic faith or the role of intellect (*aql*) is relevant in order to help one believe, but it is faith that has the upper hand. Faith is the ultimate tool by which to see Allah. Reason is not necessary as the truth is already known. It is accepted that that faith demands loyalty. Therefore, the truth cannot be questioned.

Here it is necessary to appreciate the fundamentalist's preoccupation with *shirk* – the sin of practising idolatry or polytheism – and its importance in Islamic faith *viz.* 'There is no God but God'. The main tension between Islam and secular thought on the notion of reason is that reason is minimally understood, thus limiting the conceptualisation of reason. Although dialogue can be had about different understandings of things, the place of reason in dialogue is to ensure true faith. It is not to ensure the wellbeing of the individual. This is seen in the way the idea of reason in Islam restricts personal autonomy and the modification of ideas and thoughts. Although Islam does allow for dialogue, it limits it and can in some extreme cases hinder it. Despite Akhtar's suggestion that it need not be a hindrance to dialogue, the premise that only reason can preserve faith and, more importantly, his argument that reason is important for the wellbeing of faith, there are still questions as to whether this can be acceptable in a substantive sense as 'reason'. In conclusion, it can be said that the fundamentalist's preoccupation with *shirk* and its importance in Islamic faith *viz.* 'There is no God but God' is a major obstacle to personal autonomy, and hence to the meaning and possible extent of reason for Muslim students from RICE.

The idea of reason in the Islamic faith suggests that a person has limited personal autonomy. They can choose what is considered acceptable but cannot make a choice. There is a limit to what a person can choose because they are bound by some rule that they must choose it, so there is no real choice. Real choice does not mean a person is free to do whatever they want. They do not have an actual opportunity to choose without compulsion as choice is limited to those who are acceptable within the faith's understanding. Choosing what is acceptable is not having a reason to do something. It is about being told what to choose. This conceptualisation of reason is problematic when it comes to teaching Muslim students to reason in the humanities classroom. Smeyers (2012) in his critique of Waghid's (2012) use of the word 'reason' in the pre-Islamic Arabs' embracing of Islam as an example of reason being accepted in Islam, points out that the word 'reason' refers to more than just this. Although persuasion can be part of that 'reason', he points to the Islamic understanding of reason as ignoring an individual's dignity as a person. Reason is open to interpretation, and reason, especially when it is about the self-worth of a person (Taylor, 1994), means more than just a process. Waghid's (2012) response is that it is 'reasons of faith' when people embrace a religion. However, this perspective suggests that reasons are limited to what makes them choose and not what choices they make. It moves the locus of control from the individual to others such as faith. Constructing reason in this manner ignores the idea that an individual is a rational being. The individual's capacity to think and consider what is acceptable as a justification for something is not based on the individual's own thinking. It is based on what has been decided is good. It lowers the dignity of the person and removes the right to make a decision from their hands. This interpretation of reason suggest that choice is about making the right choice, which endorses what the Islamic faith considers is right and good. To reason is to come to a realisation and acceptance that the truth is belief in God and his truth and to avoid *shirk*. In this sense, it is not the wellbeing of the person that is the purpose of education but the religion.

Questions for discussion

Based on the argument made in this section, why do you think humanities teachers face difficulties in getting Muslim students from a strong RICE to consider reason which are contradictory to Islam in discussion and debates on issues in humanities classroom?

An implication for pre-service teachers

One important implication from the preceding section is that humanities teachers should consider other ways to help Muslim students from a strong RICE to appreciate the idea of reason to a fuller extent. Of course, from a multicultural education perspective, the faith of students and its influence on their ways of understanding should be respected and provided for in the curriculum and pedagogy of humanities. The problem can only be resolved by framing humanities education on an Islamic philosophy of education (Halstead, 2007). However, I argue that such a conceptualisation only serves to limit the idea of humanities subjects and restricts Muslim students' exposure to ideas that may stand in conflict with Islamic faith and its precepts. In this way it affects their wellbeing and their ability to live in a multicultural society, as they lack experience of discussion and debate with those who may not share similar ideas. It also restricts those not from such an environment from considering an Islamic perspective on issues. However, the ultimate goal of humanities education should be to ensure that the dignity of the student as a person in a polity is provided for through education. Humanities teachers may need to explore approaches that can reach the aim of humanities without alienating or neglecting Muslim students.

Conclusion

The problem of teaching Muslim students to reason in a humanities classroom is a pedagogical problem. It requires clarity, and a philosophical consideration of the problem offers this. With clarity, pre-service humanities teachers can properly understand what informs this problem. In the process they can think about what approach might be suitable in a multicultural classroom with Muslim students in meeting the aims of humanities classroom. By doing so, they can meet the need of the humanities classroom, which is to help all students contribute to the wellbeing of themselves and society by empowering the individual to engage in discussion and debate to safeguard the selves as individuals.

However as shown in the preceding section, there is a challenge when we consider that the problem for Muslim students from a strong RICE rests in something that is fundamental to their religion. It informs their attitudes and disposition to reason in the humanities classroom. Therefore, a challenge for pre-service humanities teachers is to consider what approach may help avoid conflict between faith and the individual. One possible way is to consider adopting approaches that allow greater flexibility of thought while promoting discussion that allow all students to consider different and conflicting reasons in a fuller manner.

Summary

- The problem for humanities teachers in getting some Muslim students from strong religious Islamic cultural environments to adequately reason in discussion and debates on issues in humanities is situated in the understanding of philosophy and notion of reason within it.
- Based on an account of a conservative fundamental understanding of philosophy in Islam, there are limits to the idea of reason and how it can be applied in discussion and debates that involve issues of human wellbeing.
- Some Muslim students, particularly those from religious Islamic cultural environments that adhere to conservative Islamic tenets, are reluctant to engage in a full manner in discussion and debates on issues in the humanities classroom.
- Restrictions such as this could affect the humanities teachers in helping all their students to achieve their wellbeing in a polity.
- Pre-service teachers should ensure that their approach to pedagogy adequately engages with the problem faced by these students while ensuring the nature of humanities is maintained for their wellbeing.

Recommended reading

Banks, J. A. and Banks, C. A. M. (eds.) (2007) *Multicultural Education: Issues and Perspectives* (7th edition). New York: Wiley.

Rissanen, I. (2014) *Negotiating Identity and Tradition in Single-Faith Religious Education: A Case Study of Islamic Education in Finnish Schools.* New York: Waxmann.

Zukerman, R. and Shook, J. R. (eds.) (2017) *The Oxford Handbook of Secularism.* New York: Oxford University Press.

References

Akhtar, S. (1990) *A Faith for All Seasons: Islam and the Challenge of the Modern World.* London: Bellew.

Aminuddin H., Asmawati S., Zainal Abiddin N., Habsah I., and Haziyah H. (2010) The role of Islamic philosophy of education in aspiring holistic learning. *Procedia Social and Behavioral Sciences* **5**: 2113–2118.

Anderson, C. and Day, K. with Michie, R. and Rollason, D. (2006) Engaging with historical source work: practices, pedagogy and dialogue. *Arts and Humanities in Higher Education* **5**(3): 243–263.

Arthur, J. (2017) Secular education and religion. In P. Zukerman and J. R. Shook (eds.), *The Oxford Handbook of Secularism.* New York: Oxford University Press.

Au, W., Brown, A. L. and Calderón, D. (2016) *Reclaiming the Multicultural Roots of Multicultural Education.* New York: Teachers College Press.

Banks, J. A. (2007) Multicultural education: characteristics and goals. In J. A. Banks and C. A. M. Banks (eds.), *Multicultural Education: Issues and Perspectives* (7th edition). New York: Wiley.

Bérubé, M. (2003) The utility of the arts and humanities. *Arts and Humanities in Higher Education* **2**(1): 23–40.

Bérubé, M. (2006) *What's Liberal About the Liberal Arts?* New York and London: Norton.

Brighouse, H. (2005) *On Education.* New York: Routledge.

Carr, D. (2005) Personal and interpersonal relationships in education and teaching: a virtue ethical perspective. *British Journal of Educational Studies* **53**(3): 255–271.

Eagleton, T. (2001) 'For the hell of it'. Review of N. Bobbio (2000) *In Praise of Meekness:* Essays in ethics and politics. *London Review of Books* **23**(4): 30–31.

Gilliat, S. (1994) *Perspectives on the Religious Identity of Muslims in Britain.* PhD Thesis. University of Wales, Lampeter.

Halstead, M. (2004) An Islamic concept of education. *Comparative Education* **40**(4): 517–529.

Halstead, J. M. (2007) Islamic values: a distinctive framework for moral education? *Journal of Moral Education* **36**(3): 283–296.

Hussain, A. (2004) Islamic education: why is there a need for it? *Journal of Beliefs & Values* **25**(3): 317–323.

Martin, P. (2009) Aspects of teaching and learning in arts, humanities and social sciences. In H. Fry, S. Ketteridge and S. Marshals (eds.), *A Handbook for Teaching and Learning in Higher Education* (3rd edition.). New York: Routledge.

McCreery. E., Jones, L. and Holmes, R. (2007) Why do Muslim parents want Muslim schools? *Early Years: An International Research Journal* **27**(3): 203–219.

Memon, N. (2011) What Islamic school teachers want: towards developing an Islamic teacher education programme. *British Journal of Religious Education* **33**(3) pp. 285–298.

Memon, N. and Qaiser, A. (2006) The pedagogical divide: toward an Islamic pedagogy. Available at: https://farooq.files.wordpress.com/2007/05/nadeem_memon_and_qaiser_ahmad_2006_-_the_pedagogical_divide.pdf (Accessed 20 August 2018).

Niyozov, S. (2010) Teachers and teaching Islam and Muslims in pluralistic societies: claims, misunderstandings, and responses. *Journal of International Migration and Integration* **11**(1): 23–40.

Nussbaum, M. (2010) *Not for Profit: Why Democracy Needs the Humanities.* New Jersey: Princeton University Press.

Ozgur, N. (2005) *Top Ten Hot Issues for Islamic Schools.* Paper presented at ISNA Education Forum March 2005. Available at: www.isna.net/conferences/educationforum/2005downloads.html (Accessed 20 August 2018).

Rissanen, I. (2014) *Negotiating Identity and Tradition in Single-Faith Religious Education: A Case Study of Islamic Education in Finnish Schools.* New York: Waxmann.

Rissanen, I. (2015) Finnish teachers' attitudes to Muslim students and Muslim student integration. Available at: http://tampub.uta.fi/bitstream/handle/10024/96413/GRADU-1418288702.pdf;sequence=1 (Accessed 20 August 2018).

Shah, S. (2018) 'I am a Muslim first…'. Challenges of *Muslimness* and the UK state schools. *Leadership and Policy in Schools*, 24 January 2108.

Smith, D. (2011) Teaching humanities in the Arabian Gulf: toward a pedagogical ethos. *Learning and Teaching in Higher Education: Gulf Perspectives* **8**(2): 1–12.

Smeyers, P. (2012) Review of Yusef Waghid, 'Conceptions of Islamic education: pedagogical framings'. *Studies on Philosophy of Education* **31**: 91–98.

Taylor, C. (1994) The politics of recognition. In A. Gutmann (ed.), *Multiculturalism: Examining the Politics of Recognition.* Princeton: Princeton University Press.

Waghid, Y. (2011) Conceptions of Islamic education: pedagogical framings. In *Global Studies in Education. Volume 3.* New York: Peter Lang.

Waghid, Y. (2012) Response to Paul Smeyers's review of 'Conceptions of Islamic education'. *Studies in Philosophy and Education* **31**(1): 99–101.

Waghid, Y. (2014) Islamic education and cosmopolitanism: a philosophical interlude. *Studies in Philosophy and Education* **33**(3): 329–342.

Waghid, Y. (2018) Reconceptualising Madrasah Education: towards a radicalised imaginary. In Mukhlis Abu Bakar (Ed.) *Rethinking Madrasah Education in a Globalised World.* London: Routledge.

Walker, M. (2009) Making a world that is worth living: humanities teaching and the formation of practical reasoning. *Arts and Humanities in Higher Education* **8**(3): 231–246.

5 Children's epistemic rights and hermeneutical marginalisation in schools

Lisa McNulty and Lucy Henning

Introduction

This chapter introduces concepts to help educators reflect on children's status as knowers in schools. In particular we are concerned with how adults in schools understand children's capacity to know and make decisions about what is worth knowing. In schools, adults evaluate children's knowledge. This knowledge includes curriculum knowledge, the child's knowledge that they bring from home, and their knowledge about their experience of being schooled. From a schooled perspective, children cannot evaluate this knowledge for themselves.

The main concept we introduce is that of 'hermeneutical marginalisation', which we have borrowed from feminist literature. In philosophy, the term 'hermeneutical' is concerned with how something might be interpreted. The term was coined by Miranda Fricker in her influential book *Epistemic Injustice* (Fricker, 2007). Hermeneutical marginalisation occurs when a group of people are unable to access knowledge resources that frame the way their experiences can be interpreted. In this chapter, the group of people we are concerned with is children, who are unable to access knowledge resources – for example, teaching textbooks, curriculum outlines and education policy documents – that frame the way their school experiences are interpreted. Children rarely have access to these powerful resources; yet they are used to define what they should know, do and understand at each stage of their school careers. Without such access, children's social experiences can only be understood from the perspective of those who *do* have access to such knowledge resources; that is, adults.

In short, we suggest that hermeneutical marginalisation is embedded in the structures and systems that are found in schools. Such marginalisation might seem necessary; after all, children have had far less experience than adults and have had less time to acquire knowledge. However, we suggest that hermeneutical marginalisation can become an injustice if it leads to an avoidable disadvantage for the child. As Karin Murris (2013: 248) puts it, the potential harm here is that 'the power relations and structural prejudice [concerning the child as a knower]… undermine child's faith in their own ability to make sense of the world, and constrain their ability to understand their own experiences'. We suggest that an ethical consideration for teachers is whether and when hermeneutical marginalisation might amount to an injustice and what their role might be in avoiding it.

To explore this, we start from the position that hermeneutical injustice is inevitable in schools. We do this because Fricker suggests that there are philosophical gains in 'concentrating on the normality of injustice' and goes on to argue that 'one of the gains [of recognising the normality of injustice]... might be that we achieve a better grasp of what is required in practice to operate in a way that works against it' (Fricker 2007: 7). To suggest that hermeneutical injustice is inevitable in schooling is not to attribute blame to any individual, but to offer those working in education a philosophical tool for thinking about the systems of schooling in which they work in critical ways. We therefore begin by showing how hermeneutical injustice can be seen to be embedded in systems of mass schooling before introducing further tools and concepts to help teachers think critically about the ethical implications of how children and their knowledge practices are perceived in everyday classroom life.

Hermeneutical injustice in education

In this chapter, when we talk about 'schools' and 'systems of schooling', we are referring to mainstream state education institutions that emerged in Europe in the eighteenth and nineteenth centuries and are found throughout the world. Authors studying children and childhood have argued that, in order to justify the introduction of such systems of mass schooling, changes were needed to public opinion about the place of children in society. Significantly, Hendrick (1997: 46) argues that 'the school played a pivotal role in the making of a new kind of childhood'. He discusses how, in late nineteenth-century Britain, young children were no longer to be seen as valuable workers or wage earners for their families but as dependent, ignorant and vulnerable, requiring socialisation into the world rather than already being a part of it (Hendrick, 1997). If children were understood in this way, then the role of the school, and of the adults who worked in it, could be seen as moving children from this state of ignorance to one of knowledge. The point here is that embedded in schools is the notion that children are ignorant, and it is only adults who can make them knowledgeable.

It is helpful here to turn to the work of Michel Foucault, who wrote about what he calls the 'disciplinary technologies' of institutions of state such as schools. His concept of 'seriation' helps us to understand how schools are structured to move children from ignorance to knowledge. For example, in *Discipline and Punish* Foucault (1977: 159) describes how, within nineteenth-century European schools, the 'time of training... [was] detach[ed] from the adult time, from the time of mastery'. He takes an example of the division of the process of learning to read into levels that children would move through until they reached a terminal point. In short, children would progress towards knowledge, accumulating it in stages defined by adults. This means that adults in systems of schooling understand children to be 'learning' rather than 'doing', always lacking some element of knowledge until a point in the future is reached when adults judge that the knowledge has been acquired. As children proceed towards this point, further judgements are made by adults. These include the aspects of knowledge the child should acquire, the stages in their schooled life at which children should acquire this knowledge, and what 'knowing' this knowledge will look like.

This seriation is seen in the structure of current school curricula. For example, in England the current National Curriculum for English defines what children should be taught with respect to reading in each year (or two years) of their school careers from the ages of five to 11 in primary schools. This document stresses that the relationships to sounds in spoken words (phonemes) and letters on the page (graphemes) must be taught first. So at age five (Year 1) children should be taught to: 'apply phonic knowledge and skills as the route to decode words' (DfE, 2014: 10), and at age six (Year 2) children should be taught to 'continue to apply phonic knowledge and skills as the route to decode words until automatic decoding has become embedded and reading is fluent' (DfE, 2014: 17).

In England, the children's proficiency in this word-reading skill is tested at the end of Year 1 and children who do not demonstrate this proficiency must retake the test in Year 2. Thus, the use of phonics to read is a stage all children in English primary schools must pass through on their route from 'ignorance' about reading to 'knowledge' as they progress through the education system, regardless of what those children themselves might find useful when reading. Adults therefore determine what is helpful in supporting a child's reading and how successful or otherwise the children are in developing this knowledge, based upon their efficiency in using phonics. Judgements of children's phonic knowledge can inform how they are grouped with other children for teaching, and whether or not they need special tuition to help them 'catch up' with their peers. It can also determine the reading matter they have access to for teaching purposes. For example, to return to the National Curriculum, in Year 1 children are to 'read aloud accurately books that are consistent with their developing phonic knowledge and that *do not require them* to use other strategies to work out words' (DfE, 2014: 10, emphasis added). In terms of reading then, within the institution of schooling, the seriation of the reading curriculum by adults determines what children should read, how they should read it, where they should read it and who they should read it with.

This is not to criticise phonics as a method of teaching reading. Rather it is to demonstrate the presence of hermeneutical marginalisation in schooling. In terms of reading, young children are considered 'ignorant' and must progress through a series of carefully defined stages of teaching before they can be considered to have knowledge. These stages are controlled by adults and children have no say in how they are determined, regardless of how useful they might find other strategies and approaches for reading. Children cannot assess their own progress in official tests, cannot write curriculum documents, and cannot suggest teaching methods that they feel will support their further progress. In schooling, children receive knowledge, they do not create it.

Questions for discussion

Can you think of examples from your own experience of schooling that could be understood as 'hermeneutical marginalisation'? Do you think they were avoidable?

An ethical question is whether this hermeneutical marginalisation can be seen as an injustice. After all, with their limited experience of the world, how could children know more about what is good for them than adults? An example here may be of use. This observation is drawn from our experience of observing children reading in schools. The child observed, Maurice (pseudonym), adopts strategies for reading that are helpful to him as someone actively engaged in the process of learning to read. However, these strategies do not conform to those that adults expect him to use.

> Whilst reading with his group, Maurice realised he could swivel all the way around on his seat and did so every time he got stuck on a word. When the child sitting next to him had difficulty reading the word 'I'm', Maurice helped him by explaining that it was the same as another word on the page. Maurice also repeated each sentence out loud to himself once the group had read it.

Here Maurice displays an understanding of what is required to read. He repeats sentences back to himself to check he has understood what he reads. He helps other children in his group and recognises key words in the text. And he has found a way of making the experience enjoyable, swivelling around on his seat whenever he needs to think about a word he does not initially recognise.

This is not to suggest that all children should be taught the same strategies as Maurice for reading, or that Maurice' approach is the most efficient or effective for tackling the text. But it is to suggest that these reading strategies, working with other children, physical movement, word recognition and repeating sentences, are helpful to Maurice at this point in his life. This is the knowledge Maurice brings to reading. However, while curriculum documents and assessment materials prepared by adults value some of these strategies, in this case recognising individual words and repeating sentences back to check for understanding; others, such as working with another child and physically moving during the reading process, are not mentioned. Furthermore, Maurice's positioning within schooling as an 'ignorant' child requiring beneficial adult intervention in his reading does not allow assessing adults to consider the active engagement Maurice takes in the practices of developing his own reading and supporting those of his friend. Thus, Maurice is hermeneutically marginalised in that the value of his own knowledge practices is not recognised in the way the English school curriculum frames learning to read; and he cannot access these knowledge resources in ways that would support a change in this framing.

We argue that in this example of a child's reading practices, marginalisation does amount to an injustice. Adults' choices of how to assess Maurice's reading can affect him in all the ways described above, such as the type of teaching he receives and the books he has access to. If such assessments do not recognise Maurice's own knowledge and experience of reading then he may be disadvantaged in his access to particular curriculum materials, the type of educational support he is offered or judgements made concerning his success at learning to read. It is also worth considering whether Maurice is disadvantaged while the more powerful group – the adults – is *advantaged*. In this instance, in classrooms where adults must maintain their status as knowledge authorities, as well as maintaining an orderly and calm learning environment, Maurice talking to a fellow pupil and swivelling on his seat might be viewed as 'disruptive' and 'disorderly'. The group reading task would run much more smoothly were Maurice to sit still and listen to the teacher. It is therefore advantageous to the adult as a teacher of reading if Maurice behaves in ways expected within school. This example therefore illustrates what we mean when we suggest that hermeneutical marginalisation of children in schools can become hermeneutical injustice if young children's knowledge practices are not recognised and understood.

We argue that the concepts of hermeneutical marginalisation and hermeneutical injustice are therefore useful tools to support teachers in reflecting on the ethics of their classroom practice. To support such reflections, we now introduce some further concepts to support teachers' reflection on their educational practices. The first of these is 'epistemic norms', a term from Thomas Green's work which we suggest is an important concept when considering how children, within their peer culture, weigh up the potential value of new knowledge before deciding whether or not to accept it. The second is that of epistemic 'rights in trust', which is concerned with the tensions between children's rights in the present and those of their future selves.

Epistemic norms

The term 'epistemic' means pertaining to knowledge and knowing. For the purposes of this argument, our understanding of epistemic norms is informed by Green's (1999) discussion of social norms in relation to the formation of conscience in his book *Voices: The Educational Formation of*

Conscience. We suggest that children, not in general but as a group of children in a particular class in school, might hold their own epistemic norms against which they judge the knowledge and skills that adults teach them. Epistemic norms are to do with the evaluation of knowledge. For example, a group may have norms regarding standards of evidence, an agreement as to what counts as a good reason to believe or do something, and a shared understanding of who or what counts as an authoritative source of knowledge. They might also have norms regarding the appropriate boundaries of the task set and an agreement as to which questions, ideas or methods are central and/or relevant. We have discussed the assumption within schooling that adults have epistemic authority and thus count as the only authoritative source of knowledge in schools. This might be seen as an epistemic norm of systems of mass education. However, here we present an example that suggests that children's in-school peer cultures might also have epistemic norms against which they evaluate the knowledge that adults teach them.

This example is drawn from an ethnographic study of a class of five-year-old children being taught to read and write in a London primary school (Henning, 2017). This class had been together within the institution for 16 months, so had had ample time to form a peer culture. In the example here, a teacher is taking a group reading session. The teacher is not the children's usual teacher: she is the researcher conducting the study. The children have been taught to read using the phonics method outlined in the English National Curriculum documents described above. Thus, they have learnt to decode each word on the page, grapheme (letter) by grapheme and then blend it together to form a word. So, in the example of reading the word 'cat' the children would look at each grapheme separately in the first instance, saying /c/ then /a/ then /t/ before blending it together to make 'cat'. In the teaching system the children are familiar with, performing this 'blending' takes priority and questions about the meaning of what they are reading are only addressed once this process has been completed.

In this instance, the teacher has asked the children to complete this blending process, but each time they read a sentence they are told to go back and read the whole sentence again, without decoding each word – like Maurice was doing in the reading example above. The children were told this would help them read 'like a story'. The teacher's aim was that the children would read back each sentence with flow, helping them to gain more of a sense of the meaning of what they were reading. After the teaching input of this reading session, the children began reading in pairs. During the reading this exchange was heard between two of them – Daniella and Alison (pseudonyms). The word 'Unison' means that Daniella and Alison are reading together and letters between slashes (e.g., /b/) mean the children are sounding the word out:

1	Unison:	He
2	Alison:	looked /b/ /u/ /c/
3	Unison:	buck
4	Daniella:	back
5	Alison:	back
6		at the
7	Unison:	big /b/ /oys/
8	Alison:	[We have to read it again?
9	Daniella:	[after
10		because we don't have time?

Children's epistemic rights 59

The children begin (lines 1–7) with the practice of reading that they have been taught within their usual lessons, blending the words 'back' and 'boys'. However, when Alison reminds Daniella that the teacher has asked them to read it back – the new practice – Daniella refuses on the grounds that they 'don't have time'. We suggest that Daniella has two reasons not to accept the new practice. First, her existing experience of reading in school has determined the appropriate boundaries and central methods of reading – in this case the application of phonic knowledge – and this new practice lies outside of them. Second, in order to re-evaluate this new practice, Daniella might want an explanation from someone she already regards as an authoritative source of knowledge; that is, her usual teacher. In this instance the new task boundaries are proposed by someone who is not the children's usual teacher and this may demotivate Daniella from accepting the change.

We argue that a third reason for Daniella's reluctance to try the new practice lies in the children's in-school peer culture. US sociologist William Corsaro observed children in kindergartens and elementary schools in Italy and the US. He described how young children produce peer cultures within which they work to reproduce practices that enable them to make sense of the world around them. In schools, children are gathered together in similar age groups over extended periods of time. These institutions are therefore places where peer cultures can flourish. As Corsaro (2015: 23) explains, children 'strive to interpret or make sense of their culture and to participate in it. In attempting to make sense of the adult world, children come to collectively produce their own peer worlds and cultures.' To return to Green's discussion of 'epistemic norms', we suggest that the peer cultures that form in classes of children in schools develop their own epistemic norms in order to make sense of the adult world. In this case, data from the wider PhD study shows the children in Daniella and Alison's class valued producing a *quantity* of literacy work. For example, in writing lessons, the children counted up how much they had written and compared the total with their peers. In handwriting they valued producing as many lines of letters as possible. When reading with a group, the children liked to keep up with their peers, and not fall behind in the book. An epistemic norm within the peer culture was therefore that children should produce sizeable quantities of work and keep up with the wider class in literacy lessons. If Daniella followed the cover teacher's suggestion that she and Alison read each sentence twice, she would be sacrificing this quantity of literacy work and thus would deviate from the epistemic norms of her peer culture; that is to say, of the group's understanding of what is important in engaging with literacy activities in school.

Questions for discussion

What epistemic norms might you expect to observe in schools?

Thus, in this case, Daniella and Alison were aware that their in-class peer culture recognised three epistemic norms that may have applied to the situation. First, the perception that reading consists of sounding out the phonemes of each word, as they had been taught. Second, the need for reference to the class teacher, the authoritative source of knowledge for literacy learning in the classroom. Third, the accepted peer culture norm that it was desirable to complete the greatest quantity of literacy work in the time allotted. Both children were aware of these norms and their disagreement centred around which one should be prioritised. To return to Green, we note here that he uses the term '*voices* of conscience' in the plural. In this case, the different epistemic norms the children are aware of are 'speaking' against one another, and the children have to decide which to 'listen' to. Here we return to the notion of hermeneutical marginalisation. The following aspects of children's schooled experience are not usually recognised in adult framings of that experience: first, that children may form peer cultures that hold their own epistemic norms; second, that these epistemic norms may differ from those of schooling; and third, that peer culture epistemic norms may frame the children's choices about how to engage with teaching.

In the case of Daniella and Alison, we suggest that the hermeneutical marginalisation of children in schooling places both the teacher and the children at what Fricker (2007: 151) terms a 'cognitive disadvantage'. The teacher is at a cognitive disadvantage because she lacks the conceptual tools – in this case the notions of epistemic norms and children's peer cultures – to form an adequate assessment of the children's knowledge practices. The children are at a cognitive disadvantage because they are only offered the adults' tools for understanding and ascribing value to their own knowledge practices. Their experience of reading can therefore only be seen, in Fricker's terms, 'through a glass darkly' with 'at best ill-fitting meanings to draw on in the effort to render them intelligible' (Fricker, 2007: 148). Neither the children nor the adults have the conceptual tools to discuss their differing perceptions of the task in hand. In particular, the lack of recognition of children's epistemic norms means that teachers may not have the appropriate concepts needed to understand children's collective knowledge practices.

We have already suggested that hermeneutical marginalisation can become an injustice if it leads to an avoidable disadvantage for the child. In this instance, the injustice may arise in terms of the assessment of Daniella's abilities as a reader. Daniella's status as an 'unknowing' child within the system of schooling means that her own knowledge can only be evaluated in terms of what adults consider important, and within adult framings of her experience of what it is like to read as a child. If Daniella is only assessed according to her ability to meet the stated learning intention of the lesson – to repeat each sentence – then in schooled terms she does not fulfil the assessment criteria, regardless of the processes she engaged in to reach her decision to reject the new knowledge practice.

It is useful here to return to the work of Karin Murris (2013), as she offers the concept of 'epistemic modesty', which teachers may find helpful when making considered decisions about whether they hold enough information to make a viable assessment of the child's knowledge practices. Murris (2013: 250–251) suggest that teachers have 'epistemic modesty' when they

> accept that their (and all) knowledge is limited and that they can also learn from children. They need to be open to what they have not heard before, and to resist the urge to translate what they hear into the familiar.

We therefore suggest that an ethical consideration for teachers working within schooled epistemic norms is to have epistemic modesty when confronted with unexpected challenges to their authority as knowers. An aspect of this modesty would involve thinking about the child's own epistemic experience, including the norms they are accustomed to draw on when evaluating the new knowledge practices that teachers offer them.

Epistemic rights in trust

Here, we introduce another concept that may help educators reflect on children's status as knowers in schools. In the previous two sections, we have argued for the existence of children's own

Children's epistemic rights   61

knowledge practices, which may differ from those expected by teachers, and that these should be respected. We are claiming therefore that children in schools have epistemic rights, including the right to be recognised as knowers both as individual children and within their in-class peer cultures; and as capable of creating and disseminating knowledge. We claim that these are important ideas that teachers can use to reflect upon the ethical aspects of their pedagogical practices.

In this final section, we introduce a note of caution. Our discussion so far may suggest that children should make their own decisions about how to engage with educational materials, rather than deferring to the preferred epistemic norms of their teachers and schools. However, at the beginning of the chapter we suggested that hermeneutical marginalisation might seem necessary in schools because children have had far less experience of the world than adults and thus have had less time to develop their knowledge practices. It is important to remember that children's knowledge practices are in a constant state of development as they encounter new information. To emphasise this, we return to William Corsaro, whom we used to explain the idea of children's peer cultures. Corsaro argues that children engage in processes of 'interpretive reproduction', through which they reproduce peer cultures. We have argued that the peer cultures that children form in school may involve the formation of epistemic norms, which the children use to evaluate the knowledge and skills that they are taught. However, in Corsaro's work these peer cultures are linked to children's development which involves 'a reorganisation of knowledge that changes with children's developing cognitive and language abilities and with changes in their social worlds' (Corsaro and Eder, 1990: 200).

Thus, as children grow and change, and the world around them grows and changes, their epistemic norms might grow and change. Therefore, the criteria they use to evaluate knowledge at the age of five may not be the same as that which they use at the age of six. Teachers then must consider carefully whether respecting the epistemic norms young children hold in the present might work against their longer-term epistemic rights.

This caution about children's development means that, as with children's rights in general, it might be defensible to grant children epistemic rights that are different from those granted to adults. Typically, children are granted fewer freedoms, and more protections, than adults. This is because of their currently limited capacity to exercise some freedoms safely and appropriately. It is generally agreed that the right to drive, or drink or marry can wait until children are older and their capabilities have developed. Children are granted more protections than adults because of their greater vulnerability. For example, most people concede that children have the right to be provided with certain goods such as food, shelter and protection, which adults are generally expected to provide for themselves (unless there are circumstances preventing them from doing so). Given that children's intellectual capacities are still developing, these differences plausibly apply to epistemic rights, too.

One valuable insight comes from the ethicist Joel Feinberg, in his influential article 'The child's right to an open future' (2007). Feinberg argues for the existence of a specific category of children-only rights, which he refers to as 'rights in trust'. These are rights that the child cannot exercise until they are older, but which could be violated in advance, in which case the child will never be able to exercise them properly. Feinberg demonstrates the concept rather gruesomely, as follows:

> the right to walk freely down the public sidewalk [is already held by] an infant of two months, still incapable of self-locomotion. One would violate that right in trust now, before it can even be exercised, by cutting off the child's legs.
>
> (Feinberg, 2007: 113)

It is plausible for us to include certain epistemic rights as 'rights in trust'. Education can be conceived as developing epistemic autonomy for the future. Having received a suitable education, the child grows into an adult who can make informed and independent evaluations and decisions. Part of this must involve the child being encouraged to practise making such evaluations and decisions. Nonetheless, it might be justifiable to limit their current autonomy if their choice is a potential threat to their future autonomy.

Significantly, this idea is present in the United Nations Convention on the Rights of the Child (1990). Article 12 (Respect for the Views of the Child) states that when adults are making decisions that affect children, children have the right to say what they think should happen and have their opinions taken into account. However, the Convention 'encourages adults to listen to the opinions of children and involve them in decision-making – not give children authority over adults' (UNICEF, n.d.: 2). The caveat that the children are not to be given authority over adults is not a limitation of the child's rights, instead, it forms part of the right in question. The child has a right to be involved in the decision-making process; however, this involves 'the views of the child being given due weight in accordance with the age and maturity of the child' (United Nations, 1990: 5). This requires that adults retain ultimate responsibility, while making a considered judgement of how far the child can contribute to the decision-making process. The child is then able to gradually learn about decision-making and therefore make better decisions as an adult. Had they been excluded from the decision-making process altogether, they would not have developed this skill. Had they been given sole responsibility for the decision, without guidance from an adult, then they would *also* not have developed this skill. The balance exists to protect their *future* autonomy.

It seems plausible that when a teacher has a choice between respecting a child's current intellectual autonomy and their future intellectual autonomy, the latter ought to take priority. One powerful example of this is offered by Ladson-Billings of a child who refuses to come to the writing table in their US elementary school classroom.

> In one of the combination kindergarten and first-grade classrooms, a little African-American girl, Shannon, regularly refused to participate in the literacy activities. Daily the students were required to come up with one sentence about some question or activity that was the result of the opening morning exercises. The teachers called the children together on the carpet and discussed various things – what they did over the weekend, what they were planning for Halloween, what their favourite meal was. After the discussion the students were instructed to talk with the children at their tables to select one sentence they would all attempt to write. Many children could not accurately write the sentences they chose, but most could put down a beginning sound or a beginning and ending sound. Indeed, students were encouraged to use invented spellings so that teachers could see how close their writing paralleled what they heard and knew. Shannon could not write because she could make no sense of the sound-symbol relationship. Shannon did not know how to match sounds with letters and rather than be embarrassed about her inadequacies, she became defiant. 'I ain't writin' nuthin'' was a familiar refrain from her. Each day, the response of the teacher was to say, 'All right, Shannon, maybe you will feel like writing tomorrow'. Were we witnessing an act of racism?
>
> (Ladson-Billings, 2005: 140–141)

Shannon's repeated decision not to participate in schooled writing activities was 'respected' by the teacher, and the decision was left in her hands as to whether it was worth her effort to learn to write. This decision would mean that Shannon's difficulties with sound–symbol relationships at the age of six could severely restrict her intellectual freedom as an adult. Ladson-Billings posits that, in the instance described above, the teacher's decision to leave Shannon be may have been influenced by a racist assumption: an unjustified yet self-fulfilling scepticism about her potential for future epistemic autonomy. Ladson-Billings suggests that such decisions made by educators can, in effect, give children 'permission to fail'. In this instance then, the teacher's judgement of how far Shannon could contribute to the decision-making process might be seen as a violation of Shannon's epistemic rights in trust.

Questions for discussion

How might educators think about the specific nature of children's epistemic rights and ensure that these rights are respected?

We suggest that the concept of epistemic rights in trust can help educators balance their respect for the child's own epistemic norms and practices with a concern for their future epistemic autonomy. In instances such as that described above, a consideration of children's epistemic rights in trust can justify limiting a child's epistemic rights temporarily, to ensure that they have the greatest possible intellectual independence as adults.

Conclusion

In this chapter, we have argued that educators should reflect on children's status as knowers in schools. We conclude that the hermeneutical marginalisation of children in schools might be mitigated if teachers were to apply the tools and concepts discussed in this chapter to their peda-gogical practices. These tools include: Fricker's concept of hermeneutical marginalisation and its potential to become an injustice; Green's concept of epistemic norms and how these might develop in the in-class peer cultures that William Corsaro describes; Murris' concept of epistemic modesty, which may support teachers in respectfully recognising children's epistemic norms; and, finally, Feinberg's concept of 'rights in trust', which can help educators balance children's epistemic rights in the present against their potential intellectual autonomy as adults. In particular we suggest it is important for teachers to recognise that there is a diversity of epistemic norms in the classroom, which must be recognised and accounted for when choices are made about how to impart new knowledge and skills to children. This will help teachers ensure the educational experiences they offer children meet the requirements enshrined in the United Nations Convention on the Rights of the Child – in particular that adults should listen to the opinions of children when making decisions, specifically those that are concerned with how to evaluate young children's knowledge practices.

Summary

- The structure of schools makes hermeneutical marginalisation an inevitable part of children's school experience.

64   *Lisa McNulty and Lucy Henning*

- This can become hermeneutical injustice if educators do not reflect carefully on their knowledge practices and those they observe in the children they teach.
- This reflection should include a consideration of epistemic norms, both those within schools and those held within children's' peer cultures.
- Educators can exercise epistemic modesty, by which they remain open to the ideas and knowledge practices of children.
- This work needs to be balanced with a concern for children's epistemic rights in trust.

Recommended reading

Corsaro, W. (2015) *The Sociology of Childhood* (4th edition). Sage: London.
Feinberg, J. (2007) The child's right to an open future. In R. Curren (ed.), *Philosophy of Education: An Anthology.* Oxford: Blackwell Publishing.
Fricker, M. (2007) *Epistemic Injustice: Power and the Ethics of Knowing.* Oxford: Oxford University Press.
Murris, K. (2013) The epistemic challenge of hearing child's voice. *Studies in the Philosophy of Education* **32**(3): 245–259.

References

Corsaro, W. (2015) *The Sociology of Childhood* (4th edition). London: Sage.
Corsaro, W. and Eder, D. (1990) Children's peer cultures. *Annual Review of Sociology* **16**: 197–220.
DfE (2014) *English Programmes of Study: Key Stages 1 and 2.* National Curriculum in England. Available at: www.gov.uk/government/uploads/system/uploads/attachment_data/file/335186/PRIMARY_national_curriculum_-_English_220714.pdf (Accessed 27 March 2018).
Feinberg, J. (2007) The child's right to an open future. In R. Curren (ed.), *Philosophy of Education: An Anthology.* Oxford: Blackwell Publishing.
Foucault, M. (1977) *Discipline and Punish.* London: Penguin.
Fricker, M. (2007) *Epistemic Injustice: Power and the Ethics of Knowing.* Oxford: Oxford University Press.
Green, T. (1999) *Voices: The Educational Formation of Conscience.* Notre Dame, IN: Notre Dame Press.
Hendrick, H. (1997) Constructions and reconstructions of British childhood: an interpretive survey, 1800 to the present. In A. James and A. Prout (eds.), *Constructing and Reconstructing Childhood.* Abingdon: Routledge.
Henning, L. (2017) *Young Children, Schooling and Literacy: An Ethnographic Study of Literacy Practices in a London Primary School.* PhD Thesis, Kings College, London, Maughan Library.
Ladson-Billings, G. (2005) Reading, writing and race: literacy practices of teachers in diverse classrooms. In T. McCarty (ed.), *Language, Literacy, and Power in Schooling.* New Jersey: Lawrence Erlbaum Associates Inc.
Murris, K. (2013) The epistemic challenge of hearing child's voice. *Studies in the Philosophy of Education* **32**(3): 245–259.
United Nations (1990) *The United Nations Convention on the Rights of the Child.* New York: UNICEF. Available at: https://downloads.unicef.org.uk/wp-content/uploads/2010/05/UNCRC_united_nations_convention_on_the_rights_of_the_child.pdf?_ga=2.93123165.1778062091.1522148837-2072015468.1511718707 (Accessed 27 March 2018).
UNICEF (n.d.) *Fact Sheet: A Summary of the Rights Under the Convention on the Rights of the Child.* New York: UNICEF. Available at: www.unicef.org/crc/files/Rights_overview.pdf (Accessed 27 March 2018).

6 Consciousness, physicalism and vocational education

Terry Hyland

Introduction

A perennial problem in vocational education and training (VET) concerns the vocational/academic divide and the subordinate, second-class status of vocational pursuits. Commentators have examined the causes of this core problem – historical, cultural, economic, structural and philosophical – in some detail, and suggested remedies for bridging the divide and upgrading vocational studies have been proposed by educators from a wide range of disciplines (Silver and Brennan, 1988; Pring, 1995). Approaching the principal issues in this domain from within philosophy of mind and consciousness studies, this chapter examines the possibility of healing the divisions by means of arguments such as those by Chalmers (1996) and Strawson (2006, 2016) which seek to address the 'hard problem' of consciousness by suggesting that all material phenomena incorporate a mental or experiential component.

Supplementing this collapsing of the mind–body dichotomy, the importance of embodied learning – drawing on the work of Merleau-Ponty and Dewey (O'Loughlin, 1995; Gibson, 2016) – will be employed to emphasise the vital role of the physical, the manual aspects of human experience in gaining knowledge and understanding in all domains. Against this background, it will be suggested that recent work on craft and craftworking – both empirical and theoretical – can provide a valuable source of support for attempts to heal the vocational/academic divide and enhance the status of vocational pursuits. The foregrounding of the manual and physical aspects of craftwork are of the first importance since they point to a domain of activity which is, as Marchand (2016: 3) puts it, 'one that is ethical, guided by high standards of quality, and characterised by direct, unmediated connections between mind, body, materials, and the environment'.

Consciousness and hard problems

Susan Blackmore (2011: 25) has defined the so-called 'hard problem of consciousness' in terms of the question: 'how can objective, physical processes in the brain give rise to subjective experience?' Within philosophy of mind, this 'mind–body problem' goes back at least as far as Descartes and his infamous dualist analysis of the mental and physical worlds which leaves unexplained exactly how they may be connected (Searle, 2004). More generally it results in the longstanding problem of how to explain subjective mental phenomena such as hopes, wishes, intentions, etc. – or simply what it is like to be something (Nagel, 1974) – in a world that, according to science, consists

66   *Terry Hyland*

only of material objects, forces and processes. A number of solutions in the form of reconciliation strategies have been proposed in relation to the hard problem, including the idea that there is no serious problem since the mind and mental events are simply what the brain does (hence a form of extended materialism; see Dennett, 1991) or, alternatively, that all material objects are imbued with forms of consciousness which evolve more fully within complex systems (Chalmers, 1995, 1996). On this latter model, Strawson's special version of 'panpsychism' (2006) – which argues for the primacy of conscious experience in our understanding of all features of the material world – provides some fascinating insights of direct relevance to the educational enterprise.

Having rejected dualism and materialism as solutions to the mind–body problem, Searle (2004: 110) suggests that:

> The general character of the relation of consciousness to the brain, and thus the general solution to the mind-body problem is not hard to state: consciousness is caused by microlevel processes in the brain and realized in the brain as higher-level or system features. But the complexity of the structure itself, and the precise nature of brain processes involved, remains unanalyzed by this characterisation.

However, the problems set out by Searle here have been described by Chalmers (1995) as merely the 'easy' problems of consciousness, that is, how to map brain functions onto human thinking and behaviour. Such 'easy' problems include the integration of information by a cognitive system, the focus of attention, and the reportability of mental states, but such essentially functional processes leave us with the question of 'why the performance of these functions is accompanied by experience' (Chalmers, 1995: 5). This is labelled by Chalmers the 'central mystery' (1995: 5) of consciousness and gives rise to the 'hard problem' of how to understand and explain the undisputed existence of subjective mental states in a world that science tells us consists only of physical objects.

In tackling this latter problem, Chalmers has advanced a number of speculative solutions, such as that the fundamental building blocks of the universe utilised by science – space, time and mass, for example – may have to be extended to include consciousness as a primary entity or universal property of everything in the cosmos. This is described as a 'nonreductive psychophysical' notion, which supplements physical theories by explaining how 'physical processes are connected with and dependent upon the "properties of experience"' (Chalmers, 1995: 17). In more recent work, Chalmers (2013: 1), utilising arguments originally considered by Hegel and Russell, has reflected on theories of 'panpsychism' – the thesis that some 'fundamental physical entities have mental states' – and concluded that they merit 'serious and sustained attention' (2013: 20).

These speculations are very similar to Strawson's (2006) attachment to such solutions of the hard problem, which he describes as forms of 'real physicalism'. Real physicalists, according to Strawson, 'must accept that experiential phenomena are physical phenomena' (2006: 1), and he supports the assertion concerning the emergence of experiential or consciousness properties from physical, non-experiential characteristics through, *inter alia*, the analogy of the emergence of the liquidity of water from non-liquid H_2O molecules. A core aspect of the, admittedly speculative and hypothetical, argument is that we do not know enough about the nature of the physical to argue – as dualists since Descartes and most post-Cartesian philosophers have held – that the physical and the mental are irrevocably distinct and irreconcilable. Making use of arguments by Eddington and Russell, Strawson asks 'on what conceivable grounds do so many physicalists simply assume that

Consciousness and vocational education   67

the physical, in itself, is an essentially and wholly non-experiential phenomenon?' (2006: 3). Citing Eddington:

> 'To put the conclusion crudely', he says, 'the stuff of the world is mind-stuff'—something whose nature is 'not altogether foreign to the feelings in our consciousness'. 'Having granted this', he continues, 'the mental activity of the part of the world constituting ourselves *occasions no surprise*; it is known to us by direct self-knowledge, and we do not explain it away as something other than we know it to be – or, rather, it knows itself to be. It is the physical aspects [i.e., non-mental aspects] of the world that we have to explain.
>
> (Strawson, 2016: 13, emphasis in original)

In later writings drawing on recent work in quantum physics, Strawson (2016) re-asserts the position that, although we all know intimately and at first-hand what mental experience and consciousness is, the 'nature of physical stuff, by contrast, is deeply mysterious, and physics grows stranger by the hour'. He goes on to observe that:

> The nature of physical stuff is mysterious *except insofar as consciousness is itself a form of physical stuff*. This point, which is at first extremely startling, was well put by Bertrand Russell in the 1950s in his essay *Mind and Matter*: 'We know nothing about the intrinsic quality of physical events,' he wrote, 'except when these are mental events that we directly experience.' In having conscious experience, he claims, we learn something about the intrinsic nature of physical stuff, for conscious experience is itself a form of physical stuff.
>
> (Strawson, 2016: 1–2, emphasis in original)

Such solutions to the hard problem of consciousness advocated by Chalmers and Strawson – particularly in the non-dualist connections made between the physical and the mental aspects of experience – may be employed to highlight aspects of the hard problem of vocationalism, since they question the mental/physical dualism that is at the heart of intellectualist prejudices which divide thinking from doing, theory from practice and value the former more highly than the latter (Crawford, 2009; Marchand, 2016).

The hard problems of vocational education and training

A recent article in *The Economist* exploring the background to the McKinsey Report (2014) on the high rate of European youth unemployment noted the fact that many students pursuing academic courses would have preferred vocational ones but were discouraged by the 'low status' and 'lack of prestige' of vocational options on offer (Schumpeter, 2014). In a similar vein, a presumed 'bias against vocational education' was cited in a recent piece praising the current Finnish approach to tackling youth unemployment through systematic technical education (Subrahmanyam, 2014). Of course, none of this is new, for the problems of the vocational/academic divide and the inferior status of the vocational go back at least as far as the last quarter of the nineteenth century when the Royal Commission on Technical Instruction was convened to make recommendations for the improvement of the English system in the light of superior European models (Musgrave, 1964).

68 Terry Hyland

> **Questions for discussion**
>
> Examine recent policy documents on education at either school or post-school level. Can you detect any bias against the vocational or in favour of the academic in any of the policy recommendations?

In spite of what Keep (2006: 47) has described as a 'permanent revolution' in VET policy initiatives in recent times, the central problems are still with us and – according to recent research reports (Coughlan, 2015) – the 'recurrent theme' of low status and investment in vocational programmes prevails as a global problem. Coughlan expresses the position in graphic terms:

> Everyone says it's a good thing and it's vital for the economy. But – and there is always a but, it's still the academic pathway that has the higher status. As the saying goes, vocational education is a great thing… for other people's children. Another side of this conundrum is that there is more need for vocational education than ever before. Youth unemployment, particularly among those without training or qualifications, is a scourge in many countries. But at the same time employers are warning about skills shortages and not being able to find the right staff.
>
> (Coughlan, 2015: 1)

Given the importance of the vocational in education systems throughout the world, how can we explain such anomalies? A wide range of reasons has been offered to explain the intractability of these problems, in addition to a vast array of suggested solutions. The following (necessarily overlapping) list is representative, although by no means exhaustive:

Structural – rigid curriculum divisions between vocational and academic subjects (Walsh, 1978; Hyland, 2014a); centralist planning and control in England as opposed to the state partnership models on the Continent (Keep, 2006).

Historical – aristocratic ethos derived from ancient Greek ideas held by powerful interests which defined and established state education systems, and still control their direction (Castle, 1967; Schofield, 1972).

Cultural – social class interests differentiating curricula in terms of intellectual and manual pursuits (Kenneth Richmond, 1945; Hyland, 1999).

Biological – manual pursuits directly linked to evolutionary survival became less valued than intellectual/aesthetic activities far removed from everyday toil (Pinker, 1997; Hyland, 2002).

Philosophical – deriving from the ideas of Plato and Aristotle, the intellectualist thrust (with its attendant devaluing of practical studies) of much of mainstream Western philosophy upon which modern education systems were built (Curtis and Boultwood, 1970; Wilds and Lottich, 1970).

Reconciliation strategies designed to bridge the divide are legion and their principal prescriptions follow from which particular form of diagnosis of the problem is favoured. An interesting early example can be found in Sir John Adams' (1933: 50) *Modern Developments in Educational Practice*, which insists that 'all education must affect our future life either adversely or favourably, and to that extent all education is vocational, as preparing us for the vocation of life'. A more recent example of this sort of strategy is Silver and Brennan's (1988) advocacy of 'liberal vocationalism' in higher education, which involves the introduction of hybrid courses combining arts and science subjects, in addition to the incorporation of liberal/general educational elements in vocational programmes in fields such as engineering and business studies (not unlike the general/liberal studies introduced into British further education vocational programmes from the 1950s to the 1980s: e.g., Hyland, 1999; Simmons, 2014). Pring (1995: 189) has also suggested a number of similar remedies for bridging the gap in this domain, arguing that:

> 'Liberal' is contrasted with 'vocational' as if the vocational, properly taught, cannot itself be liberating – a way into those forms of knowledge through which a person is freed from ignorance, and opened to new imaginings, new possibilities; the craftsman who finds aesthetic delight in his craft, the technician who sees the science behind the artefact.

In the past few decades, suggested remedies for the chief ills in this sphere have come thick and fast in the form of UK government reports or think-tank reviews and prescriptions and – since they have been examined at length elsewhere (Winch, 2000; Wolf Report, 2011) – I will not rehearse them all again here. As mentioned at the outset, the chief concern of the present analysis – while not denying the relevance of the other characteristics of the hard problem listed above – is with the broadly philosophical aspects of the vocational/academic divide, and to this end it is suggested that recent work on craft and craftworking has much to offer in terms of both theoretical insights and suggestions for the reform of educational practice.

Craft and education

According to Marchand (2016: 3, 8), craft is said to belong to a 'polythetic category' of concepts that are messy and 'not absolutely fixed'; such a category 'is one in which any of its members possess some, but not necessarily all, the properties attributed to that category'. This description seems to owe a great deal (although unacknowledged) to Wittgenstein's (1974: 32) notion of 'family resemblances', which explains how omnibus conceptions ('games' is Wittgenstein's famous example) may belong to a common group – not by virtue of any common characteristic, but by features that 'overlap and criss-cross' as with 'various resemblances between members of the same family'. Thus, one type of craft may involve meticulous planning and systematic execution, another spontaneous creation, another novel use of materials, and yet another theoretical inventiveness and imagination. Noting the fact that 'craft, crafting and crafted are commonly employed to describe or praise ideas well-conceived, activities well-executed, or things well made', Marchand moves from denotation to connotation in the ironical observation that contemporary usages of craft (typically employed by advertisers) tend to 'rouse longing for an alternative, idealised way of living and working – one that is ethical, guided by high standards of quality, and characterised by direct, unmediated connections between mind, body, materials, and the environment' (Marchand, 2016: p.3).

Broadly similar accounts are offered by Sennett (2009: 20), who suggests that 'all craftsmanship is founded on a high degree of skill' typically involving 'about ten thousand hours of experience', and that craftspeople 'are dedicated to good work for its own sake'. Crawford (2009: 20) also makes much of the idea of craftworking as 'being good at something specific [...] dwelling on a task for a

70 Terry Hyland

long time and going deeply into it, because you want to get it right'. Moreover, both these accounts refer in different ways to the hard problem in this sphere which – in Sennett's (2009: 11) description of the 'troubled craftsman' – regrets the fact that:

> History has drawn fault lines dividing practice and theory, technique and expression, craftsman and artist, maker and user; modern society suffers from this historical inheritance. But the past life of craft and craftsmen also suggests ways of using tools, organizing bodily movements, thinking about materials that remain alternative, viable proposals about how to conduct life with skill.

Crawford (2009: 21) is concerned to emphasise the 'cognitive demands of manual work' and, within the context of craftwork, explains that:

> Skilled manual labour entails a systematic encounter with the material world, precisely the kind of encounter that gives rise to natural science. From its earliest practice, craft knowledge has entailed knowledge of the 'ways' of materials – that is, knowledge of their nature, acquired through disciplined perception. At the beginning of the Western tradition, *sophia* (wisdom) meant 'skill' for Homer: the technical skill of a carpenter, for example.

Contemporary conceptions of craftwork seek to challenge such dualistic thinking – and their philosophical underpinnings – in a number of ways.

Problem-solving

Marchand (2016) argues that solving problems of various kinds is at the heart of craftwork, and its central place is illustrated by reference to a wide range of accounts of the multifarious and ingenious ways in which problems are conceived and solved in different craft domains. Solving problems in the production of digital videography – explains Durgerian (2016: 94), for example – involves technical knowledge of recent innovations in the field, in addition to having a grasp and feel for the history of film-making and a heightened sensitivity to diverse audiences. Often solutions to problems in the field call for 'stargazing breaks', which allow 'unconscious processes to work' on non-linear difficulties. The field of bike mechanics, on the other hand, is described by Martin (2016: 73) as

> An interesting case for the craft paradigm because the problems that the bike mechanic works with are not the result of his or her own processes going awry; rather, problems are the starting point from which the mechanic approaches the craft.

Martin provides a fascinating account of how workers go about repairing the many faults that can befall cycles and how – in the workshop – there can be 'severe limitations of language as a basis for problem solving' (2016: 83). In the context of the 'social habit of work in the mechanics' workshop' a form of 'group problem solving' emerges in which communication about faults and problems is conveyed through diagrams, direct interaction with tools and bike components and, at times, 'fruitful misunderstandings' (Martin, 2016: 80, 84).

Consciousness and vocational education 71

This apparently *ad hoc* and context-independent aspect of craftwork – which Crawford (2009: 21ff.) suggests gives a 'cognitive richness' to skilled physical work– arises from the need to constantly adapt tools and materials (and our own bodily functions) to the ever-changing demands and requirements of making, altering and repairing objects. It is also connected with what Pye (1968: 5) has called the 'workmanship of risk' which is inherent in processes that often (as in designing, manufacturing and repairing) involve techniques and skills that are adaptive and emergent as the craftsperson responds to problems encountered. Sennett's (2009: 55ff.) historical account of the craft 'workshop' from the medieval guilds to the Industrial Revolution provides a graphic illustration of how uncertainty and risk have shaped the development of work in a wide range of craft fields.

Intellectual versus manual work

Crawford's (2009: 38) fond and careful description of his own journey from PhD and think tank to motorcycle repair shop was partly an attempt to escape the uniformity of a deskilled post-Fordist society which had led to the 'degradation of blue-collar work'. His response to this – described as an attempt to show how 'manual work is more engaging intellectually' than 'knowledge work' (2009: 5) – takes the form of a critique of the divisions between intellectual and manual work against the background of the way Taylorist scientific management and automation has degraded the nature of so much productive work. A strand of this thesis takes the form of the attempt to challenge the assumptions that 'all blue-collar work is as mindless as assembly-line work and […] that white-collar work is still recognisably mental in character' (Crawford, 2009: 31). Crawford questions relentlessly the standard educational distinctions between propositional/theoretical and practical/ operational knowledge and – by examples drawn from the activity of chess players, firefighters and electricians – demonstrates the importance of tacit, personal and intuitive knowledge in all human activity so that 'thinking and doing' are inseparable not distinct processes (2009: 161ff.).

Sennett (2009: 280ff.) offers similar observations in his description of 'operational intelligence', and Marchand, in a recent dialogue with Nigel Warburton for the *Big Ideas in Social Science* collection of readings (Edmonds and Warburton, 2016), defines his role as a craft worker, researcher and writer in terms of addressing the misguided and harmful distinction (attributed here to Leonardo da Vinci) between manual labour and intellectual work reflected in the division made between 'craft-work' and 'fine art'. Criticising an education system in which 'working with the hands is perceived as a fallback position – a second choice', he defines his mission in terms of 'challenging the mind-body dichotomy' and explains that his 'research aims to explore and expose the complexity of knowledge that is actually involved in handwork, and thereby raise its status in the eyes of educationalists, the government, and the general public' (Marchand in Edmonds and Warburton, 2016: 124). This holistic view of knowledge – which is very similar to Dewey's (1916/1966: 306) instrumentalist conception employed in his attempts to break down the 'antithesis of vocational and cultural educa-tion' based on the false oppositions of 'labour and leisure, theory and practice, body and mind' – is well illustrated in the collection of accounts of craftworkers edited by Marchand (2016), in which practitioners operating in diverse fields describe their activities.

Describing the relationship between designer, artist and gaffer (the glassblower) in glass produc-tion, for instance, O'Connor and Peck (both glassblowers at New York Glass) explain how contem-porary craftworkers in the field now take on multiple roles in imagining and designing 'prototypes'

72   Terry Hyland

of objects (Marchand, 2016: 33–49). Craftwork is thus foregrounded as being essentially a 'process [...] anchored in the gaffer's tacit knowledge of the craft, the organisation of labour, and the product end-goal'. The process from imagination and prototype design to final production is complex, drawing on many forms of knowledge and experience, and one in which 'discovery and the generation of new problems can be part of the problem-solving process in prototyping' (Marchand, 2016: 48). Similarly, Gowlland's (2016: 183–196) account of the work of ceramics manufacturing in Yingge, Taiwan, explains how 'embodied problem solving' serves, in practice, to break down the 'distinction between design and workmanship' since the 'intellectual' and the 'pragmatic' aspects of ceramics production are realised at all stages of the process. The experience led Gowlland to conclude that:

> It is striking that the discourse in Yingge resembles so closely the distinctions made in Europe and North America concerning the dichotomy between the work of the mind and that of the hands. It is important for scholars (and artisans) to deconstruct such discourses to reveal the relations of power revealed within.
>
> (Gowlland, 2016: p.195)

Recent research by Vaughan (2017) on craft apprentices in the field of carpentry revealed similar findings. As Vaughan observed about the apprentices participating in the project: 'Their vocational thresholds were based on getting to grips with an increasingly sophisticated interplay between their minds, bodies, cross-trade interactions, and their physical environment of climate, tools and materials' (2017: 547).

Handwork, learning and education

As indicated earlier, various forms of working with the hands are at the core of the theory and practice of craftwork. Dewey's 'theory of occupations' (DeFalco, 2010) places various forms of craft and handwork activities – wood and metalwork, designing, making and using tools – at the centre of a project designed to break down the antagonisms between liberal and vocational pursuits. The overriding importance of the hand in human development generally is now widely acknowledged and has broad implications for all forms of learning. Noting Kant's famous remarks that the 'hand is the window on to the mind', Sennett (2009: 149ff.) devotes a whole chapter in his study of craftsmanship to the role of the 'intelligent hand' in human evolution in general and human achievement in the arts, humanities and sciences in particular. The extraordinary versatility and flexibility of the hand – in terms of prehension, sensitivity of touch, opposable thumb dexterity, hand-wrist forearm capability and hand/eye coordination – is described in painstaking detail and demonstrated to be a primary component in human achievement and progress. Sennett (2009: 178) concludes that 'the unity of head and hand [...] shaped the ideals of the eighteenth-century Enlightenment: it grounded Ruskin's nineteenth century defence of manual labour'.

Crawford (2009: 21) similarly asserts the importance of manual work in that it 'entails a systematic encounter with the material world' which is at the heart of the search for knowledge in all its forms. Recent work by Leader (2016) on the role of the human hand throughout history serves to supplement and consolidate the foregrounding of handcraft in learning and education. Our hands, observes Leader, 'serve us' in countless ways:

Consciousness and vocational education   73

They are the instruments of executive action, our tools. They allow us to manipulate the world so that our wishes can be fulfilled. We show our hands to vote, to seal an agreement, to confirm a union, to such an extent that the hand is often used to stand for the human agent that bears it.

(Leader, 2016: Kindle loc. 55)

Leader takes us on a fascinating kaleidoscopic tour of a broad sweep of history and culture to show the importance of the hand in shaping the human story, which includes recent changes in the use of our hands in response to digital technology and the communications revolution.

In the light of the crucial importance of working with the hands, we may ask why handwork and related manual skills seem to have so little prominence in contemporary education systems. Indeed, as Crawford (2009: 27) wryly observes: 'Given the intrinsic richness of manual work – cognitively, socially, and in its broader psychic appeal – the question becomes why it has suffered such a devaluation as a component of education.' The general answer to this question can, of course, be found in the standard explanations for the vocational/academic divide and inferior status of vocational pursuits examined above. However, there are more particular factors at work here as well, and they may be located in another general divide in education: that between mind and body or, using old-fashioned curriculum terminology, divisions between the cognitive, affective and psychomotor domains of education.

Although curriculum planners and designers have had access to the detailed descriptions of the cognitive, affective and psychomotor components of learning since they were analysed systematically in the construction of taxonomies of educational objectives by Bloom *et al.* (1956) and Krathwohl *et al.* (1964), mainstream educational textbooks – having mentioned the affective and psychomotor domains – tend to quickly forget them in their concentration on purely cognitive aims (Weare, 2004; Hyland, 2011). This oversight has generated a cognitive/affective divide as wide as the vocational/academic divisions and led to an overly intellectualist conception of the educational task, which marginalises values and emotions in teaching and learning (Hyland, 2014b). Moreover, the neglect of the psychomotor domain – the importance of the body and physical operations in the learning process has reinforced such false dualisms and perpetuated the undervaluation of handwork and the practical nature of vocational studies.

Questions for discussion

Have a look at the curriculum research and writings that refer to the cognitive, affective and psychomotor domains of education. Why do you think the psychomotor domain concerning the manual and physical aspects of learning has been marginalised and neglected in contemporary education systems?

Recent work within philosophy of education – drawing mainly on the writings of Merleau-Ponty (1962) – has attempted to bring the 'embodied subject' back into educational discourse as a way of remedying the undermining of the physical in the learning/teaching encounter. O'Loughlin (1995: 8), for example, asserts that:

It seems to me that bringing bodies back into the picture has been crucial for education. As teachers, educational theorists and the like, we need to direct our attention to the realities of

74 *Terry Hyland*

bodies in discursively constituted settings. Western philosophy can be seen as the history of successive periods of Western humanity's cultivation of its own 'mind'.

In attempts to embody the cultivation of mind, similar arguments have been proposed in terms of the role of bodies in relation to language learning (Okui, 2013), and all this serves to underscore the arguments of Crawford and Sennett noted above that it is largely through our physical acting on the world that we may develop knowledge, understanding and skill. Such a conception may be used to justify Crawford's (2009: 31) idea of manual work which involves the 'learning of aesthetic, mathematical and physical principles through the manipulation of material things', and has echoes in Marchand's (2016:12) interpretation of craftworking as one that 'counters the classical emphasis on internal "mind" operations and challenges the separation drawn between the mental arithmetic and the physical doing, by making the sensing, feeling, acting, and socialised body the locus of its enquiry'.

Embodied learning and the vocational curriculum

Such a perspective that foregrounds the crucial role of craft and handwork in learning can provide a solid philosophical foundation for a re-imagining and reframing of the roles of the mental and the physical, the theoretical and the practical in educational activity and, thus, help to pave the way for a long-overdue resolution of the hard problem of VET and the potential dissolution of the vocational/academic divide. However, the segmentation of vocational and academic learning is deeply entrenched in educational systems from school to university (Webb *et al.*, 2017) and the source of inequality of esteem – or as Billett (2014: 3) puts it 'the societal standing of occupations and the means of their preparation' – has historically been in the hands of 'privileged others'. In order to challenge this entrenched privilege, there is a need to explain how the suggested philosophical realignment of vocational/academic studies might be translated into policy and practice.

Drawing on the ideas of Crawford, Sennett and Merleau-Ponty outlined above, it is suggested that a Deweyan conception of 'embodied learning' may be useful in translating this philosophical perspective into practical curriculum proposals. Baldwin (2004: 130) explains how, in his later writings, Merleau-Ponty came to see the 'body, as a "chiasm" or crossing-over (the term comes from the Greek letter chi) which combines subjective experience and objective existence', and it is this notion of the importance of bodily experience which is found in Dewey's philosophy of vocational education. As Gibson (2016: 121) suggests, both Dewey and Merleau-Ponty viewed understanding, experience and the self in terms of 'activity which comes to know itself through its actions in the world'. However, although Dewey's instrumentalist notion of vocational education through 'occupations' – with an occupation understood as any 'mode of activity [...] which reproduces or runs parallel to some form of work carried on in social life' (Dewey, 1965: 132) – fits well with the ideas of craft and manual work discussed earlier, such activity would need to take account of contemporary developments in leisure, work and society.

Recent work in philosophy of education on technology education has referred to a 'transformative epistemology' in which technology is viewed as 'an extension of human capability' through the manipulation of technical artefacts which ultimately 'rests upon the social interactions that arise through engagement with the process of their development' (Morrison-Love, 2017: 29). This echoes the more practical, operational perspectives offered by Marchand and Crawford referred to earlier, concerning the importance of the physical – especially manual handwork – in coming to know the world. Both Sennett and Leader emphasise the importance of the intelligent hand in human evolution and progress, and Leader in particular investigates the changing use of hands in the digital age of the internet, smartphone and personal computer. He relates fascinating anecdotes about the impact of the newly acquired requisite hand movements of scrolling, pinch-to-zoom and multi-touch gestures (which the Apple corporation tried but failed to patent, since patents already existed!), along with the attendant 'massive increases in computer- and phone-related hand problems, as the hand and wrist are being used for new movements that nothing has prepared them for' (Leader, 2016: Kindle loc. 31). Against such physical teething problems must be placed the incredible increase in physical dexterity displayed in particular by young people – riding bicycles or carrying loads with one hand while texting effortlessly with the other – which are seemingly acquired with very little practice or formal tuition. Motivation for learning is, of course, crucial here and this is supplied by the increasing need to gain access to social media and video games, a need that now appears to be as basic as food, water and security (Harari, 2017).

Strawson's panpsychism is founded on a monistic thesis that there is only one sort of 'stuff', i.e., physical stuff, in the universe, and this incorporates an emergent experiential or mental element (hence his claim to be a 'real physicalist' in accounting for subjective consciousness). The claim is that 'consciousness is itself a form of physical stuff' (Strawson, 2016: 1) and is out there in the world. If we add to this the related argument proposed by Clark and Chalmers (1998: 18) about the 'extended mind' – the notion that human cognition does not end with the brain/body but is connected with its environment through an 'active externalism' linking us to data and algorithmic sources located in devices of all kinds (digital resources, tools of all kinds, and the internet) – then we can interpret social media in terms of an extremely powerful instance of this cognitive extension. Moreover, embodied learning takes on a crucial role in this story since we can only gain access to the extended mind located in smartphones and computers through particular physical operations in which minds and hands are inextricably conjoined. (These links are explored by Bostrom (2016) in his hypotheses about the evolution of 'superintelligence'). The notion that the world is at our fingertips should remind us that fingertips are connected to hands manipulated by bodies and minds. (Indeed, Barad's (2007) discussion of Bohr's philosophy-physics shows how knowledge at the fundamental quantum level depends on the physical arrangements and operations executed through the agency of the human body–mind.)

Given all this, it is natural that educators in general – and vocational educators in particular – would take an active interest in exploiting the learning potential of social media. Most of the studies in this field have examined ways in which social media can facilitate learning (Callaghan and Bower, 2012), or how, in vocational contexts, the development of social media skills can help students to select, interpret and manage data of all kinds (Valentin et al., 2015). However, given the vast range of content incorporated in diverse fields, there is also enormous scope for accessing and utilising data on craft- and handworking of the kinds recommended by Marchand (2016: 27) in his project of transforming 'the widespread undervaluation of manual work into recognition and appreciation for the creative intelligence and ingenuity involved in craft'. Leaving aside the superficial and fashionable marketing gimmicks for craft coffee, craft beer and the like, the coverage of worthwhile crafts and craft-like activities – such as interior decorating, repairing and renovating, gardening, cooking, painting, pottery, videography, game construction, playing musical instruments and so on – on television and digital platforms such as YouTube has never been so widespread or easily accessible.

76   *Terry Hyland*

Utilisation of such material – in either formal curriculum modules such as art, design and technology or, ideally, as a free-standing dimension of all subjects – offers unlimited potential for realising the ideals of craft and manual work recommended by Crawford and Marchand.

Question for discussion

Given the importance of the physical and manual emphasised by writers on craftwork, can you think of ways of introducing more handwork into the curriculum areas you are most concerned with?

Conclusion

Historically entrenched privilege and innate educational conservatism have militated against the achievement of such an ideal in the past, but attempts to enhance the status of VET for the majority of the generally underachieving and most disadvantaged students who predominate on vocational courses are still high on the agenda of educators and policy-makers (Avis and Orr, 2016; House of Commons Education Committee, 2014). The recent report on the transition from school to work by the House of Lords Select Committee on Social Mobility (2016: 49) decried the 'unspoken snobbery in favour of academic qualifications rather than vocational qualifications', and made a raft of worthy recommendations for the improvement of this state of affairs. However, like countless similar proposals by educators and policy-makers since the establishment of compulsory education in Britain in 1870, such recommendations are likely to remain at the level of pious and hopeful rhetoric until there are radical cultural and attitudinal shifts in educational philosophy and practice of the sort espoused by the writers on craft and manual work outlined above.

Summary

- Relevance of the mental/physical dichotomy to vocational studies and its suggested solution in recent work in consciousness studies.
- Causes of the vocational/academic divide and subordinate status of vocational pursuits.
- Examination of craftwork as a means of bridging the vocational/academic divide and enhancing the status of the vocational.
- The importance of the manual and physical in education and its realisation in embodied learning.
- Re-asserting the importance of the physical and the embodied learning typified in craftwork in vocational education and training.

Recommended reading

Fuller, A. and Unwin, L. (2011) Apprenticeship as an evolving model of learning. Special Issue of the *Journal of Vocational Education and Training* **63**(3): 261–266.

Hager, P. and Hyland, T. (2003) Vocational education and training. In N. Blake, P. Smeyers and P. Standish (eds.), *The Blackwell Guide to the Philosophy of Education*. Oxford: Blackwell.

Pilz, M. (ed.) (2017) *Vocational Education in Times of Crisis: Lessons from Around the World*. Dodrecht: Springer.

References

Adams, J. (1933) *Modern Developments in Educational Practice.* London: University of London Press.

Aristotle (1962) *The Politics.* Trans. T.A. Sinclair. Harmondsworth: Penguin.

Avis, J. and Orr, K. (2016) HE in FE: vocationalism, class and social justice. *Research in Post-Compulsory Education* **21**(1–2): 49–65.

Baldwin, T. (ed.) (2004) *Maurice Merleau-Ponty: Basic Writings.* London: Routledge.

Barad, K. (2007) *Meeting the Universe Halfway: Quantum Physics and the Entanglement of Matter and Meaning.* London: Duke University Press.

Billett, S. (2014) The standing of vocational education: sources of its societal esteem and implications for its enactment. *Journal of Vocational Education and Training* **66**(1): 1–21.

Blackmore, S. (2011) *Zen and the Art of Consciousness.* Oxford: Oneworld Publications.

Bloom, B. S., Engelhart, M. D., Furst, E. J. Hill, W. H. and Krathwohl, J. R. (1956) *A Taxonomy of Educational Objectives: Handbook I – The Cognitive Domain.* New York: Longman, Green Co.

Bostrom, N. (2016) *Superintelligence.* Oxford: Oxford University Press.

Callaghan, N. and Bower, M. (2012) Learning through social networking: the critical role of the teacher. *Educational Media International* **49**(1): 1–17.

Castle, E. B. (1967) *Ancient Education and Today.* Harmondsworth: Penguin.

Chalmers, D. (1995) Facing up to the problem of consciousness. *Journal of Consciousness Studies* **2**(3): 200–219.

Chalmers, D. (1996) *The Conscious Mind.* Oxford: Oxford University Press.

Chalmers, D. (2013) Panpsychism and panprotopsychism, *2013 Amherst Lecture in Philosophy.* Available at: http://consc.net/papers/panpsychism.pdf (Accessed 8 July 2018).

Clark, A. and Chalmers, D. (1998) The extended mind. *Analysis* **58**: 10–23.

Coughlan, S. (2015) Vocational education's global gap. *BBC News,* 16 December. Available at: www.bbc.com/news/business-35061496 (Accessed 8 July 2016).

Crawford, M. B. (2009) *Shop Class as Soulcraft: An Inquiry into the Value of Work.* New York: Penguin Press.

Curtis, S. J. and Boultwood, M. E. A. (1970) *A Short History of Educational Ideas.* London: University Tutorial Press.

Edmonds, D. and Warburton, N. (eds.) (2016) *Big Ideas in Social Science.* London: Sage.

Defalco, A. (2010) An analysis of John Dewey's notion of occupations: still pedagogically valuable? *Education and Culture* **26**(1): 82–99.

Dennett, D. (1991) *Consciousness Explained.* New York: Little Brown.

Dewey, J. (1965) *The School and Society.* Chicago: University of Chicago Press.

Dewey, J. (1916/1966) *Democracy and Education.* New York: Free Press.

Durgerian, P. (2016) Crafting solutions on the cutting edge of videography. In T. H. J. Marchand (ed.), *Craftwork as Problem Solving.* Farnham: Ashgate.

Gibson, G. (2016) *Experience, Education and Subjectivity: A Comparison of John Dewey's and Maurice Merleau-Ponty's Conceptions of Experience and their Implications for Education.* Kingston, Ontario: Queens University. Unpublished MA dissertation.

Gowlland, G. (2016) Thinking through materials: embodied problem solving and the values of work in taiwanese ceramics. In T. Marchand (ed.), *Craftwork as Problem Solving.* Farnham, Surrey: Ashgate.

Harari, Y. N. (2017) *Homo Deus.* London: Vintage.

House of Commons Education Committee (2014) *Underachievement in Education by White Working Class Children.* London: The Stationery Office Ltd.

House of Lords Select Committee on Social Mobility (2016) *Overlooked and Left Behind: Improving the Transition from School to Work for the Majority of Young People.* London: The Stationery Office Ltd.

Hyland, T. (1999) *Vocational Studies, Lifelong Learning and Social Values.* Aldershot: Ashgate.

Hyland, T. (2002) On the upgrading of vocational studies. *Educational Review* **45**(3): 287–296.

Hyland, T. (2011) *Mindfulness and Learning: Celebrating the Affective Dimension of Education.* Dordrecht, Netherlands: Springer Press

Hyland, T. (2014a) Reconstructing vocational education and training for the 21st century: mindfulness, craft, and values. *Sage Open* **4**(1): 1–15.

Hyland, T. (2014b) Mindfulness-based interventions and the affective domain of education. *Educational Studies* **40**(3): 277–291.

Hyland, T. (2017) Mindful working and skilful means: enhancing the affective elements of vocational education and training through the ethical foundations of mindfulness. In M. Mulder (ed.), *Competence-based Vocational*

78 Terry Hyland

and Professional Education: Bridging the Worlds of Work and Education. Switzerland: Springer International Publishing.

Hyland, T. and Winch, C. (2007) A Guide to Vocational Education and Training. London: Continuum.

Keep, E. (2006). State control of the English education and training system: playing with the biggest train set in the world. Journal of Vocational Education and Training 58(1): 47–64.

Kenneth Richmond, W. (1945) Education in England. Harmondsworth: Penguin.

Krathwohl, D. R., Bloom, B. S. and Masia, B. M. (1964) A Taxonomy of Educational Objectives: Handbook II – The Affective Domain. New York: David McKay Co.

Leader, D. (2016) Hands: What We Do with Them – and Why. London: Penguin.

Marchand, T. H. J. (ed.) (2016) Craftwork as Problem Solving. Farnham: Ashgate.

Martin, T. (2016) Making 'sense' in the bike mechanic's workshop. In T. H. J. Marchand (ed.), Craftwork as Problem Solving. Farnham: Ashgate.

Merleau-Ponty, M. (1962) Phenomenology of Perception. London: Routledge.

Morrison-Love, D. (2017) Towards a transformative epistemology of technology education. Journal of Philosophy of Education 51(1): 23–37.

McKinsey Report (2014). Education to Employment: Getting Europe's Youth into Work. Available at: www.mckinsey.com/industries/social-sector/our-insights/converting-education-to-employment-in-europe (Accessed 18 January 2019).

Nagel, T. (1974) What is it like to be a bat? Philosophical Review 83: 435–450.

Musgrave, P. W. (1964) The definition of technical education, 1860–1910. The Vocational Aspect of Secondary and Further Education 34(1): 105–111.

Okui, H. (2013) Subject, language and body: Merleau-Ponty's phenomenology in educational studies. Record of Clinical-Philosophical Pedagogy 12(1): 58–62.

O'Loughlin, M. (1995) Intelligent bodies and ecological subjectivities: Merleau-Ponty's corrective to postmodernism's "subjects" of education. 1995 Philosophy of Education Yearbook. Sydney: University of Sydney.

Pinker, S. (1997) How the Mind Works. London: Penguin Books.

Plato (1965) The Republic. Trans. H. P. D. Lee. Harmondsworth: Penguin.

Pring, R. (1995) Closing the Gap: Liberal Education and Vocational Preparation. London: Hodder and Stoughton.

Pye, D. (1968) The Nature and Art of Workmanship. Cambridge: Cambridge University Press.

Searle, J. (2004) Mind. Oxford: Oxford University Press.

Sennett, R. (2009) The Craftsman. London: Penguin Books.

Schofield, H. (1972) The Philosophy of Education: An Introduction. London: Allen and Unwin.

Schumpeter, A. (2014) Got skills? Retooling vocational education. The Economist, 23 August. Available at: www.economist.com/news/business/21613279-retooling-vocational-education-got-skills (Accessed 18 January 2019).

Silver, H. and Brennan, J. (1988) A Liberal Vocationalism. London: Methuen.

Simmons, R. (2014) Civilising the natives? Liberal studies in further education revisited. British Journal of Educational Studies 62: 85–101.

Strawson, G. (2006) Consciousness and its Place in Nature: Does Physicalism entail Panpsychism? Available at: www.philosopher.eu/others-writings/strawson-physicalism-entails-panpsychism/#sthash.ItxWXvhc.dpuf (Accessed 18 January 2019).

Strawson, G. (2016) Consciousness isn't a mystery. It's matter. New York Times, 16 May. Available at: www.nytimes.com/2016/05/16/opinion/consciousness-isnt-a-mystery-its-matter.html (Accessed 18 January 2019).

Subrahmanyam, G. (2014) Vocational education: why the Finns do it best. The Guardian, 15 January. Available at: www.theguardian.com/global-development-professionals-network/2014/jan/15/youth-unemployment-vocational-training-finland (Accessed 18 January 2019).

Valentin, C. D., Emrich, A., Lahann, J., Werth, D. and Loos, P. (2015) Adaptive social media skills trainer for vocational education and training. 48th Hawaii International Conference on System Sciences. Available at: www.computer.org/csdl/proceedings/hicss/2015/7367/00/7367b951.pdf (Accessed 18 January 2019).

Vaughan, K. (2017) The role of apprenticeship in the cultivation of soft skills and dispositions. Journal of Vocational Education and Training 69(4): 540–557.

Walsh, P. D. (1978) Upgrading practical subjects. Journal of Further and Higher Education 2(3): 58–71.

Weare, K. (2004) Developing the Emotionally Literate School. London: Paul Chapman.

Webb, S., Bathmaker, A-M., Gale, T., Hodge, S., Parker, S. and Rawolle, S. (2017) Higher vocational education and social mobility. *Journal of Vocational Education and Training* 69(1): 147–167.

Wilds, E. H. and Lottich, K. V. (1970) *The Foundations of Modern Education*. New York: Holt, Rinehart and Winston.

Wittgenstein, L. (1974) *Philosophical Investigations*. Oxford: Basil Blackwell.

Winch, C. (2000) *Education, Work and Social Capital*. London: Macmillan.

Wolf Report (2011) *Review of Vocational Education*. London: Department for Education.

7 Emotion and effective learning

Alexandros Tillas

Introduction

The human mind is a learning machine. New-borns can form mental representations that have properties of a general schema or prototype 'in less than one minute after their birth' (Walton and Bower, 1993: 203). Furthermore, the human mind is versatile enough to allow us to reuse existing mental processes that developed over millions of years as part of novel routines for new-fangled purposes, like algebraic calculations (Goldstone *et al.*, 2017).

Despite these fascinating features of the human mind, however, we are not always in a position to fully exploit its learning capacities. For instance, we are biased against certain things or mistakenly overlook specific aspects of the environmental stimuli that we seek to learn about. This chapter looks into ways in which we can unlock our learning potential. In doing so, learning is construed rather broadly as a process at the end of which we acquire knowledge that we did not possess prior to it, while the focus is on enhancing human learning capacities by appealing to the role of emotion in the learning process.

Emotion is closely related to learning to the extent that it sharpens our perceptual abilities allowing us to focus on what is important (Thagard and Nussbaum, 2014). Furthermore, emotion provides a scaffolding for the learning process to the extent that it allows for fast formation of associations between bits of novel information. For instance, a young child does not usually have to go through the same painful experience in order to learn that high drops are to be avoided (single-trial memory). Nevertheless, emotion can also impede learning by dampening existing associations which ground thinking patterns routinely deployed in reasoning. In turn, emotion drives selective attention to stored representations or external cues that are different from what the subject would have attended to without this emotional influence. In this sense, emotion can impede learning by not allowing a learner to build upon previously acquired knowledge.

A further aspect of the relation between emotion and learning, which is the main focus of this chapter, concerns affective responses to a learning task like boredom and anxiety. The present view suggests that emotion can help us 'navigate through' boredom and anxiety and maintain a constant 'flow', to use Csikszentmihalyi's (1990) famous concept that couches experience of 'full-engagement' in terms of an emotional state.

In order to highlight how emotion can enhance learning, the suggested view adheres to Prinz's view of emotion according to which emotions are valenced representations of bodily states (Prinz, 2004). Valence is the psychological term for the character of emotions, in the sense that the difference between positive and negative emotions concerns a difference in their valence. Furthermore, Prinz argues that even though emotions are under the control of the environment, we also have conceptualised versions of emotions that we can activate in the absence of the appropriate environmental stimulus. Building upon Prinz's view, this chapter suggests that we can put (conceptualised versions of) emotion to work and benefit from their influences on our bodies and minds with regard to learning in terms of nourishing flow. In doing so, the chapter builds upon established emotion-regulation techniques and suggests a novel way to control (the physiological, behavioural, as well as experiential aspects of) affective responses and ultimately enhance learning.

As already mentioned, the chapter focuses on boredom and stress as two cases of affective responses to a learning task. Starting from the latter, it is suggested that we can manage stress and maintain a constant 'flow' by associating states of stress with propositional knowledge about methodical approach to hard problems, examining ways in which others have dealt with similar problems and so forth. Boredom, on the other hand, is regulated by applying the information read in a task to issues that are of more interest to the learner (knowledge transfer), applying information about gravitational forces to bungee jumping for instance, or searching for multiple ways to deal with a given task. In this sense, emotions (valenced representations) are deployed in order to recalibrate our system of interconnected representations which ultimately grounds our knowledge.

The chapter starts by introducing the notion of 'flow', whether flow can be externally induced and whether emotion can nourish it. On the assumption that flow enhances learning, and on the further assumption that flow-nourishing conditions can be manipulated, a suggestion is made about how deploying emotion can help us maintain flow. Finally, an assessment of how these suggestions can inform current learning practices and ultimately enhance learning is offered

Feeling the flow

Recently Sky Sports F1 sport television in collaboration with Tobii Tech conducted a real-life eye-tracking recording on a Formula 1 driver (Nico Hülkenberg of Force India Formula 1 Team) in an attempt to get a realistic driver's perspective while driving a race car on a track. When asked whether he thinks about or consciously analyses what he is looking at while driving a race car on a circuit, Hülkenberg replied, 'Not really to be honest, […] this is something very natural to us and [something that] you do instinctively'. In a similar fashion, professional basketball player Pat Garrity describes an experience wherein 'the ball feels so light, and your shots are effortless' (reported in Moller *et al.*, 2010). This is in line with a well-documented view that expert task execution is most often not followed by reflective exercise (Dreyfus and Dreyfus, 1986).

Interestingly, the aforementioned state of full engagement is not limited to experts. For instance, a number of studies (e.g., Massimini and Delle Fave, 2000) show that when optimally challenged, i.e., when the agent's skills are matched to the challenges posed by the task they execute, people find the task at hand not requiring effort (Moller *et al.*, 2010). In particular, for these studies subjects are provided with pagers that randomly beep several times a day over the course of a number of weeks and subjects are asked to report on their experience at the moment of beep, allowing a gathering of information from a wide range of contexts (e.g., athletic, academic, etc.) about the subjects' subjective experience of their performance. This state of effortless performance is known in the extant literature as 'flow', a term coined by Csikszentmihalyi (1975). It is worth clarifying at

82 Alexandros Tillas

this point that flow experience does require objectively measured effort even though this effort is not subjectively noticed by the subject. The reason why this effort goes unnoticed is because the subject's mind is occupied with the task at hand (Csikszentmihalyi, 1990).

Nakamura and Csikszentmihalyi (2002) characterise a flow state as having at least the following six qualities: (1) the acting agent is fully concentrated on the task at hand, (2) action and awareness are merged, (3) the agent loses her reflective self-consciousness, (4) the agent has an enhanced sense of control of actions and environment, (5) time perception is distorted – usually subjects perceive time as passing more quickly than normally, (6) autotelic or intrinsic motivation, in the sense that the activity *per se*, rather than its outcome, is seen as rewarding, and subjects most often opt to repeat such rewarding tasks. In this sense, flow not only enhances performance directly by matching challenges and skills, but also indirectly in the sense that agents become motivated to repeat the performed activity. On repetition of a given task, subjects find greater challenges in it, which in turn further develops the agent's skills (Csikszentmihalyi and Larson, 1987; Wong and Csikszentmihalyi, 1991). The focus of this chapter is mainly on intrinsic motivation, while a way to manipulate emotion in order to 'externally induce' flow is also suggested.

Externally induced flow?

Given the obvious benefits of high levels of concentration and engagement that subjects in a state of flow experience, it seems intuitive to attempt to enhance learning by providing learners with conditions that nourish flow. This chapter builds upon evidence showing that flow conditions can be manipulated (e.g., task design), while focusing on the psychological states that an individual experiences during task execution. It is argued that these psychological states can also be conditioned in a way that makes flow states more easily accessible as well as more durable and, in this way, enhances participants' psychological involvement.

One such condition that nourishes flow is 'task design'. Tasks designed with flow in mind provide, among other things, adjustable levels of difficulty in the light of the individual skills, mirrored in the individual's performance in the task at hand. This constant adjustment helps the individual avoid boredom and stress. Boredom and stress, the psychological states on which this chapter focuses, are construed here as the two extremities of a continuum in the centre of which lies flow. Roughly the underlying hypothesis is 'make the task too hard and the learner becomes overladen, frustrated and ultimately stressed; make it too easy and the learner gets bored'. In either of the two extremities, flow, and in turn learning, suffers. The relation between challenge and flow is curvilinear in the sense that challenge increases flow but only up to the point where skill is roughly equal to challenge, while flow decreases as challenge becomes greater than skill (Csikszentmihalyi et al., 2005).

According to Csikszentmihalyi and his colleagues, there are two basic aspects of a flow state. First, the aforementioned optimal challenge or the matching between skills and challenge posed by the task. Second, subjects enter more easily into a state of flow when the task is structured in a way that provides proximal goals as well as direct feedback about one's progress (Csikszentmihalyi and Rathunde, 1993, reported in Moller et al., 2010).

Cabo et al. (2004) focus on the relation between mood and flow and experimentally induce positive and negative moods to players of Tetris – the famous tile-placing puzzle video game. They report that negative moods prevented subjects from entering a flow state, while positive ones did not significantly promote it. In a similar study, Keller and Bless (2008; also reported in Moller et al.,

Emotion and effective learning   83

2010) describe an adaptive condition in which the level of difficulty is a function of the player's performance, i.e., game speed increases as a result of good performance (in the adaptive condition). In turn, the moods induced were a function between levels of difficulty. For instance, players playing at a very low level of difficulty (low game speed – slow falling tiles) were led to boredom and thus did not enter a flow state. Similarly, extremely high speed (overload) also deterred flow conditions.

Despite its significant role for flow, the matching between skills and challenge is not the only factor influencing a flow state. Specifically, Engeser and Rheinberg (2008) show that the external utility of the task (task-instrumentality) plays an equally important factor and show that during activities with higher instrumentality, such as an obligatory statistics course, subjects experienced high levels of flow, even when their skills were greater than the levels of perceived difficulty, which should normally lead to boredom. They also found that the matching between skill and challenge was more relevant when task instrumentality was low (reported in Moller *et al.*, 2010).

Keller and Bless report that after playing Tetris for eight minutes, subjects in the adaptive playing mode performed better, completed more lines, perceived that they were playing for less time than they actually were, reported greater control, involvement and enjoyment in comparison to boredom and overload conditions. In this sense, even if positive moods do not promote flow (Parks and Victor, 2006), negative moods seem to deter flow conditions. To this extent, and in the interest of making flow more easily accessible and extend its duration, preventing negative moods nourishes flow. This will play a key role later on in the chapter when conditions to maintain flow are examined.

Question for discussion

What does it take to enter into a state of flow?

Emotions as promoters of flow

In suggesting that emotion can nourish flow, the present chapter builds upon the hypothesis that our conceptual repertoire forms a 'network of connections'. Networks are construed here rather loosely as constellations of interconnected concepts but without committing to connectionism – a movement in cognitive science that aims at explaining human intellectual abilities in terms of artificial neural networks (Bechtel and Abrahamsen, 1991). Nevertheless, it is assumed that interconnected nets of concepts and representations are ultimately grounded in inter-neural connections. In turn, learning is seen as conditioning the connection weightings between (groups of) neurons, which essentially ground concepts.

One way to shed light upon the above hypothesis is to couch it in terms of the principles of the widely accepted Hebbian rule of learning implemented by Long-term Potentiation (e.g., Martinez *et al.*, 2002). Briefly, Hebb (1949) examined how the environment alters or in any case conditions the human brain, and specifically the connections between neural groups that underpin certain experiences, and famously suggests that 'neurons that fire together, wire together'. The more frequently two (groups of neurons) become activated simultaneously, the greater the connection weighting between them. In turn, the greater the connection weighting between two neurons, the greater the probability that activation of one will trigger (activation of) the other.

84 *Alexandros Tillas*

In this light, learning is construed as the conditioning of connection weightings between representations or bits of information stored in the human mind. This is significant for nourishing flow as it explains how emotion can scaffold learning by allowing for faster formation of stronger connections between cues in a given task and stored information (propositional knowledge) about the task's instrumentality, in the manner explained below.

In order for emotion to contribute to nourishing flow, emotion has to be available on demand, which seems to be in tension with the fact that emotion is largely exogenously controlled (Prinz, 2004). In particular, Prinz argues that emotion is essentially registrations of bodily states deriving from perceptual experiences and that, unlike concepts that can be activated endogenously, emotion is generally under the 'control' of the environment. That is, we experience certain emotional states as a reaction to a given external stimulus – we feel happy when meeting a friend, and so forth.

Despite normally being under environmental control, however, we also have conceptualised versions of emotional states. That is, we can recall how it is to feel sad even without being sad at a specific given moment. Building upon this, activating on demand (and in the absence of the appropriate environmental stimulus) conceptualised versions of emotion can provide suitable conditions for flow.

Flow can be nourished by force-tokening or activating conceptualised versions of emotion alongside concepts couching a given task's external utility or instrumentality. During participation in a seemingly dull task, which seems to hinder flow, the learner can force flow by consciously thinking about the task's instrumentality, its end goal and the benefits of this task for her. For instance, consider a fairly advanced martial arts practitioner performing her routine. At several points during her training she is asked to perform basic movements. Being an advanced martial artist suggests that she has gone through this basic routine numerous times before. In order for this subject to enter a state of flow, it is useful to consciously think about the task's instrumentality, how useful this simple routine is for her and how it will help her develop as a martial arts practitioner: that repeating basic moves is essential in order to become faster, and so forth. In addition, she can deploy inner motivation strategies, which is the main focus here, and think how proud of herself she would feel once she is a *better* martial arts practitioner. Moreover, she can recall the emotional states she was in during earlier parts of her training and how hard these currently-perceived-as-easy moves have felt, and in this way realise that practice is key for learning and developing skills.

Repetition of this process leads to the strengthening of the connection weightings between the conceptualised version of the appropriate emotion and concepts that couch the task's instrumentality by the principles of Hebbian learning. Once conditioned, the associated concepts and emotional states that couch the motivational strategy become more readily activate-able when participating in similar tasks. This inner motivation process is seen as a scaffolding for entering into a state of flow that can after a while become less salient and ultimately part of the task syntax, to use Bruya's (2010) terminology. As a result, the subject will progressively become less dependent upon consciously engaging in motivational processes similar to the one described above and will be in a position to start relishing various stages of her routine almost automatically.

The suggestion that utilising conceptualised versions of emotion as way to force flow is in line with evidence showing that flow satisfies our psychological need for autonomy or freely endorsing our actions as opposed to feeling coerced by internal or external forces (Deci and Moller, 2005). For instance, Moller *et al.* (2010) stress that when describing the task to participants it is more beneficial to flow to use language that puts emphasis on the participants' choice, e.g., 'may' or

Emotion and effective learning   85

'can', rather than control (e.g., 'must' or 'have to'). In this line, the thought 'If I complete this basic routine, I can then become better at performing more complex X-martial-art-moves', to use the example described above, alongside a recollection of the feeling of pleasure or satisfaction after completing a task can be more persuasive for participating in this task than the direction 'complete this task in order to gain X reward' or 'you must complete this task'.

At a glance, the claim that manipulation of conceptualised versions of emotion can nourish or bring about states of flow seems to be in tension with one of the basic characteristics of being in a state of flow. Namely, while in a state of flow, subjects lose their conscious reflective self, which is rather a requisite for conscious manipulation of conceptualised versions of emotion. Nevertheless, the conscious manipulation of emotion is a requisite for the process that brings about the conditions that promote (generation of) a state of flow. Once a state of flow is reached, no conscious manipulation of emotion is required. At the same time, the next point where such a manipulation will be required to kick in and help an individual navigate through boredom and stress will be precisely when the individual experiences either boredom or stress and is once again out of the state of flow. Think of the suggested emotion regulation as a safety net that helps the individual bounce back into the state of flow. In this sense, conceptualised versions of emotion are not deployed while in a state of flow but merely in order to get (back) in. The above suggestions about inner motivation and flow can plug into existing evidence about various factors that influence flow.

Emotion, empathy and flow

As mentioned above, it is more beneficial to stress the participant's choice when couching task instructions as opposed to putting emphasis on control. The effects of wording of task instructions for flow can become even more apparent when seen through the perspective of emotion and empathy and when combined with the well-known effects of persuasive psychology. Regarding the latter, results show that subjects are more prone to imitate true social norms or behaviours that most of an individual's peers, in the broad sense of the term, practice. For instance, environmentally sensitive hoteliers, or at least hoteliers interested in keeping their business running costs low, prompt their customers to reuse their towels and bed linings by putting up signs containing messages like 'Reuse your towels'.

Goldstein, Cialdini and Griskevicius (2008) famously examined the effectiveness of wording of signs like the one in the previous example that prompt hotel guests to participate in an environmental conservation programme. They report that communicating the social norms boosts the likelihood of towel reuse by 26 per cent. For instance, messages like 'the majority of guests reuse their towels' proved superior to the aforementioned standardised message, 'Please reuse your towels'. Furthermore, they show that normative appeals were most effective when the described group behaviour occurred in a setting that matched the guests' immediate situational conditions, e.g., 'The majority of guests in this room reuse their towels'. Without getting into the details of whether and why this kind of behaviour could be irrational, it is largely rational to follow norms that closely match our circumstances. Consider for instance visiting a public library and complying with the norms of remaining quiet and carefully browsing through the book collections.

A further reason why wording that communicates social norms is more effective is also that it promotes the hotel guest's autotelic motivation: reusing towels becomes in itself a satisfying activity as it makes the guest feel better about herself. Importantly, this is not in tension with the

86 *Alexandros Tillas*

aforementioned psychological need for autonomy (as opposed to feeling coerced by internal or external forces). For in this example the individual feels in charge of choosing the 'less pampering' but more environmentally friendly option.

Projecting this to the previous discussion about flow, task participants can become more motivated and in turn get closer to a state of flow when presented with information like '85 per cent of participants who completed this task exhibited increased cognitive versatility in subsequently performed tasks'. Analogous effects can be gained by appealing to an authority. To return to the martial arts example, consider the following wording as an alternative for task instruction: 'Bruce Lee always focused on execution of simple movements during his training.'

Keller and Bless (2008) stress that a number of personality traits may also interact with contextual features in generating flow in lab conditions such as the volatility-persistence component of action orientation (in Moller *et al.*, 2010). Subjects higher in volatility and lower in persistence are less influenced by the compatibility of skills and task demands. As a result, such action-oriented subjects were more readily experiencing flow when engaged in a demanding task, and experience this task as less effortful. Furthermore, individual differences in achievement motivation also contribute greatly to flow generation. Specifically, hope for success and fear of failure moderates the relation between difficulty–skill balance and flow. Subjects with high implicit hope for success report that they experience greater flow when difficulty and skill are balanced, while subjects higher in explicit fear of failure report experiencing less flow under the same balanced difficulty–skill conditions.

This becomes important when considering the role of emotion in generating or maintaining flow. That is, conceptualised versions of emotion, such as the emotional state of satisfaction after successful completion of a task, can be utilised to induce persistence, 'If I finish this task I will become a better problem-solver' – associated emotion of satisfaction. Accordingly, the fear of failure can be managed by force tokening conceptualised versions of feeling confident and a general positive attitude alongside concepts couching the task's end goal and the individual's progress. In this way, deploying versions of emotion that are available on demand nourish flow, either by promoting persistence or by diminishing the effects of personal traits such as volatility.

Question for discussion

Can we talk ourselves into a certain emotional state?

Learning to flow

Nourishing flow depends equally upon inner motivation and external utility of the task, as well as task structure. This section focuses on the interface between these factors. Namely, it investigates a potential way to teach learners how to learn by focusing on the flow-friendly aspects and 'cues' in the task. In doing so, an appeal is made to techniques of perceptual learning (Goldstone *et al.*, 2017).

Perception is extremely versatile and adaptable to our environment, allowing us to extract information about environmental regularities. As Goldstone and colleagues (2017) point out, we reuse brain systems that have developed for different purposes in order to convert originally demanding, strategically controlled cognitive tasks into learned, automatically executed perception-action

Emotion and effective learning 87

routines. In the case of mathematical regularities, the visual-attentional system learns to give higher priority to notational operators with higher precedence: e.g., the notational symbol for multiplication (×) attracts more attention than the lower precedence addition operator (+) even when subjects do not have to solve mathematical problems. In addition, algebra-literate subjects tend to fixate for longer on × in comparison to +. Importantly, learning mathematics does not simply make notational objects more salient but also allows the learner to group them together. Perceiving different parts of the visual world as belonging to the same object allows the learner to compare them more efficiently than when comparing parts that come from different objects. In addition to tuning up our perceptual systems, tuning of mathematical notation in order to fit our perceptual system is of equal importance. Consider for instance the historic transition from '3 times the variable b plus 5' to '3´b+5' to later '3•b+5', and more recently as '3b+5', which shows a consistent trend towards decreasing the spacing between operands that should be combined together earlier. In this way, mathematical notation directs our perceptual grouping.

The above suggestions are about educating perception on how to give higher priority to certain notational operators than others in order to convert complex cognitive tasks into perception-action routines. They can be used to shed light upon how we can educate learners to use aspects of the task as cues that highlight task instrumentality and task structure, and ultimately induce flow. Admittedly, it is not always easy to find 'cues' in the task that highlight instrumentality and structure. For cues of this kind do not stand out in the same way that a doorknob on a door does, for instance. Nevertheless, there are several aspects of a task that are themselves salient and that can be used as cues and associated with instrumentality and structure. For instance, 'executing simple/boring movements', a *bona fide* flow hindrance in the martial artist example, can be construed as a proxy that leads the individual to recall instrumentality-related (propositional) knowledge. As soon as the individual starts experiencing boredom and makes thoughts like 'This task is boring', she can force thoughts containing information about the task instrumentality. In this sense, the salient features of a task that have been repeatedly associated with hindering flow can be recast into cues for the distal flow-inducing propositional knowledge about task instrumentality.

Engeser and Rheinberg (2008) focus on task instrumentality and show that it can moderate the difficulty–skill balance, which is in turn important for flow. Specifically, they report that difficulty–skill balance was most relevant during tasks with low instrumentality, such as playing a game of Pacman. In contrast, subjects experienced high levels of flow during task with high instrumentality, e.g., an obligatory course of statistics, even when subjects exhibited higher skills than perceived difficulty.

On these grounds, stressing task instrumentality can be used as a 'cure for boredom', as it were, by becoming incorporated in inner motivation techniques. For instance, recall the martial artist example. Task instrumentality can have a lasting effect on nourishing flow by stressing the importance of going though drills that are perceived as 'easy to complete' for becoming faster at responding to an attacking opponent. This lasting effect can be further complemented by the positive effects that recalling conceptualised versions of emotion has for flow. That is, while the subject recalls the benefits awaiting her if she continues practising a seemingly boring routine she can also recall how proud she will be of herself once she is in a position to effectively defend herself against opponents, how she will be able to progress in tournaments, and so forth. Thus, associating knowledge about task instrumentality and conceptualised version of the appropriate emotional state provides sufficient material for inner motivation strategies.

Flow and the classroom

The balance between task difficulty and skill can be further moderated by task structure and clarity of goals. Results show that participants in highly structured tasks report greater psychological involvement and flow (Mannell and Bradley, 1986). However, highly structured tasks can ultimately deter flow as they diminish creativity (Moller *et al.*, 2010). In this way, the relation between structure and flow can also be seen as curvilinear to the extent that high levels of structure increase flow but only up to the point that structure does not impede creativity, while flow decreases as structure restricts creativity further.

One of the most ubiquitous learning settings that systematically uses highly structured tasks is traditional schooling. In light of the above evidence, traditional schooling seems ironically rather orthogonal to flow. In addition to using structured tasks, a further reason why traditional schooling environments impede flow can be the large number of students in the average classroom. This entails a significant amount of external distractions, but mainly highly diverging degrees of skill-levels and skillsets. Of course, students in a single classroom are usually of approximately the same age and should in principle have the same skillset, which would allow them to approach a given problem that has been designed for students/learners of their age without any problem. However, not all students are equally good at all subjects, neither are they all interested in studying that specific topic in a specific point in time. Without going into further details about the problems that traditional schooling structure poses for learning (see Tillas, 2017 for an extended discussion), it suffices to say that given individual skillsets and interests, a learner's attention level is very likely to plummet even only after a few minutes in a given class.

Finally, task instrumentality in traditional schooling normally means having a marking and/or a(n associated) credit system. As Moller *et al.* (2010) show, even though making extrinsic rewards, like course credit, contingent upon a learner's performance can increase instrumentality, it actually undermines flow whenever difficulty and skill are evenly matched. Upon these grounds, they suggest that performance-contingent rewards should be downplayed for the sake of preserving flow. The importance of marking and grading systems for traditional schooling makes flow ever-more elusive for learners in a traditional setting.

The difficulties in restructuring current educational systems are numerous and well documented and are thus not discussed here in further detail. However, this chapter suggests that a number of these problems, especially those related to flow nourishment, can be surmounted by focusing on inner motivation techniques to which individuals of all ages and across educational settings can appeal in order to enter a flow state. Flow can be further nourished by classrooms that stimulate learners and attract their attention. As Tillas (2017) points out, the most inexpensive and at the same time effective way in which this can be done is by letting students of different ages co-exist and mingle together freely. Importantly, learners should be allowed to choose freely the topics they want to investigate at a particular point in time, under the discrete yet essential guidance of trained instructors. In this way, the fact that individuals of different backgrounds, skillsets and skill levels will mingle together does not pose an obstacle for experiencing flow and greater psychological involvement. For simply, different individuals will *choose* from a variety of activities according to their interests or can simply focus on what other individuals do. Either way, their psychological need for autonomy will be satisfied. Following something that is of importance for the beholder is key for maintaining high levels of attention, great psychological involvement and flow. Importantly, inner motivation techniques can prove instrumental for force-inducing flow, even outside of a learning environment like the one described here.

Activity

Would you agree that free mingling with peers of different ages nourishes flow?

Conclusion

This chapter focuses on emotional responses normally associated with learning tasks and shows how emotion can help us enhance learning. In particular, it focuses on boredom and anxiety and suggests an inner motivation technique on the basis of which learners can navigate through these emotional responses. Steering clear from boredom and anxiety enhances psychological involvement in the learning task and can in principle enhance learning.

According to the theoretical model offered here, we can use aspects of a given task as 'cues' to signpost our inner motivation strategy in order to nourish learning conditions. Flow can be achieved by activating conceptualised versions of emotion or emotion that are not controlled by the environment and are not mere responses to external stimuli.

Summary

- Flow refers to experience of 'full-engagement' in terms of an emotional state.
- Boredom and anxiety can be seen as the two extremities of a continuum of emotional responses to a learning task. Flow lies in the middle of this continuum.
- We experience emotional states as a response to external stimuli. Yet we can also activate versions of emotional states endogenously (in the absence of the appropriate stimulus). These 'conceptualised' versions of emotion can be deployed as part of an inner motivation technique and help us induce a state of flow.
- We can learn to single out 'cues' in a task that signpost our inner motivation and, in turn, greater psychological involvement in the task at hand.
- A number of factors can influence flow, including the balance between difficulty and skill, task instrumentality, task structure and clarity of goals.

Recommended reading

Bandura, A. (1977) *Social Learning Theory*. Englewood Cliffs, NJ: Prentice-Hall.
Bruya, B. (2010) *Effortless Attention: A New Perspective in the Cognitive Science of Attention and Action*. Cambridge, MA: MIT Press.
Gray, P. (2013) *Free to Learn: Why Unleashing the Instinct to Play Will Make Our Children Happier, More Self-Reliant, and Better Students for Life*. New York: Basic Books.
Hurley, S. and Chater, N. (2005) *Perspectives on Imitation: From Neuroscience to Social Science*. Cambridge, MA: MIT Press.

References

Bechtel, W. and Abrahamsen, A. (1991) *Connectionism and the Mind: An Introduction to Parallel Processing in Networks*. Cambridge, MA and Oxford: Blackwell.
Bruya, B. (2010) *Effortless Attention: A New Perspective in the Cognitive Science of Attention and Action*. Cambridge, MA: MIT Press.

90 *Alexandros Tillas*

Cabo, R., Kleiman, M., McCauley, A. and Parks, A. C. (2004) *May. Mood and flow.* Poster presented at the 16th Annual Convention of the American Psychological Society.

Csikszentmihalyi, M. (1975) *Beyond Boredom and Anxiety: The Experience of Play in Work and Games.* San Francisco: Jossey-Bass.

Csikszentmihalyi, M. (1990) *Flow: The Psychology of Optimal Experience.* New York: Harper and Row.

Csikszentmihalyi, M. and Larson, R. (1987) Validity and reliability of the experience sampling method. *Journal of Nervous and Mental Disease* **175**: 526–536.

Csikszentmihalyi, M. and Rathunde, K. (1993) The measurement of flow in everyday life: toward a theory of emergent motivation. In J. J. Jacobs (ed.), *Nebraska Symposium on motivation. Vol. 40. Developmental perspectives on Motivation.* Lincoln: University of Nebraska Press.

Csikszentmihalyi, M., Abuhamdeh, S. and Nakamura, J. (2005) Flow. In A. Elliot and C. Dweck (eds.), *Handbook of Competence Motivation.* New York: Plenum Press.

Deci, E. L. and Moller, A. C. (2005) The concept of competence: a starting place for understanding intrinsic motivation and self-determined extrinsic motivation. In A. Elliot and C. Dweck (eds.), *Handbook of Competence Motivation.* New York: Plenum Press.

Dreyfus, H. L. and Dreyfus, S. E. (1986) *Mind Over Machine: The Power of Human Intuition and Expertise in the Era of the Computer.* New York: Free Press.

Engeser, S. and Rheinberg, F. (2008) Flow, Performance and Moderators of Challenge – Skill Balance. *Motivation and Emotion* **32**(3): 158–172.

Goldstein, N. J., Cialdini, R. B. and Griskevicius, V. (2008) A room with a viewpoint: using social norms to motivate environmental conservation in hotels. *Journal of Consumer Research* **35**(3): 472–482.

Goldstone, R. L., Marghetis, T., Weitnauer, E., Ottmar, E. R. and Landy, D. (2017) Adapting perception, action, and technology for mathematical reasoning. *Current Directions in Psychological Science* 1–8. Available at: d1o0i.1or1g7/170/.01197673/70926134712717410747808488 (Accessed 18 January 2019).

Hebb, D. O. (1949) *The Organization of Behavior.* New York: John Wiley.

Keller, J. and Bless, H. (2008) Flow and regulatory compatibility: an experimental approach to the flow model of intrinsic motivation. *Personality and Social Psychology Bulletin* **34**: 196–209.

Mannell, R. C. and Bradley, W. (1986) Does greater freedom always lead to greater leisure? Testing a Person X Environment model of freedom and leisure. *Journal of Leisure Research* **18**: 215–230.

Martinez, C., Do, V., Martinez, J. L. and Derrick, B. E. (2002) Associative long-term potentiation (ltp) among extrinsic afferents of the hippocampal CA3 region in vivo. *Brain Research* **940**: 86–94.

Massimini, F. and Delle Fave, A. (2000) Individual development in a bio-cultural perspective. *The American Psychologist* **55**: 24–33.

Moller, A. C., Meier, B. P. and Wall, R. D. (2010) Developing an experimental induction of flow: effortless action in the lab. In B. Bruya (ed.), *Effortless Attention: A New Perspective in the Cognitive Science of Attention and Action.* Cambridge, MA: MIT Press.

Nakamura, J. and Csikszentmihalyi, M. (2002) The concept of flow. In P. R. Snyder and S. J. Lopez (eds.), *Handbook of Positive Psychology.* Oxford: Oxford University Press.

Parks, A. C. and Victor, H. A. (2006) *Are Positive and Negative Moods Causes or Correlates of Flow?* Poster presented at the 18th Annual Convention of the American Psychological Society.

Prinz, J. (2004) *Gut Reactions: A Perceptual Theory of Emotion.* New York: Oxford University Press.

Thagard, P. and Nussbaum, D. (2014) Fear-driven inference: mechanisms of gut overreaction. In L. Magnani (ed.), *Model-Based Reasoning in Science and Technology: Theoretical and Cognitive Issues.* New York: Springer.

Tillas, A. (2017) Hacking our brains for learning. *Humana.Mente: Journal of Philosophical Studies* **33**: 83–102.

Walton, G. E., and Bower, T. G. R. (1993) Newborns form 'prototypes' in less than 1 minute. *Psychological Science* **4**(3): 203–205.

Wong, M. M. and Csikszentmihalyi, M. (1991) Motivation and academic achievement: the effects of personality traits and the duality of experience. *Journal of Personality* **59**: 539–574.

8 The social, the natural and the educational

Koichiro Misawa

Introduction

In his lecture for his inauguration to the chair of the philosophy of education in 1963 at the London Institute of Education, R. S. Peters, a principal founder of the Philosophy of Education Society of Great Britain and the first editor of the *Journal of Philosophy of Education*, insisted that: 'education is not an autonomous discipline, but a field, like politics, where the disciplines of history, philosophy, psychology, and sociology have application' (Peters, 1963/1980: 273, cited in McCulloch, 2002: 100). The four so-called 'foundation disciplines' (Hirst, 1983/2014) were well established by the mid-1970s (McCulloch, 2002: 111) and exerted hegemony over other intellectual resources as well as over a more unitary and autonomous notion of 'educational research'. Beginning in the 1980s, however, the dominance of the 'foundation disciplines' became eroded by increasing socio-economic-political pressures, 'leading to a growing emphasis on "practical" approaches at the expense of "theory"' (McCulloch, 2002: 112), a trend that has clearly set the direction for the current prevalence of empiricist 'evidence-based' policy, practice and research in education. Nonetheless, caution is needed here. Not all of the 'foundation disciplines' have been side-lined in these rapidly changing educational and other contexts by more recently established educational (sub-)disciplines and research, such as curriculum studies, the economics of education and comparative education. It is the history and philosophy of education that have lost much of their appeal within the education community. It does seem that the cardinal reason for this is that they, unlike the other two 'foundation disciplines', are not necessarily scientific in character, and the current climate both within and outside of academia is increasingly marginalising non-scientific disciplines.

Questions for discussion

Is philosophical inquiry still relevant to actual educational issues? If your answer is 'yes', do you think that it is not surprising that the philosophical study of education is giving way to more scientific educational disciplines and research?

This chapter aims to articulate the proposal that philosophical inquiry can improve, deepen and advance our understanding of education in ways that differ from those of social and natural scientific research, because philosophy is concerned not only with the educational but also with the

92 Koichiro Misawa

'social' and the 'natural' in their own right. The way that the chapter opens by articulating the significance of philosophical thinking in the study of education, while being simply one strand among many philosophical alternatives, helps illustrate the ineliminable quality of the *educational* from our investigation into the social and the natural at the most fundamental level. In other words, it is made apparent that the educational is a necessary, constitutive part of the way we live our lives as human beings who are social and natural animals simultaneously inhabiting a world that is at once social and natural.

To this end, the chapter investigates some influential ideas around the question of whether different conceptual schemes carve up the world differently. Examples are social constructivism and the philosopher Richard Rorty's proposal to abandon the notions of conceptual schemes and the world. Insightful as they are to some degree, they still fail to bring the nature of social reality to light in a way that allows the question of whether there is one reality or multiple realities to make no sense. One way to dissolve the nagging problem with realism is to recast the relation between mind and world along the lines of the philosopher John McDowell's less restrictive conceptions of human experience and the natural, which thereby enable us to see the essential role that the educational plays in the fabric of the world human beings inhabit.

Questions for discussion

Do you think different conceptual schemes carve up the world differently? If your answer is 'yes', in what ways and to what extent?

The flourishing of social constructivism

In one ordinary sense, different conceptual schemes carve up the world in multiple ways. Social norms, cultural habits and shared histories and beliefs vary from one social group to another. All such variations constitute, and are constituted by, different conceptual schemes, and through them, people recognise the world differently. Educational practices and systems in a society are, of course, under the sway of those different schemes since such a diversity in terms of, for instance, how to lead a (non-)religious life and even how to eat (with fork and knife, with chopsticks or with hands) may well affect how (best) to educate children in each society. As education is a socially embedded enterprise, heightened awareness in educational research and disciplines of social dimensions of education that can be vastly different among societies should come as no surprise. The suspicion that educational studies that seeks to lay claim to universally applicable and generalisable guides to actual practices cannot fulfil its promise has, therefore, paved the way for the idea of 'social construction', which is in tune more with 'the local', 'the particular', 'the contextual' and 'the timely' than with 'the universal', 'the general', 'the de-contextualised' and 'the timeless', as well as for a plethora of 'post-' isms such as post-modernism, post-positivism and post-structuralism (*cf.* Derry, 2008).

In fact, since the appearance of *The Social Construction of Reality* (1966) by Peter Berger and Thomas Luckmann, the term 'social construction' has been widely dispersed in social science disciplines and other relevant areas. In the education community too, the idea of social construction

The social, natural and educational   93

(of, say, mind, meaning, knowledge and reality) evidently has gained intellectual currency. There is no shortage of literature consonant with social constructionist ideas. *Knowledge and Control* (1971), edited by the sociologist of education Michael Young, *Fourth Generation Evaluation* (1989) by the methodologist and educational researcher Egon Guba and Yvonna Lincoln, and *The Culture of Education* (1996) by the psychologist Jerome Bruner are just a few of the representative works that have exerted a profound influence on the education community, both as an approach to educational studies and as the substance in teacher-training courses.

Yet something has, for all their richness and importance, been left out of the idea that different conceptual schemes carve up the world differently and of the flourishing of social constructionist approaches that often accompany the tempting idea. What remains unacknowledged is a fuller grasp of the social nature of reality or social reality, which adherents of those approaches are supposed to spell out. There are, of course, many variants of social constructionist approaches (for a thorough account, see Gergen, 1999), such as 'radical constructivism' (by Claude Levi Strauss and Ernst von Glasersfeld), 'constructivism' (Jean Piaget and George Kelly), 'social constructivism' (Lev Vygotsky and Jerome Bruner), 'social constructionism' (Kenneth Gergen) and 'sociological constructionism' (Henri Giroux and Nikolas Rose). In this chapter, however, the term '(social) constructivism' is practically employed to cover the range of those isms that, with varying degrees but commonly, lack a substantial analysis of the nature of social reality because the term 'constructivism' is now used most frequently in discussions of reality construction.

The lack of a meticulous treatment of the nature of social reality has prolonged or even fortified the life of the lingering issue of *realism* and *anti-realism*, thus impeding a more comprehensive development of educational research by creating many unnecessary dualisms such as quantitative and qualitative research in which a researcher steeped and trained in one side of the dualism is liable to close off from the other side. The philosopher of education Richard Pring condemns typical bipolar paradigms towards which much current work in educational studies still tends, despite its claims to the contrary, to fall; 'Paradigm A' is positivist, embracing 'an objective reality' and 'Paradigm B' is constructivist, taking reality to be a 'social construction of the mind' (Pring, 2000/2004: 232). Classifying contemporary educational inquiry as Paradigms A and B may be an over-simplified travesty, but it is instructive here to ask whether widely accepted alternatives are really anything more than a middle position somewhere between them. Pring's own position might be one such alternative:

> Far from individually constructing the world, we acquire those constructions which (although socially developed) are possible because of *certain features of reality* which make them possible. It is not that there are multiple realities. Rather are there different ways in which reality is conceived, and those differences may well reflect different practical interests and different traditions.
>
> (Pring, 2000/2004: 236, emphasis added)

This is a well-balanced outlook that avoids going to the extremes. Someone sympathetic to Paradigm B, however, could object that Pring implicitly prioritises a realist stance by rejecting 'multiple realities' since 'certain features of reality' he refers to actually do not make sense without some individuation of properties of beings, both material and immaterial. And the crucial point is that such an initial individuation may *already* be a social construction. The issue, it might be added,

94 *Koichiro Misawa*

is just thrown back into the question of whether initial individuations are impressed by or immune to social factors. (For more on this, see Misawa, 2016.)

What is important to notice here is the possibility that exploring the social at such a funda-mental level might not be an entirely empirical issue. Attempts to find an appropriate position along the spectrum of the realism/anti-realism framework underlying the positivist-constructivist dualism cannot, at least from a *philosophical* perspective, break genuinely out of the unprofitable frame-work, for they, often unwittingly, commit themselves to the dualism of *scheme* and *content*, the dualism identified by the philosopher Donald Davidson as the 'last dogma' of empiricism (Davidson, 1974/2001).

Questions for discussion

Do you find the idea that empirical content appears depending on the conceptual scheme under consideration to be plausible? If your answer is 'yes', do you think that the primary task of educational disciplines and research is to do case studies about various contexts that frame diverse conceptual schemes?

The lure and pitfall of the ideas of scheme and content

Empiricism in philosophy is the idea that experience (commonly sense experience) is 'the ultimate source of all our concepts and knowledge' (Markie, 2017). Such a foundationalist approach that aspires to ensure that we can achieve empirical knowledge with no need for anything independent of our (sense) experience is all too easily gripped by the dualism of scheme and content. In an oft-cited passage, Davidson argues: 'I want to urge that this… dualism of [conceptual] scheme and [empirical] content, of organizing system and something waiting to be organized, cannot be made intelligible and defensible' (Davidson, 1974/2001: 189). Under this dualism, schemes are construed as 'systems of categories' through which content takes shape, i.e., the world is (empirically) carved up; and such schemes are not in place prior to forms of human activity. In other words, schemes are socially – including culturally and historically – conditioned, and content shows up or comes into being through such schemes. If scheme and content are understood this way, a clear parallel can be drawn with the basic idea of social constructivism, the idea that what we live with is always (socially) schematised content.

And yet, while it is tempting to associate scheme with 'organising system' and content with 'some-thing waiting to be organised', neither scheme nor content can be formulated in the way described above. For one thing, a scheme cannot be a worldview since the latter is an immediate outcome of both constituents of the scheme-content dualism. John McDowell writes: 'A scheme would be, not a world view, but what is left when content is subtracted from a world view' (McDowell, 1999/2009: 119). In short, a scheme is, by definition, a worldview devoid of content. But such a vacuous notion is unintelligible. (Supposed candidates for a scheme such as language and shared beliefs in a society cannot meet the requirement, for they always already embody worldviews.)

Second, content cannot be empirical content or 'representational content' (to use a modern philosophical term) since the latter also commits both parties to the dualism in question. Another candidate for what stands over against the supposed scheme is something like (part of) the world in itself (in Immanuel Kant's sense), which is waiting to be interpreted or discovered. This is what many philosophers call 'the Given', namely, that which has no internal connection with thought. In this conception of content, it is only through an external or causal transaction that content is given empirical form; that is, thought is precluded from such a 'natural' transaction, making unintelligible the process through which content as 'the Given' interacts with non-contentful scheme in such a way that a thinking being can have a worldview.

The discussion thus far tells us that the idea that our worldview is founded on schematised content is fundamentally misguided, for it is question-begging. This indicates that in order for theories about scheme and content to be developed, we need to first address the more primitive question, the significance of which both classical empiricists and social constructivists fail to fully appreciate. This question is how we come to have a worldview at all. This is not as much an empirical question as a *philosophical* one about the very idea of worldviews, involving a philosophical analysis of the very idea of what we call the world, which, as implied, can no longer be simply identified as 'the Given'. Seen this way, the challenges we face are in effect one of modern philosophy's central problematics: the seemingly unintelligible divide between mind and world, between reason and nature, and between the social and the natural. The dualism of scheme and content is by no means of a new kind.

Davidson suggests dropping empiricism and scheme-content dualism altogether, proposing his well-known, non-foundationalist 'coherentism', the thrust of which is well epitomised by the statement that 'nothing can count as a reason for holding a belief except another belief' (Davidson, 1983/2001: 141). This idea, however, means that experiences themselves, *contra* empiricism, do not justify beliefs, thus leaving open a possibility that the nature of reality that we think we know may be all the more vulnerable because it seems unwarranted that our conception of reality – our worldviews – in justificatory relations puts us in contact with reality itself. It seems, in other words, that the question of how it is possible for us human beings to have a worldview at all never attracts the more detailed attention it deserves in Davidson's coherentism.

Richard Rorty and John McDowell both highly appreciate Davidson's work in general, but their responses to his proposal here stand in stark contrast to each other. Whereas Rorty goes so far as to recommend discarding not just empiricism, epistemology and conceptual schemes but also the notion of the world itself, McDowell attempts to rehabilitate them in a way that sheds new light on the relation between the social, the natural and the educational. Drawing attention to their views in turn helps to illuminate the essential context in which we come to have our views of the world in the first place, the context where the social, the natural and the educational inextricably intertwine.

Question for discussion

Do you think educational disciplines and research can do away with the notions of conceptual scheme and the world?

Rorty's denial of the notions of conceptual framework and the world

Rorty's well-known *Philosophy and the Mirror of Nature* (1979) has been widely read beyond the philosophical community and has had a considerable impact on educational discourse in ways

96 *Koichiro Misawa*

that call many Enlightenment values and ideals into question (e.g., Carr, 2004, 2006). Rorty, who boldly and eagerly straddles the analytic–continental divide in philosophy and even incorporates post-modernist and post-structuralist thinking, is at pains to convince the reader that epistemology-centred philosophy, in its search for foundations of knowledge as a mental or linguistic mirroring of a mind-independent world to which modern philosophy has been captive, should come to an end.

In his early essay, 'The world well lost' (1972/1982; unless otherwise specified, the page references in brackets in this section refer to this work), Rorty suggests that the Kantian notion of a 'conceptual framework' and its correlative notion of 'the world', in other words, the Kantian background that is the germ of constructivist thinking (Winch and Gingell, 2008: 39), should be removed altogether. We can put the argument like this: The question of whether 'different conceptual schemes carve up the world differently', a question that remains a matter of concern for those engaged in the perennial realism/anti-realism debate, is a pseudo one. Relief will come if the Kantian distinctions above – the distinction between given and non-given (i.e., receptivity and spontaneity in Kant's terms) and the distinction between necessary and contingent truths – are dismissed, for they make the question look plausible and serious, thereby generating the sterile controversy. Rorty writes:

> Since Kant, we find it almost impossible not to think of the mind as divided into active and passive faculties, the former using concepts to "interpret" what "the world" imposes on the latter. We also find it difficult not to distinguish between those concepts which the mind could hardly get along without and those which it can take or leave alone – and we think of truths about the former concepts as "necessary" in the most proper and paradigmatic sense of the term.
>
> (3)

With recourse to the work of Wilfrid Sellars and W. V. Quine, Rorty vehemently rejects these distinctions. In an early part of 'The world well lost', Rorty offers a conclusive overview of his point, arguing that 'without the notions of "the given" and of "the a priori" there can be no notion of alternative experiences, or alternative worlds, to be constituted by the adoption of new a priori concepts' (5).

Rorty then mainly exploits Davidson's coherence theory of truth (a variant of coherentism mentioned in the previous section) to diminish, more directly, the effectiveness of the notion of 'alternative conceptual frameworks' and of its interrelated notion of 'the world'. The typical objection to the coherentist view that 'nothing can count as a reason for holding a belief except another belief' comes from the defender of the so-called 'correspondence theory of truth', for whom the representationalist mirror-imagery between mind and world that Rorty denounces is in play. The exponent of the correspondence theory complains that 'although our only *test* of truth must be the coherence of our beliefs with one another, still the *nature* of truth must be "correspondence to reality"' (12, emphasis in original). For those who hold such a realist view, coherentism appears to 'perform the conjuring trick of substituting the notion of "the unquestioned vast majority of our beliefs" for the notion of "the world"' (13), since the coherentist presupposes their being 'in touch with the world' – i.e., their having worldviews – simply on the grounds that 'most of a person's belief must be true' (Davidson, 1983/2001: 146). In other words, the realist, since she thinks "it is the *world* that determines the truth" (12, emphasis in original), doubts whether our conception of reality in jus-tificatory relations only among beliefs puts us in contact with *reality itself*. Rorty allows no room for this scepticism, averring that 'the realistic true believer's notion of the world is an obsession' (13); for Rorty, the notions of the world and truth in the sense attached by the realist are two sides of the same obsession with the mirror-imagery between mind and world that he is attacking: '"Truth" in the sense of "truth taken apart from any theory" and "world" taken as "what determines such truth" are notions that were... made for each other. Neither can survive apart from the other' (15). Rorty sees no good reason to give them a chance of survival.

Toward the end of 'The world well lost', Rorty indicates 'the equivocation in the realists' own use of "world"' (14): one is innocuous and the other noxious. In the innocuous sense, which Rorty accepts, the world is 'just whatever that vast majority of our beliefs not currently in question are currently thought to be about' (14). This is quite in line with the Davidsonian position, where the world 'will just be the stars, the people, the tables, and the grass – all those things which nobody... thinks might not exist' (14). In other words, 'The fact that the vast majority of our beliefs must be true will, on this view, guarantee the existence of the vast majority of the things we now think we are talking about' (14). So, in this innocent sense of the world, '(except for a few fringe cases like gods, neutrinos, and natural rights) we now know perfectly well what the world is like and could not possibly be wrong about it – *there is no argument about the point that it is the world that determines truth*' (14, emphasis added).

The realist, however, is not content to accept this 'trivial sense in which "truth" is "correspondence to reality"' (14). Indeed, the sense that the realist envisages is the other sense of the world, which Rorty insists is exactly the Kantian noumenal world, the world as it really is independent of the way that human beings are. Rorty claims: 'The notion of "the world" as used in a phrase like "different conceptual schemes carve up the world differently" must be the notion of something completely unspecified and unspecifiable – the thing-in-itself, in fact' (14, emphasis in original). As we have seen, Rorty suggests giving up this vacuous sense of the world that the realist virtually embraces, complete with the Kantian distinctions between spontaneity and receptivity and between necessity and contingency. Rorty also instructs us to *not* care about the other trivial sense of the world because it is literally trivial. He sees no point in trying to furnish philosophical expositions to the notion of the world that ordinary people understand it to be, and he does not see epistemology (especially in the Kantian framework) as being worth pursuing. In the concluding part of 'The world well lost', he argues that 'if we can come to see both the coherence and correspondence theories as noncompeting trivialities, then we may finally move beyond realism and idealism' (17).

Questions for discussion

Do you think there is a clean break between the realm of causation and the realm of justification? If your answer is 'yes', which realm do you think educational studies should be more concerned with?

Singling out 'the logical space of reasons'

There is, on Rorty's view, no point in worrying that we might merely be making judgements on a case-by-case basis regardless of how things really are, for the notion of truth finds no important place in his picture. On the basis of his reading of Davidson's work, Rorty contends that 'nobody should even try to specify the nature of truth' (Rorty, 1998: 3), holding that truth is, if anything, neither stable nor

98 *Koichiro Misawa*

convergent but, rather, context-based and even *ad hoc*. This view is elevated in his remark that 'the only criterion we have for applying the word "true" is justification, and justification is always relative to an audience' (Rorty, 1998: 3). As long as there is nothing that is true once and for all, 'truth is not a goal of inquiry' (Rorty, 1998: 3). It is notable that 'justification' in Rorty's conception takes a different shape from that in the philosophy-as-epistemology that he is keen to denounce; Rorty protests that 'justification is not a matter of a special relation between ideas (or words) and objects, but of *conversation, of social practice*' (Rorty, 1979/1980: 170, emphasis added).

Rorty's conversationalist conception of philosophy as a social practice that sees the notion of world as a non-issue emphasises the significance of making ourselves answerable to one another rather than to the world. His inclination is explicitly found in his interpretation of Sellars' passage, which has itself been made well-known by his quote in *Philosophy and the Mirror of Nature*. In the passage, Sellars writes:

> The essential point is that in characterising an episode or a state as that of *knowing*, we are not giving an empirical description of that episode or state; we are placing it in the logical space of reasons, of justifying and being able to justify what one says.
>
> (Sellars, 1956/1997: 76, emphasis in original)

Rorty takes this passage to mean that our correct starting point is ongoing conversations in the space of justifying and being able to justify what one says and not metaphysical questions about how one occupies a position in that space:

> If we see knowing not as having an essence, to be described by scientists or philosophers, but rather as a right, by current standards, to believe, then we are well on the way to seeing *conversation* as the ultimate context within which knowledge is to be understood.
>
> (Rorty, 1979/1980: 389, emphasis in original)

There is an intuitive appeal in Rorty's conversationalist view, and it has clear affinities with social constructivist thinking. Rorty rejects as a philosophical red herring the addressing of metaphysical questions about the position we occupy in the logical space of reasons and about how we are also inhabitants of a space that is amenable to 'empirical description' because, for him, the sheer fact that conversations are being performed here and now is the correct starting point.

There is thus no need, Rorty thinks, to care about whether and how we thinking and minded beings are in touch with the world. Drawing on Davidson's notion of 'triangulation' – a 'three-way relation among two speakers and a common world', i.e., 'the mutual and simultaneous responses of two or more creatures to common distal stimuli and to one another's responses' (Davidson, 2001: xv) – Rorty argues that *causal* impacts suffice for our being in the world and that this sort of intersubjective agreement through conversation takes the place of the traditional notion of objectivity. The lesson he learns from Sellars' critique of the 'Myth of the Given' is to guard against confusion between the realm of causation and the realm of justification. Once we have become, owing to a causal chain of events, a denizen in the space of reasons, what matters exclusively is human affairs in the space of justifying and being able to justify what one says; no story other than that of causal impingements needs to be told about the relation between the causal space and the normative space.

The social, natural and educational   99

Still, such a causal story is not a full story of how we have the world in view at all, precisely because elements regarded generally as belonging in the space of reasons (such as the social and the normative) in the most fundamental sense figures much earlier than ongoing conversations. The world's intelligibility cannot be a one-sided story; it requires a far-reaching one that crosses the boundary between the realm of causation and the realm of justification. McDowell tells us such an encompassing story, which, while highlighting the distinctiveness of the space of reasons, sustains our answerability to the world – i.e., to how things are in the world. The line of thinking he elaborates casts light on the way that we live our lives as human beings, who are social and natural animals simultaneously inhabiting a world that is both social and natural, as well as on the essential role that the educational, in the deepest sense possible, plays in the way our lives are lived.

McDowell's expanded view of experience and the natural

John McDowell, who is now regarded as a major figure in philosophy, applauds Rorty for trying to extricate us from foundationalist epistemology. But, along Kantian lines, McDowell sharply objects to Rorty's call to depart from the idea of answerability to the world, for Rorty throws some viable babies out with the bathwater, such as objectivity in the sense of our thinking's being directed at reality, i.e., at how things are thus and so in the world (e.g., McDowell, 1994/1996, 2000a).

The foundational characteristic of modern philosophy, first-person authority, *ipso facto* makes us afraid that our minds might be out of touch with (the rest of) the world. McDowell calls this a 'transcendental worry' (which constitutes modern epistemology's question of how knowledge is possible) and offers a way out of the worry by providing a detailed analysis of the question of 'how empirical content is possible' (McDowell, 1994/1996: xxi), an analysis that reorients our understanding not only of the logical space of reasons but also of the other space in Sellars' images. In fact, the contrast McDowell draws is not, as Rorty does, between the space of *causes* and the space of reasons. What is contrasted with the space of reasons is 'the realm of law' (McDowell, 1994/1996: 71, n. 2) or 'the logical space of natural-scientific understanding' (McDowell, 2000b: 7). Noteworthy here is that McDowell refuses to equate what stands opposed to the space of reasons with the space of *nature*, thereby allowing room for natural occurrences that are not foreign to the normative space of reasons. McDowell claims: 'Contrary to what Rorty's contrast implies, reasons might *be* causes' (McDowell, 1994/1996: 71, n. 2, emphasis in original). This is not to be taken as a species of constructivist thinking, for McDowell's view does not contradict the fact that 'a *merely* causal relation cannot do duty for a justificatory relation' (1994/1996: 71, n. 2, emphasis in original). What he is resisting is the prevailing view bolstered by the modern *disenchanted* conception of nature that experiences themselves do not justify beliefs – that is, the view that is also inherent in Davidson's coherentism extolled by Rorty. McDowell offers a salutary corrective to this view by casting perceptual experience not as 'a merely causal relation' between minded beings and a mind-independent world but as belonging already in the logical space of reasons. Perception, McDowell says, is 'the capacity for knowledge through impacts of reality on the senses' (McDowell, 2018: 89).

According to the prevailing view that generates the transcendental worry, empirical content seems impossible for a pair of thoughts that are incompatible with each other: first, sense experience must play a juridical role if our thinking is answerable to the world; second, nonetheless,

100 *Koichiro Misawa*

sense experience, as the impact that the world makes on a possessor of sensibility, cannot play such a juridical role because that transaction occurs as a natural phenomenon in the natural world, which, as Davidson and Rorty see it, allows for only causal connections and not justificatory relations. McDowell challenges this dominant frame of mind by proposing what he dubs 'minimal empiricism' or, in some instances, 'transcendental empiricism', according to which the content of experience is always *conceptual* rather than the Given (something waiting to be conceptualised), as perceptual experience in which conceptual capacities are already actualised (although not necessarily exercised) plays the role of the tribunal (McDowell, 1994/1996, 2000b). This minimal form of empiricism, McDowell argues, enables us to see the way in which our thinking has empirical content; that is, how things are in the world. In other words, it explains how we can have the world in view at all – without either ignoring not just the causal but also rational constraint the world exerts on our thinking or forgetting the bearing of thought on reality.

To complement his seemingly enigmatic argument, McDowell reminds us of the Aristotelian idea of 'second nature' (McDowell, 1994/1996), which a normal human being acquires through initiation, primarily via the acquisition of language, into traditions of thought and reasoning, namely into the logical space of reasons. Taken altogether, human sensibility is permeated with our second nature, which is to mean that 'the naturalness of our sensibility can be the naturalness of second nature' and thus '[o]ur sensibility is, if you like, part of the *cultural* world' (McDowell, 2005: 201, emphasis added). This is also to suggest that the Davidsonian 'triangulation' thesis that 'the mutual and simultaneous responses of two or more creatures to common distal stimuli and to one another's responses' falls short of accounting for how we come to be as we are. The truth is, as McDowell expounds, that '[p]erceptual capacities, rational or not, are modes of responsiveness to features of an animal's distal environment that are *strikingly underdetermined* by impingements on sensory nerve endings in the animal's perceptual equipment' (McDowell, 2011: 55, emphasis added). The triangulation thesis fails to acknowledge that 'common distal stimuli' may not be 'a merely causal relation' but already have a normative dimension that is enmeshed with second nature. This failure in turn makes us recognise that the triangulation thesis is putting the cart before the horse. McDowell argues:

> By my lights, if subjects are already in place, it is too late to set about catering for the constitution of the concept of objectivity. We must take subjectivity and the concept of objectivity to emerge together out of initiation into the space of reasons.
>
> (McDowell, 1994/1996: 186, emphasis added)

If we allow McDowell's line of argument to come into the picture, we would, especially by focusing attention to the initiation into the space of reasons, have a richer conception of the social, the natural and the educational as playing an essentially fundamental part in the way that we live our lives as social and natural animals in the fabric of the world human beings inhabit.

The fundamental interweaving of the social, the natural and the educational

According to McDowell's reconceptualisaion of experience as operations of sensory receptivity *and* simultaneous actualisations of conceptual capacities, human experience at the deepest level cuts across the boundary between the realm of causation and the realm of justification. If this conception

The social, natural and educational   101

of experience is properly understood, it follows that the world that figures through our sensibility *is* different from a world in which a non-human animal dwells (if any) because the naturalness of our sensibility is *sui generis* to human beings (which thus intimates that our life-activity cannot be fully captured in natural-scientific explanations of law-governed occurrences).

However, such second-naturedness is, as the ordinal number designates, *not* an inborn equipment of human children. It needs to be acquired. McDowell makes this point rather polemically: 'Human beings are not [born at home in the space of reasons]: they are born *mere animals*, and they are *transformed* into thinkers and intentional agents in the course of coming to maturity' (McDowell, 1994/1996: 125, emphasis added). McDowell himself is reluctant to do more than stress the importance of being initiated into one's first language, invoking the German idea of *Bildung* in order to explain this transformational and emancipatory process 'from a merely animal mode of living into being a full-fledged subject' (1994/1996: 125). He may be too cautious, however, to fill in the details of this *educational* dimension of the human condition. Scientific research, natural or social, probably does not suffice to do the work, for the issue in question is concerned with our sociality and naturality, which is a *precondition* of the kind of beings that we are and thus of the way that we live our lives. The deepest sense of our being social grows out of our responsiveness to reasons in the space of reasons and that responsiveness is synchronically made second nature to human beings through the social. This process of the becoming of human animals *qua* human beings deserves the name of the educational in its most basic sense. To relocate the issues of human nature and the human condition in this interweaving between the social, the natural and the educational is certainly worth pursuing.

Although McDowell's philosophy has not been a topic to which philosophers of education have paid adequate attention, we have recently witnessed a remarkable change in the treatment of his thought-provoking ideas, most prominently in the work of the philosopher David Bakhurst (e.g., Bakhurst, 2011, 2015). Most recently, Bakhurst further explores the educational implications of McDowell's approaches in the symposium on his 2011 book and picks out four related areas that have a profound relevance to our understanding of education: 'responsiveness to reasons', 'freedom', 'initiation' and 'liberal education' (Bakhurst, 2016). The symposium-related issues have soon provoked both sympathetic and critical responses in the philosophy of education (e.g., Misawa, 2017; Williams, 2018). Yet, this promising avenue of philosophical inquiry is waiting to be brought into full flower, an avenue that would refine the context in which scientific research, natural and social, in education could also make more substantive advances.

Conclusion

This chapter has been concerned with articulating the sense that a philosophical appreciation of the fundamental context of the social and the natural encourages us to acknowledge the educational character of the kind of beings that we are whose engagement with the world is not shared with non-human animals. In the course of reaching this point, the chapter has paid heed to social constructivism, which tends to fall into the dualism of scheme and content, and to Rorty's dismissive attitude towards the notions of conceptual scheme and the world which, notwithstanding his claim, does not rid itself of the realism/anti-realism divide. As a welcome antidote to such unhelpful modern dualisms that make the question of how many realities exist look legitimate, this chapter has called attention to McDowell's expanded conceptions of experience and the natural, conceptions that

102 *Koichiro Misawa*

invite us to reshape our recognition of the dualism of reason and nature that underlies a number of ill-conceived modern dualisms. The interrelatedness between the social, the natural and the educational that McDowell's view is implying prompts us to reflect, in a new light, on the general frameworks within which the issues of education are currently addressed: the natural-scientific understanding of human beings as part of (first) nature and the social constructivist realisation of human beings as social products. McDowell's arguments suggest that once we have become an inhabitant of the space of reasons through the acquisition of second nature, even our first nature could be different in quality from what human animals as mere animals have, as we see it in the case of causal events through perception. That is, this line of philosophical argument as to the social and the natural indicates that the educational is integral to human nature and the human condition.

Summary

- The dualism of nature and reason is the root dualism underlying numerous dualisms that have impeded further development of educational research and disciplines (such as the dualism of scheme and content, constructivism and positivism, realism and anti-realism and quantitative and qualitative research).
- If we, with McDowell, conceive experience and nature along the lines suggested by this chapter, we can see ourselves as natural and social animals simultaneously inhabiting a world that is at once social and natural.
- Philosophical inquiry makes it possible to cast light on the social and the natural in ways that differ from those of social and natural scientific research, thereby bringing to light the fundamental interrelatedness between the social, the natural and the educational.
- Analysing human nature and the human condition from the perspective of such an interrelatedness opens up a promising path for those who study education and human beings.

Recommending reading

Bakhurst, D. (2011) *The Formation of Reason*. Oxford: Wiley-Blackwell.
Bonnett, M. (2004) *Retrieving Nature: Education for a Post-Humanist Age*. Oxford: Blackwell Publishing.
Standish, P. (2016) The disenchantment of education and the re-enchantment of the world. *Journal of Philosophy of Education* **50**(1): 98–116.

References

Bakhurst, D. (2011) *The Formation of Reason*. Oxford: Wiley-Blackwell.
Bakhurst, D. (2015) Training, transformation and education. *Royal Institute of Philosophy Supplement* **76**: 301–327.
Bakhurst, D. (2016) Introduction: exploring the formation of reason. *Journal of Philosophy of Education* **50**(1): 76–83.
Bruner, J. (1996) *The Culture of Education*. Cambridge, MA: Harvard University Press.
Berger, P. L. and Luckmann, T. (1966) *The Social Construction of Reality: A Treatise in the Sociology of Knowledge*. Garden City, NY: Doubleday.
Carr, W. (2004) Philosophy and education. *Journal of Philosophy of Education* **38**(1): 55–73.
Carr, W. (2006) Education without theory. *British Journal of Educational Studies* **54**(2): 136–159.
Davidson, D. (1974/2001) On the very idea of a conceptual scheme. In D. Davidson *Inquiries into Truth and Interpretation* (2nd edition). Oxford: Clarendon Press.

Davidson, D. (1983/2001) A coherence theory of truth and knowledge. In D. Davidson, *Subjective, Intersubjective, Objective*. Oxford: Clarendon Press.

Davidson, D. (2001) *Subjective, Intersubjective, Objective*. Oxford: Clarendon Press.

Derry, J. (2008) Abstract rationality in education: from Vygotsky to Brandom. *Studies in Philosophy and Education* **27**(1): 49–62.

Gergen, K. J. (1999) *An Invitation to Social Construction*. London: Sage.

Guba, E. G. and Lincoln, Y. S. (1989) *Fourth Generation Evaluation*. London: Sage.

Hirst, P. H. (ed.) (1983/2014) *Educational Theory and Foundation Disciplines*. London: Routledge.

Markie, P. (2017) Rationalism vs. empiricism. In E. N. Zalta (ed.), *The Stanford Encyclopedia of Philosophy*. Available at: https://plato.stanford.edu/entries/rationalism-empiricism/ (Accessed 18 January 2019).

McCulloch, G. (2002) Disciplines contributing to education? Educational studies and the disciplines. *British Journal of Educational Studies* **50**(1): 100–119.

McDowell, J. (1994/1996) *Mind and World* (2nd edition). Cambridge, MA: Harvard University Press.

McDowell, J. (1999/2009) Scheme-content dualism and empiricism. In J. McDowell, *The Engaged Intellect: Philosophical Essays*. Cambridge, MA: Harvard University Press.

McDowell, J. (2000a) Towards rehabilitating objectivity. In R. Brandom (ed.), *Rorty and His Critics. Philosophers and Their Critics 9*. Malden, MA: Blackwell.

McDowell, J. (2000b) Experiencing the world. In M. Willaschek (ed.), *John McDowell: Reason and Nature*. Münster, Germany: LIT.

McDowell, J. (2005). Reply of John McDowell [to Michael Williams]. In J. Boros (ed.), *Mind in World: Essays on John McDowell's Mind and World*. Pécs, Hungary: Brambauer. Available at: www.part-oldalak.hu/kutatas/Essays%20on%20John%20McDowell's%20Mind%20and%20World.pdf (Accessed 18 January 2019).

McDowell, J. (2009) *Having the World in View: Essays on Kant, Hegel, and Sellars*. Cambridge, MA: Harvard University Press.

McDowell, J. (2011) *Perception as a Capacity for Knowledge*. Milwaukee, WI: Marquette University Press.

McDowell, J. (2018) Perceptual experience and empirical rationality. *Analytic Philosophy* **59**(1): 89–98.

Misawa, K. (2016) Rethinking the 'social' in educational research: on what underlies scheme-content dualism. *Ethics and Education* **11**(3): 326–337.

Misawa, K. (2017) Humans, animals and the world we inhabit – on and beyond the symposium 'Second nature, *Bildung* and McDowell: David Bakhurst's *The Formation of Reason*'. *Journal of Philosophy of Education* **51**(4): 744–759.

Peters, R. S. (1963/1980) Education as initiation. In P. Gordon (ed.), *The Study of Education*. London: Woburn.

Pring, R. (2000/2004) The 'false dualism' of educational research. In R. Rorty (ed.), *Philosophy of Education: Aims, Theory, Common Sense and Research*. London: Continuum.

Rorty, R. (1972/1982) The world well lost. In R. Rorty, *Consequences of Pragmatism: Essays, 1972–1980*. Minneapolis: University of Minnesota Press.

Rorty, R. (1979/1980) *Philosophy and the Mirror of Nature*. Princeton: Princeton University Press.

Rorty, R. (1998) Introduction. In R. Rorty, *Truth and Progress: Philosophical Papers, Volume 3*. Cambridge: Cambridge University Press.

Sellars, W. (1956/1997) *Empiricism and the Philosophy of Mind*, introduction by R. Rorty, study guide by R. Brandom. Cambridge, MA: Harvard University Press.

Williams, E. L. (2018) 'To catch at and let go': David Bakhurst, phenomenology and post-phenomenology. *Journal of Philosophy of Education* 52(1): 87–104.

Winch, C. and Gingell, G. (2008) *Philosophy of Education: The Key Concepts* (2nd edition). London: Routledge.

Young, M. F. D. (ed.) (1971) *Knowledge and Control: New Directions for the Sociology of Education*. London: Collier-Macmillan.

9 The teacher–student relationship
An existential approach

Alison M. Brady

Introduction

The teacher–student relationship, and how to define it, has often been an area of interest for educational researchers, perhaps because it is so central to the very notion of education itself. Indeed, how might one conceive of the process of education without considering *who it is* that is being educated, and *who it is* that is educating? And yet, while there are various conceptions of what the role of the teacher is in relation to the student, there is arguably far less discussion around the *lived experience* of this relationship. Furthermore, the ways in which the teacher–student relationship is defined seems to rest on a somewhat rigid separation of the two seemingly distinct roles. But how are we to understand what a teacher is without the students she is teaching? And how are we to understand what a student is, in strict terms, without the presence of some form of teaching? These questions are central to understanding what constitutes the teacher–student relationship on the one hand, but also, in considering what it actually *feels like* to be in such a relationship, and what effects this might have for the ways in which we understand ourselves and our roles as either teachers or students.

What are some of the main ways in which we understand this relationship? It is worth clarifying here that a number of different kinds of schooling will be referred to throughout this chapter. While these contexts are arguably quite different, the chapter attempts to chart the notion of 'freedom' that is essential for understanding the relationship, and to think about the ways in which this notion has been installed (and distorted) in different educational regimes, and throughout different educational stages.

First, let us consider what might be called the currently dominant 'neoliberal' conception, and in particular, how this might affect the roles that are envisioned for both teachers and students. Subsequently, an image of the progressivist teacher–student relationship will be explored, followed by a consideration of what the philosophy of existentialism can offer to the discussion.

The neoliberal teacher–student relationship

Neoliberalism has been identified in recent decades as a discourse deeply affecting the education sector in a myriad of ways. As an economic and political ideology, neoliberalism is primarily concerned with creating a free market economy, where the regulation of public services is seen as best devolved to the level of the market. The needs for the supply of such services are based on demand, with increased quality of services managed through the creation and maintenance of greater competition between providers. Minimal state control is perceived as necessary to allow

The teacher–student relationship   105

such competition to flourish. This is the neoliberal society that was envisioned by the economists Hayek and Friedman (Grek and Lindgren, 2015) in the light of the perceived failures of the welfare state. However, in an age of globalisation, the competitive playing field between such services has increased immensely, and it is often argued that neoliberalism has become the dominant, and thus inescapable, way in which various providers function globally.

What does this mean for education? Like many so-called developed nations, the United Kingdom is what is known as a *knowledge-based economy* (Castells, 1996). This means that, unlike other countries whose economy might rely on natural resources, the UK's greatest resource is its qualified, highly educated workforce. This puts education at the centre of concerns around economic growth. With such pressures on education sectors needing to meet the demands of industry and of the economy, various regulation mechanisms (with the explicit aim of increasing competition) have been introduced. Thus, although neoliberalism seems to favour 'de-regulation', literature suggests that, rather, neoliberalism results in a kind of 're-regulation' (Ball, 2003). This 're-regulation' takes the form of a governance under which the conditions necessary for the market to flourish remain unhampered by restrictions and constraints.

Through mechanisms such as student–teacher feedback and evaluation, increased parental school choice, benchmarking and league tables, and various accountability measures such as school inspection systems, the education sector has been reconceptualised in quasi-market terms, based on the belief that increased competition leads to increased quality of output. Educational institutions, indeed, are forced to compete with one another, vying for increased student numbers through the strategic use of marketing and ensuring that the students are satisfied with the level of service provided (thereby increasing student turnover). As a result, there is a heightened pressure on teaching to continually demonstrate improvement in order to meet the requirements of student and parent satisfaction. As a result, whereas traditionally, the teacher may have been seen as an 'authority figure' in the classroom, through neoliberalism, students, and indeed the wider public, have been given new powers that have shifted this balance of authority considerably.

This has been, perhaps, most notably witnessed in the higher education sector. Since 2005, not without controversy, final-year undergraduate students have been requested to fill in the National Student Survey (NSS), a questionnaire that allows them to grade their level of satisfaction on a number of aspects related to their university experiences, one of which includes the quality of teaching and learning (HEFCE, 2018). The NSS is significant since the results partly impinge upon where universities stand in relation to others, since once such information is made publicly available it is used by various agencies as part of a systematic benchmarking system that allows universities to be compared and ranked accordingly, increasing levels of competition.

What does this imply about the teacher–student relationship? Many authors argue that neoliberalism, either directly or indirectly, places the teacher in relation to the student as a service provider stands in relation to his clients (Molesworth *et al.*, 2011). There are numerous ways in which this is achieved. Unlike many countries where university fees are heavily subsidised by the government, most students in the UK pay upwards of £9,000 a year, and thus it seems obvious that they would expect a certain level of service to be provided to them, and that certain levels of satisfaction be met in relation to their course. More recently, there have been moves to base university fees on the extent to which it provides a 'return' to students, the idea being that universities will be able to charge students different fees based on the level of 'value-for-money' that their degree courses provide (e.g., *The Times*, 2017).

106 *Alison M. Brady*

In turn, students 'rate' their university experience through mechanisms such as the NSS. Indeed, the university sector (but also other forms of schooling) run very much on a model that is similar to the service industry – where students have purchasing power, where teachers are merely providing them with a service, and where the emphasis on 'student satisfaction' leads to greater levels of teacher accountability.

A direct result of this is the commodification of knowledge – something that Lyotard (1979) warned us against in his highly influential book, *The Postmodern Condition*. Students are offered pre-packaged courses with seemingly direct routes to employment, or at least the anticipation that their university degree will allow them to attain a high level of 'employability'. The role of the teacher is reduced to ensuring that such skills are being acquired through the knowledge they provide, skills that have been invariably labelled as 'twenty-first-century', ranging from 'critical thinking' and 'creativity' to 'multicultural literacy' and 'perseverance' (DfES, 2003). These twenty-first-century skills have been promoted as 'broad foundation skills needed for sustainable employment', and seem to apply to all levels of schooling (including higher education), albeit in terms of 'making more sense of what is already there, integrating what already exists and focusing it more effectively'. Effectiveness here is defined in terms of ensuring 'that everyone has the skills they need to become more employable and adaptable' (DfES, 2003: 1–12). Thus, it is not so much 'knowledge' that is being imparted to students in the traditional sense, but sets of entrepreneurial skills that ensure that students are ready to take an active role in the economic growth of the country.

These 'twenty-first-century skills' serve to promote a consumerist notion of the *freedom of choice*, loosely based on the idea that educational institutions can impart the necessary skills (creativity, entrepreneurialism, employability) in order for this 'freedom to choose' (a university course, a career) to be realised. Indeed, universities are often complicit in promoting this idea, perhaps partly due to their need to 'market' themselves to students along lines that would secure higher levels of student turnover. But this notion of 'freedom of choice' is a much debased (re)conception of the notion of freedom that is outlined in progressivist theories of education, and as we will see later, is even further removed from the existentialist usage of the term. The resulting factor, however, is a somewhat impoverished understanding of teaching, which has been promoted with the phrase 'teacher as facilitator'.

It is, perhaps, difficult to think of the purpose of universities outside of this framework, since these seemingly inexorable neoliberal trends have been evident in education for quite some time (Harvey, 2007). But if we think about the teacher–student relationship in particular, isn't there something about it that goes beyond this client–service provider construction? Before considering these questions, it is worth thinking about another model of the teacher–student relationship, which may help highlight some of these issues further, and perhaps even mitigate against them.

Questions for discussion

What other ways is this 'client–service provider' relationship visible in education? The focus has been on higher education here, but can this model be seen in other contexts?

What are the potential harms of this relationship? Doesn't it, in fact, give more power to students? Why might this be a bad thing?

Is there anything in the teacher–student relationship that is not captured by this 'client–service provider' relationship model?

The progressive teacher–student relationship

Moves towards a more progressivist understanding of the teacher's role in relation to the student can be traced at least as far back as Rousseau (1979 [1763]) in his highly influential book *Emile*. Contrary to his contemporaries, Rousseau conceived of childhood and of the education of children in a radically different way from the dominant theory of the time, which was based on the religious tenet of Original Sin. Rousseau believed that all children were born 'good' but are later corrupted by society. He indicates this in the first few lines of *Emile* when he states that 'everything is good as it leaves the hands of the Author of things; everything degenerates in the hands of man' (Rousseau, 1979 [1763]: 37).

Rousseau's theory of education is based partly on his wider theory of the self in relation to society, wherein he differentiates two kinds of 'self-love'. For Rousseau, *amour de soi*, or 'self-love', is an innate quality of the human being, and manifests itself, among other things, in terms of the basic drives for human self-preservation, as well as an empathy through also wanting the self-preservation of others. Since this is innate in humans, it is also good, insofar as everything natural, according to Rousseau, is inherently good. *Amour propre*, or 'love of self', can be understood on a basic level as a corrupted version of the more primordial self-love. Understanding *amour propre* requires an appreciation of Rousseau's overall socio-political aims in writing this text, based on his formulation of an ideal state, pitted against the shallowness of the aristocratic class he witnessed at the time, from which his philosophy of education was drawn. In *Emile*, the basic premise of *amour propre* is that, should this 'love of self' develop too early in a child, he may become too preoccupied with what others think, with the recognition others confer on him, a recognition that becomes a calculation of the worth of himself and others. It causes the child to turn away from his natural inclinations, which are not only good, but which also allow for a non-superficial and non-instrumental responsiveness to others. All of this can be understood as a metonym for his 'ideal state', rather than simply a manual for teachers, and yet it does tell us something important about the nature of education and, as we will see, the nature of the teacher–student relationship.

In *Emile*, Rousseau argues that, first and foremost, students should be educated (at least initially) in the countryside, isolated from societal ruination. Since the teacher, as an adult, may function as a perverting force against the development of 'self-love', Rousseau emphasises the necessity of experiential learning, or learning through discovery, as opposed to 'rote' or 'acquisition' learning through the teacher. Thus, the role of the teacher here is reduced to that of a facilitator: one who provides the conditions under which such learning can take place, rather than act as an authority figure or 'expert' who transmits information to students in a rigid and linear way.

Much of Rousseau's philosophy was both taken up and criticised by other philosophers, such as John Dewey, and his ideas later became influential in the 1960s in England with a series of policy changes aimed at altering the ways in which children were taught in schools. Most notable was, perhaps, the Plowden Report (Central Advisory Council for Education, 1967). Although aimed largely at primary schools, the Plowden Report was influential in all spheres of teaching and learning. It emphasised the individual nature of each child and the need for personalised forms of learning. It also recommended a reduction in class sizes so as to allow for more 'authentic' forms of learning to take place, one based on the teacher-as-facilitator model, with learners acquiring knowledge through experimentation, discovery and other so-called 'progressive' methods.

108   *Alison M. Brady*

The progressivist movement in England was influential, but it was not without criticism. It was attacked from various stances: from the so-called conservatism of the 'Black Papers in Education' first published in 1969 (Cox and Dyson, 1969), to the conservative government under the auspices of Thatcher in the late 1970s. Indeed, following the oil crisis of 1973, the progressivist movement became a scapegoat for many of society's ills. But it was also criticised by advocates of the idea of liberal education who argued that the view of the child in progressivism was excessively sentimental, that a debased notion of the happiness of the child was being emphasised, and that not enough attention was being paid to the necessity of inculcating children into intrinsically worthwhile activities (Dearden, 1968).

What is interesting here is the image of the teacher–student relationship that is promoted in progressivism, and how far this relationship has changed in recent times. It is difficult to argue against the seemingly noble motives of progressivist educators, especially those writing in reaction to the often-impoverished ways in which students were being educated at that time. Progressive educators were acutely attuned to the necessity of the freedom of the child, unshackled from the pervasive forms of traditional pedagogy. This notion of freedom is a far cry from the consumerist notion of freedom outlined above. It centred on the role of the child in its *own* education, unhampered by the corruptive forces not only of society, but of the ways in which schools were organised at the time.

The idea of liberal education also promotes freedom, despite reacting against what its advocates saw as the problematic overemphasis of progressivism in British schools. However, their idea of freedom was intimately connected to the notion of rational autonomy. It is simply not enough to allow students to behave in a free manner in the classroom, learning through exploration and discovery, with the teacher merely providing the conditions under which such kinds of learning can take place. Rather, teachers must actively cultivate autonomy in their students through engaging them in academic pursuits that are worthwhile, and through ensuring that they develop into beings capable of making rational choices, and therefore exercising their autonomy in a reasoned way.

How does this responsibility of the teacher towards her students compare with what we understand about the teacher–student relationship today? One could argue that, with its emphasis on twenty-first-century skills, teachers *are* providing the conditions under which the autonomy of the student can be realised. Indeed, without the skills of perseverance, employability, creativity and problem-solving, how can we expect students to navigate the world once they leave university? How, indeed, can we expect them to be reasonable?

And yet, the ways in which these skills function in modern universities is often through a 'marketised' lens. In neoliberalism, such skills are seen as static and transferrable to various contexts. They allow for the creation of flexible individuals, individuals who create a collective, viable workforce who work towards sustaining the knowledge-based economy. The skills come 'prepackaged', as it were, ready to be installed in the minds of students who pay for the luxury. Whereas both liberal and progressivist educators might think of education as a worthwhile pursuit in and of itself, neoliberal society sees education is only worthwhile if it can help the individual achieve in a way that is instrumental for economic growth, on both personal and on societal levels.

Thus, the language of both progressivist and liberal education has, in a sense, become usurped by the neoliberal agenda, culminating in a shift from the 'child-centred' approach in schools to a 'student-centred' one in universities. Its effects are neutralising. Indeed, who could argue against the importance of creative, entrepreneurial, critical-thinking individuals? What exactly is the matter

The teacher–student relationship 109

with an education that aims at economic growth? And thus, surely the role of the teacher in relation to the student is to ensure that this happens? In fact, it might be argued that it is not only the *role* of teacher to do so, it is their *responsibility*.

In the next section, we will diverge slightly in order to think in an entirely new way about the teacher–student relationship, and how this role plays out in practice. We will do so through the lens of existentialist philosophy. A central theme thus far has been on the notion of freedom. As we will see below, freedom is a central concept in existentialist thought. However, unlike the notions of neoliberal freedom of choice, liberal freedom as rational autonomy, or child-centred freedom through exploration and discovery, the existentialist notion of freedom is, perhaps, altogether more complex.

Questions for discussion

Rousseau's book *Emile* is often criticised for not offering a practical solution to the problem of education. Who would agree to send their child into the countryside, isolated from all others? But are there ways in which this could be adapted? Are there any examples of where this has been done?

Three conceptions of freedom of the child have been discussed so far. How might these pose (practical) problems for the role of the teacher?

Do you think the progressivist or liberal model can act as a remedy to neoliberal conceptions of education? In what way?

The existentialist approach

Before embarking on this discussion, there are a few points worth clarifying. First of all, existentialism is often defined more as a 'philosophical attitude' shared by those who might be loosely termed as 'existentialists', rather than a systematic doctrine with easily definable tenets and beliefs. Philosophers who have been labelled as 'existentialists' differ immensely in terms of their overarching positions, and indeed, many have rejected this label in turn. Some might be called 'theistic existentialists', such as the Danish philosopher Søren Kierkegaard and the French philosopher Gabriel Marcel. Others rely heavily on an atheistic worldview, including many of the French existentialists who were writing around the time of the Second World War, including Simone de Beauvoir and Albert Camus. Some philosophers who have been labelled existentialists have completely rejected the work of other existentialists, most notably Martin Heidegger in relation to Jean-Paul Sartre. Thus, existentialism is unique in that, as a philosophy, it is difficult to define in any systematic sense.

Partly this is due to something that those labelled as existentialists mostly share, and that is an inherent suspicion of what we might think of as 'abstract philosophy'. Essentially, because existentialism often starts from the point of view of the individual, it is sometimes considered to be 'anti-abstractionist'. In other words, whereas many philosophical traditions are concerned with explaining reality through the use of abstract categories, norms and classifications, existentialism finds this tendency to generalise and, thus, to avoid the 'subjective' elements that are essential for understanding the lived experience of human reality, deeply problematic.

110   *Alison M. Brady*

One of the only philosophers who readily accepted the label of existentialist was Jean-Paul Sartre. Sartre, a key member of the French Resistance movement during the Second World War, is perhaps most famous for his seminal text *Being and Nothingness*, which he wrote in German-occupied France in 1943. Sartre was also a key figure in the French literary scene at the time, so much so that he was offered, but ultimately rejected, the Noble Prize for Literature on two separate occasions. A number of his novels and plays, such as *Nausea* (1938), *No Exit* (1944) and *The Roads to Freedom* (1945) trilogy, deal with key existentialist themes, often in a much more comprehensible format than the more 'systematic' of his philosophical tomes.

One of Sartre's main foci was on the nature of human freedom, but this is quite a profound idea of freedom that does not necessarily correlate to the notions of freedom outlined so far. One can understand this emphasis, however, given the time in which he was writing. Sartre (as quoted in Barrett, 1962: 239–240) once spoke of freedom in the following way:

> We were never more free than during the German occupation. We had lost all of our rights, beginning with the right to talk. Every day we were insulted to our faces and had to take it in silence. Under one pretext or another, as workers, as Jews, or political prisoners, we were deported *en masse*. Everywhere, on billboards, in the newspapers, on the screen, we encountered the revolting and insipid picture of ourselves that our suppressors wanted us to accept. And because of this we were free. Because the Nazi venom seeped into our thoughts, every accurate thought was a conquest. Because an all-powerful police tried to force us to hold our tongues, every word took on the value of a declaration of principles. Because we were hunted down, every one of our gestures had the weight of a solemn commitment.... And the choice that each of us made of his life was an authentic choice because it was made face to face with death... And here I am not speaking of the elite among us... but of all Frenchmen who, at every hour of the night and day throughout four years, answered 'No.'

In *Being and Nothingness*, Sartre outlines two main modes of being: *being-in-itself* and *being-for-itself*. *Being-in-itself* constitutes what we might call 'inanimate objects' – they are the things that exist without consciousness, inert and, thus, exist with what we might call a 'fixed essence'. A tree is just a tree, and will always *be* a tree. Its essence is 'fixed' – it can never be anything other than a tree. On the other hand, there also exists what is called *being-for-itself*. This mode of being is often used interchangeably with consciousness and is therefore a central component of what it means to be a human since, unlike trees, humans are *conscious* beings. What's more, they are *conscious of* things. They are conscious of, for example, the fact that they are *not* a tree, but rather, that they are beings *with consciousness* (relating to what Sartre calls 'pre-reflective consciousness').

Consciousness is not 'fixed' in the way that *being-in-itself* is. Rather, it exists primarily through what Sartre calls 'negation', or 'non-being'. What this means is that the 'essence' of consciousness (and, indeed, humans) – what it is that makes consciousness what it is – is the fact that it is *conscious of not being a thing-in-itself*. It is, essentially, a 'lack'. Indeed, part of who I am resides in the fact that I *am not* this object, or thing-in-itself. And this 'negation' is perpetual, insofar as we are always conscious (of something).

So what am I, then, as a conscious being? From this point of view, Sartre (2003 [1943]: 58) argues that consciousness 'is what it is not and is not what it is'. But it is not just consciousness itself that this applies to – humans themselves, to paraphrase Heidegger (1978 [1927]), are beings

The teacher–student relationship 111

for whom Being is a question. This can be loosely connected to Sartre's (2003 [1943]) postulation that *existence precedes essence*. Unlike trees, humans do not have a fixed essence. We cannot say with certainty that we are *this* or *that*, and nothing else. Rather, our 'essence' comes about through the *process of existing in the world.* It is existence that comes first, through which we become who we are. For that reason, human beings *are not*, and therefore, they are always *becoming*.

What are they becoming, one might ask? Here lies the crux of what Sartre deems as existential freedom. Humans are, in fact, *becoming nothing.* For Sartre, there is no set path that humans must follow. Instead, humans are constituted by a dizzying level of freedom. Sartre uses the example (adopted from Kierkegaard) of walking somewhere up high. Often we feel anxious about this, and often we attribute this vertigo to a fear of falling. However, we are also anxious about the fact that we might jump – or, at least, that we *could* jump, and there is nothing anyone, including ourselves, can do to stop us, aside from *our choosing not* to jump.

This gives us a taste of the freedom that is a central component of what it means to be a human. Because we do not exist like trees (who have no other choice but to be a tree), human beings are ultimately free to project their own meaning into the world, to make choices about what they want to do, and, indeed, who they want to become. This is not to deny, however, that there are 'factual limitations' to who we can become (since we are 'embodied' or 'situated' in a way that is beyond our control). This relates to what Sartre calls 'facticity'. However, we are still free to respond to such limitations, to apply meaning to them, to resist the meaning that seems to be 'inherent' in such limitations if we so choose.

With all of this choice, however, comes the great weight of responsibility. Sartre, indeed, doesn't want to argue that this freedom is always liberating. Rather, like the vertigo example above, such freedom indicates that we are solely responsible for any (in)actions that we take. And this can leave us with an inalienable sense of anxiety, and often causes us to cower in what he calls 'bad faith', where we see our situated-ness or factual limitations as fully determining who we are, wherein which we prevent ourselves from acting otherwise.

All of this might seem to be quite different from how many of us think naturally, especially when it comes to encountering other people. Indeed, it might seem straightforward enough to think about a tree as an object with no other choice but to be a tree. But how is it that we encounter other people? Do we also, in a sense, see them as objects? How do we know that they are conscious beings? This is a central concern for Sartre, so much so that he devotes an entire section to it in *Being and Nothingness*, entitled 'Being-for-others'.

When we encounter someone for the first time, we often see them in fixed terms. When I walk into a classroom as a teacher, I know that the humans sitting at their desks in front of me are what I call 'students'. Because I know this, I automatically have certain expectations of them – that they sit quietly, that they raise their hands when they wish to speak, that they do the work I ask of them, that they are here to learn. In a sense, I am encountering the students as *fixed essences* – I have abstract categories in my mind about what a student *is*, and I apply this to the situation and to understanding those that are sitting before me.

Interestingly, the students are doing the same thing to me. When *I* walk into the classroom, not in uniform, as an older individual (most likely), with an 'air of authority' perhaps, they immediately see that I am a teacher. And with that comes certain expectations – that I am going to start speaking to everyone at once, that I will start talking about whatever subject I am there to teach, that I will stand in front of the class with some PowerPoint slides behind me. These are traits that make me

112 *Alison M. Brady*

as a teacher immediately recognisable, and these traits, in a sense, constitute a fixed essence of who I am *for others*.

Moreover, because of the ways in which we, as humans, exist in the world with other humans, who both create and maintain certain expectations of each other, we also come to impose such expectations on ourselves. These expectations serve as kinds of 'functions' of ourselves and our perceived roles that we (often complacently) submit to. According to Sartre (2003 [1943]: 59):

> Society demands that he limit himself to his function… There are indeed many precautions to imprison a man in what he is as if we lived in perpetual fear that he might escape from it, that he might break away and suddenly elude his condition.

In the chapter on bad faith, Sartre uses the example of an attentive pupil. This pupil has a fixed image in his mind about what a good pupil should look like – he focuses his eyes on the teacher, sits upright, looks engaged. Much of this comes from others – the teacher, his parents or, perhaps, society more broadly. In fact, because he becomes so fixated by the expectations that he appear attentive, he is actually disengaged from what is happening in the classroom. He performs his function well, but in doing so, he is failing to enact his freedom as a *being-for-itself*, a human who is fully present and immersed in what is going on. Thus, we can see how by performing certain roles, we act as if we are *things-in-themselves*, and thus who we are (or how it is that we *perform* who we are) is often anchored to the ways in which others perceive us.

But Sartre wonders what happens when another person *looks* at you. This, he argues, can often be quite disorientating. When people appear in front of us, it may seem easy to think of them as objects. In doing so, I am able to maintain my own subjectivity as a conscious being, the focal point in the situation in which I find myself. However, as soon as another person looks at me, I suddenly become aware that they are *also* beings with consciousness of their own, and that they are therefore *looking at me* as if I am an object. Indeed, I feel 'objectified', which I may try to resist by objectifying the person looking at me, or, indeed, the look itself. But since this is also the case for that person (who is also trying to maintain *their* subjectivity through avoiding being seen as an object), the relationship becomes trapped in a perpetual struggle.

These two modes of *being-for-others* can be understood in terms of *recognition*. In the first instance, we have what might be called a *recognition as profiling*. This is a form of recognition involves the use of (pre)constructed categories or groupings of individuals (teachers, students, woman, man) which are affixed to certain 'profiles' (authority figure, attentive, feminine, masculine). Such profiles allow us to enact expectations upon these individuals, depending upon which category they are immediately recognisable by. Furthermore, as has been argued through theories relating to the politics of recognition, often it is the case that individuals internalise such profiles and come to see themselves in this way (e.g., Fanon, 2001 [1962]). However, these profiles are severely limited. In fact, they cause us to think of individuals as having fixed essences, as opposed to understanding them as *being-for-itself*, and thus ultimately free (and responsible) to project their own meaning both into the world, and, indeed, onto themselves. Yet, Sartre's notion of the 'look' suggests that a richer sense of recognition is possible, one that surpasses the forms of fixity that we see in *recognition as profiling*. This we might call the *struggle for recognition*.

This *recognition as profiling* appears in everyday life, and often in innocuous ways. We might recognise a friend on the street, or a celebrity we have seen on television. But outside of this, the

The teacher–student relationship   113

process becomes all the more difficult. If someone in the class receives praise and recognition for working hard, we might start seeing them purely as a 'hard-working' student. This creates all sorts of expectations of them, and it makes it difficult to see them as a person *beyond* being hard-working. Indeed, this student has taken on a 'role' of the hard-working student, performs it in class and becomes 'fixed' to it as a label that constitutes their essence as a person. In doing so, we are denying the extent to which they might – and could – act differently.

This is a positive example, perhaps. But what would happen if we saw a student as lazy? Numerous studies have indicated that the ways in which teachers perceive students often become the way in which a student sees themselves (e.g., Rubie-Davis, 2010). As mentioned, the recognition that one confers on another is crucial to how that person understands, or identifies, themselves. But when a student *only* understands themselves in terms of the fixed category of 'lazy', then they are denying the extent to which they are (existentially) free to become something else entirely.

So, although recognition is unavoidable as long as we reside in the world with others, since we are free subjects, the way in which it is enacted need not be understood in fixed terms. Thus, this struggle for recognition is both a struggle *against* recognition (as profiling) as well as a struggle for a *more authentic* recognition, a recognition of ourselves as existentially free as *being-for-itself*, which involves a freedom to respond to the ways in which we might be 'fixed' through the understanding others have of us. This struggle, however, cannot be overcome, since it is intimately connected to what it means to be in the world as a free subject with other free subjects. In attending to this, we can thus start to think about the lived experience of being human with others, and indeed, of being in a teacher–student relationship.

Questions for discussion

In what ways might this struggle for recognition be visible in classroom practice? Can you think of any specific examples?

Part of the intention here is to make the teacher–student relationship more akin to what it means to be a human. In what way might the other conceptions of the teacher–student relationship be 'dehumanising'?

Sartre never specifically wrote on education in this way. Are there any issues with applying his philosophy to (a) more recent times and (b) to a field he (perhaps) never fully considered? What might this say about philosophy of education more broadly?

Conclusion: the existential teacher–student relationship

So what does this say about the conceptions of the teacher–student relationship in both the neoliberal and the progressivist approach? A number of distinctions can be drawn.

First, let us consider how each approach thinks about the nature of the relationship itself. In neoliberalism, the teacher may be seen as a service provider in the eyes of the consumerist student. Thus, certain expectations for the level of service provided also become an important way in terms of how the teacher is understood more broadly, but in particular in how the teacher understands herself, and how she sets out to behave in the classroom.

114   *Alison M. Brady*

Similarly, the progressivist approach has partly resulted in a (debased) image of the teacher as a facilitator. On the surface this may seem to at least account for the freedom of the student. But what it says about the teacher is a bit more dubious, in that it implies that the teacher is a (fixed) resource in the classroom, similar to textbooks or other kinds of equipment. Contrary to this may be the liberal approach that, despite contending that education is an end-in-itself, sees the role of the teacher as that which imparts an appreciation of worthwhile activities, with the explicit aim of creating rationally autonomous students.

Through an existentialist lens we can see that this relationship is much more complex. All three examples offer an essentialist conception of both the teacher and the student. Not only this, but such conceptions do not fully account for the lived experience of being in this relationship. Furthermore, to postulate such ideas about the student and the teacher in this way is to deny the extent to which they are free in the existentialist sense, and not *only* free in the sense that they are consumers, or that they have the capacity to be explorative, or that they are rationally autonomous. This notion of existentialist freedom is different and, arguably, more profound, and it allows us to consider this relationship not in fixed terms, but as conditioned by a perpetual struggle for recognition.

According to Kneller:

> The teacher must not be merely a kind of social-minded umpire or provider of free social activity, in the Deweyan sense, or a model personality to be imitated, as the idealists would hold. He must himself be a free personality actively engaging in such relations and projects with individual students as to leave no doubt in their minds that they, too, are *in fact* free personality and are being treated that way.
>
> (Kneller, 1958: 115, emphasis in original)

The notion of freedom and authority is, indeed, central to the discussion here. In both neoliberalism and progressivism, we see a shift of authority from the teacher to the student, albeit in very different ways. In neoliberalism, the authority of the student lies in their ability to rate, and subsequently influence, the practices of teaching. In progressivism, this authority comes from a downplaying of the significance of the teacher in the relationship in favour of the student. But to think of 'authority' in these fixed terms, as something that resides only in the student or in the teacher, denies the extent to which a struggle for recognition is palpable in the classroom context. In many ways, this struggle for recognition is also a struggle for authority.

Indeed, a battle of wills is often extant in any classroom. There is frequently an underlying tension, which can range from deep-seated, more visceral friction, to more explosive and overt contestations. This seems to be an inevitable aspect of the teacher–student relationship, but it need not be a despairing one. Indeed, often such cases of disruption can signal wider issues with schooling, or evidence of difficulty with content, or simply an echo of the misrecognition that is being inferred by one party on another. Such contestations, in this sense, are not only important, but necessary. They, and the struggle itself, are also testament to the existential freedom that is inherent in all human beings.

Finally, we might like to think about the ways in which knowledge is understood in terms of this relationship. In the neoliberal sense, there is an emphasis in the content of learning on equipping students with the necessary skills for working life. This notion of 'pre-packed' skills is arguably quite different from a progressivist understanding of content. In progressivism, one could argue that the content is, in a sense, 'external' to the learner, waiting to be discovered through explorative practices facilitated by the teacher. But none of these accounts offer a vision of the lived experience of engaging with such content. Often, it is not 'passively' ingested and applied as the skills-based model might suggest. But neither is it always 'liberating' in the way that the child-centred approach implies. It, too, involves a necessary struggle based on the model of recognition.

A good example of this comes from the more recent calls to 'liberate the curriculum' in higher education institutions (e.g., Kennedy, 2017), based on the claim that current curricula are overly Eurocentric and patriarchal, and do not fully recognise the important contributions made by other ethnic, religious, sexual and gender minority groups. The call, thus, comes as a response to the perceived misrecognition of the 'other' in the content that is imparted on students. This example serves to offer an alternative model to the 'fixed' notion of content we see in neoliberal understandings, but also (albeit to a lesser extent) progressivist approaches. And those who make such calls are therefore resisting this misrecognition in a way that might favour the existentialist approach. In putting traditional sources of authority into question in this way, it does so without denying the existential underpinnings of what it means to be human with agency. And in doing so, it suggests something crucial about the nature of the teacher–student relationship, and the central role that content plays in relation to this.

In conclusion, the existential approach to the teacher–student relationship is one that concerns itself primarily with the lived experience of that relationship in the classroom. Rather than seeing this relationship in fixed terms, it situates it within a wider struggle for recognition. This not only calls into question the dominant modes of thinking about the teacher–student relationship, it allows us to reconceptualise being a teacher or student in arguably more 'humanistic' terms, since this struggle for recognition is intimately connected to understanding what it means to exist in the world with others. Since this is a central and necessary part of being both a teacher and a student, it is something that should not be denied, nor overcome, but lived with well. The perpetual struggle may be difficult, but as Camus (1942: 37) remarks, 'being able to remain on that dizzying crest – that is integrity, and the rest is subterfuge'.

Summary

- Neoliberalism, a highly influential discourse in educational reform, is visible in the ways in which education is often focused on the extent to which it creates 'employable' individuals who can contribute to economic growth. In terms of the teacher–student relationship, which comes to be considered in 'client–service provider' terms, it also inculcates an impoverished notion of freedom as consumerism.
- A progressivist approach, with its emphasis on creating the conditions of freedom under which the child can flourish, may remedy some of these. However, it has been criticised by a number of angles, including the liberal philosophers of education, who argued that the role of the educator must, above all, be aimed at engaging students in intellectual pursuits so as to allow them to become rationally autonomous, rather than acting merely as a facilitator. Both approaches offer particular views of freedom that is, perhaps, richer than the neoliberal approach, but neither seem to address what it is that the teacher and the student actually experience in the classroom, something that can give us an entirely different understanding of freedom.

116   *Alison M. Brady*

- Existentialist philosophy can add a new dimension to our understanding of the teacher–student relationship along these lines. In attending to a richer sense of freedom, we can come to appreciate the (inescapable) struggle for recognition that comes about through the very fact of being-in-the-world-with-others. This can be thought of as a struggle *against* recognition (as 'profiling') as well as *for* recognition (a desire to be recognised as an existentially free human being, and thus, beyond fixation through profiling).
- In accepting this, an altogether more complex understanding of the teacher–student relationship is possible, one which is attuned to the concrete experiences of being in this relationship in the classroom and enriches the (arguably impoverished) notions of freedom that are central to some of the other approaches offered in the chapter.

Recommended reading

Kneller, G. (1958) *Existentialism and Education.* New York: Philosophical Library Inc.
Sartre, J-P. (1938) *Nausea.* London: Penguin Books Ltd.
Sartre, J-P. (1944) *No Exit: A Play in One Act.* USA: Vintage Books.

References

Barrett, W. (1962) *Irrational Man: A Study in Existential Philosophy.* New York: Anchor Books.
Ball, S. (2003) The teacher's soul and the terrors of performativity. *Journal of Educational Policy* **18**(2): 215–228.
Camus, A. (1942) *The Myth of Sisyphus and Other Essays.* London: Penguin Classics.
Castells, M. (1996) *The Information Age: Economy, Society and Culture.* Oxford: Blackwell.
Central Advisory Council for Education (England) (1967). *The Plowden Report: Children and their Primary Schools.* Available at: www.educationengland.org.uk/documents/plowden/ (Accessed 18 January 2019).
Cox, C. B. and Dyson, C. B. (1969) *The Crisis in Education.* London: Critical Quarterly Society.
Dearden, R. F. (1968) *The Philosophy of Primary Education: An Introduction.* London: Routledge.
DfES (2003) *21st Century Skills: Realising Our Potential: Employers, Individuals, Nation.* Available at: https://assets.publishing.service.gov.uk/government/uploads/system/uploads/attachment_data/file/336816/21st_Century_Skills_Realising_Our_Potential.pdf (Accessed 18 January 2019).
Fanon, F. (2001 [1962]) *The Wretched of the Earth.* Trans. C. Farrington. London: Penguin Classics.
Grek, S. and Lindgren, J. (2015) *Governing by Inspection.* London: Routledge.
Harvey, D. (2007) *A Brief History of Neoliberalism.* Oxford: Oxford University Press.
HEFCE (2018) *National Student Survey: Policy Guide.* Available at: www.hefce.ac.uk/lt/nss/influence/#summary (Accessed 18 January 2019).
Heidegger, M. (1978 [1927]) *Being and Time.* Trans. J. Macquarrie and E. Robinson. London: Wiley-Blackwell.
Kennedy, M. (2017) Cambridge academics seek to decolonise the English syllabus. *The Guardian*, 25 October. Available at: www.theguardian.com/education/2017/oct/25/cambridge-academics-seek-to-decolonise-english-syllabus (Accessed 18 January 2019).
Kneller, G. (1958) *Existentialism and Education.* New York: Philosophical Library Inc.
Lyotard, J. F. (1979) *The Postmodern Condition: A Report on Knowledge.* Manchester: Manchester University Press.
Molesworth, M., Scullion, R. and Nixon, E. (eds.) (2011) *The Marketization of Higher Education and the Student as Consumer.* London: Routledge.
Rousseau, J. J. (1979 [1763]) *Emile: or On Education.* Trans. A. Bloom. New York: Basic Books.
Rubie-Davis, C., Hattie, J. and Hamilton, R. (2010) Expecting the best for students: teacher expectations and academic outcomes. *British Journal of Educational Psychology* **76**(3): 429–444.
Sartre, J-P. (1938) *Nausea.* London: Penguin Books Ltd.
Sartre, J-P. (1944) *No Exit: A Play in One Act.* USA: Vintage Books.
Sartre, J-P. (1945a) *The Age of Reason.* London: Penguin Books Ltd.
Sartre, J-P. (1945b) *The Reprieve.* London: Penguin Books Ltd.
Sartre, J-P. (1949) *Iron in the Soul.* London: Penguin Books Ltd.

Sartre, J-P. (2003 [1943]) *Being and Nothingness: An Essay on Phenomenological Ontology.* Trans. H. E. Barnes. London and New York: Routledge Classics.

The Times (2017) University tuition fees could be linked to course costs and job prospects. Available at: www.thetimes.co.uk/article/university-tuition-fees-could-be-linked-to-course-costs-and-job-prospects-ffkbf6zzt (18 January 2019).

10 Educational phenomenology
Is there a need and space for such a pursuit?

Sonia Pieczenko

Introduction

This chapter assesses the usefulness of a phenomenological investigation for educational purposes. This is something that should be seen in the light of the currently domineering influence that cognitive psychological science and its many variations has on education. The cognitive approach to scientific psychology rests upon the provision of stimuli under controlled experimental circumstances allowing the experimenter to make inferences about what must be going on in the receiving mind or brain (Anderson, 2010). A further step tries to link these inferences (conceptualised as *cognitive states* and/or *cognitive structures*) to the neuronal processes or structure of the brain in the form of a cognitive neuroscience (Bear *et al.*, 2001). Cognitive neuroscience has found support by some educationalists (Oxford Cognitive Neuroscience, 2011), proposing an educational neuroscience (ENS) in which the mechanics of successful learning and teaching are to be explained with recourse to such a cognitive-biological explanatory framework (Anderson and Reid, 2009).

However, the reach of such cognitive or cognitive-neuroscientific explanations of the mind have come under increasing critique within psychology itself (Wallace, 2007; Varela and Shear, 1999; Depraz *et al.*, 2003; Feldges, 2013), but also in terms of its supposed educational application (Cuthbert, 2015; Feldges *et al.*, 2017; Feldges, 2018). It is not the aim of this chapter to follow the many arguments that have been mounted against the ENS agenda in detail. Its focus is rather upon the question as to whether – and this beside the mentioned limitations of a cognitive-neuroscientific approach to learning – there could or should be enough space for an approach to education that focuses upon the experiences of the learner and teacher.

In order to accomplish this aim, a brief overview on the current debate around the problems of a bio-psychological approach to education is needed. The second section of the chapter will introduce the systematic investigation of human experiences in the form of a philosophical tradition called 'phenomenology'. A third section will develop some aspects of Husserl's phenomenology as a structural investigation of consciousness. With all this in place, it is possible to conclude that a structural, phenomenological investigation could indeed contribute to the current understanding of education.

Cognitive neuroscience

Cognitive psychology emerged between the 1950s and 1970s as the dominant approach to the investigation of the mind in a scientific manner. This shift from a previously dominant behaviourist

Educational phenomenology 119

approach has been necessitated by a growing acceptance that the scientific assessment of displayed behaviours, while denying the existence of mental states or consciousness (Watson, 1913), could not explain human agency (Beckerman, 1998). Earlier suggestions by Smart (1962) to link specific mental states to their supposedly underlying bodily, neuronal processes in the form of an identity theory had proven to be difficult, as mental states appear to be emerging from a multitude of physical states. Hence, it remained difficult to pin down any single causal physical state for emerging mental states (Rosenthal, 1995) and therefore to develop a sufficient explanatory theory for the mind. The psychological assessment of physical states for psychological purposes remained an important aspect of research, as for example in Hebb's (1949) development of a neuronal network theory or in Luria's (1996 [1973]) systematic approach to neuronal connectivity. However, the main focus of psychology shifted towards the cognitive approach. The main tenets of cognitive psychology are recently outlined by Feldges (2018). Without too much detail here, it is nevertheless worth explaining that cognitive psychology works on the assumption of hypothetical states and structures that must be in place for the mind to perform a certain function. Hence, in order to be able to think about anything, the mind must be organised in such a way that it can represent things that are outside itself, while it must equally be able to run the necessary processes whereby, for example, a table is represented and perceived as such. These (cognitive) structures and states are essentially hypothetical. That is, they are not directly linked to physical or neuronal structures and processes and in that way this functional theory of the mind can avoid the problem of Smart's identity theory. However, as Feldges (2018) explains in relation to the educational reality, these cognitive states are classified as functional in relation to the end-goal they serve. It is here that the concept of *causal over-determination* gains educational value. If the causation of a cognitive state is sufficiently explained with recourse to the function they serve, then these states cannot equally be caused by the individual's experiences. Hence, cognitive psychology is left with an experiential blind spot (Varela, 1996) that leaves not much room for these cognitive states to be accounted for in relation to an individual's feelings or emotions. Specifically in relation to educational neuroscience, Feldges argues that any suggested pairing of cognitive psychology with neuroscientific accounts would carry this experiential blind spot into the emerging cognitive-neuroscience and – of course – into an educational (cognitive-)neuroscience as well.

This discussion about the role of experiential states like feelings and emotions within a cognitive-scientific psychology is not new. It is probably most prominently formulated by Chalmers' (1996) notion of the *hard problem*, i.e., the problem of how to match a functional account of the mind with the experiences that are supposedly an integral part of human mental activity. It is this well-established problem that has sparked off some considerable discussion about the possibility of utilising an investigative approach that utilises human experiences to investigate human consciousness in the form of a naturalised phenomenology (Petitot *et al.*, 1999; Carel and Meacham, 2013) or a neuro-phenomenology (Varela, 1996). As the name of these projects indicates, both are intrinsically linked to a philosophical tradition that was founded by Edmund Husserl around the turn of the nineteenth and the twentieth centuries and which is known as 'phenomenology' (Smith and Smith, 1995). Although there is still a continuing debate in the literature about the potential benefits of such projects, the import of human experience, as experienced by the one who is undergoing these states, cannot be underestimated, especially in relation to education. Therefore, as a means to get a first grasp of the issue, it is time to focus upon the idea and the goal of phenomenology.

> ## Questions for discussion
>
> Can you think about instances where the learners' feelings or emotions provided support for their learning – or became an obstacle to their success?

Phenomenology: a first – and tentative – take on the issue

Writing in an educational journal in 1979, Bolton (1979: 245) claimed that phenomenology had a tenuous position in the British academic scene, 'appearing on the lunatic fringe of not one, but two, established disciplines, namely philosophy and psychology'. In relation to such a verdict, it seems warranted to say that, especially in the UK, phenomenology was not really considered to be of much use and that it was mostly ignored in terms of its potential usage for educational purposes. There are a few papers bearing a phenomenological slant, or even proposing the use of phenomenology for educational research; but it appears as if phenomenology has not (yet?) made it into mainstream theorising in relation to educational purposes. On the European mainland, the picture looks different. The Humboldt University in Berlin organises regular symposia to promote research and the dissemination of research results regarding phenomenological-informed educational studies (*Phänomenologische Erziehungswissenschaft*) with a great number of subsequent publications (Humboldt Universität Berlin, 2017) as for example Brinkmann's (2019) anthology of educationally relevant phenomenological texts. The University of Rouen, France engaged in a programme, Thinking Education, with a pronounced phenomenological leaning (Houssaye, 2005). This is not surprising as Rouen is also a centre for empirical research utilising phenomenological methods to challenge the current cognitive-scientific dominance in consciousness research (Université de Rouen, 2017). It thus appears as if the academic discipline of education has a developing interest in the utilisation of phenomenological philosophy, either as a guiding theoretical thread or as a means of developing phenomenological research approaches for educational purposes. However, it is probably fair to state that within mainstream educational academia, this educationally relevant phenomenological current has still to arrive.

However, before it is possible to engage with phenomenology at all, it is necessary to approach the topic and to gain a secure understanding of what it is about and how it differs from the cognitive or cognitive-neuroscientific approach. It is important to note here that phenomenology as such is not to be understood as a clearly fixed school or a group of philosophers committed towards one shared goal. Phenomenology is more of a movement and because of this it is impossible here to provide a comprehensive overview of all the developments since Husserl founded this phenomenological movement. Therefore, some general comments must suffice to establish what this phenomenological way of thinking or of doing philosophy is about.

Husserl (1975) started to develop the concept of phenomenology in his 1901 publication *Logical Investigations*. His initial concern was his reluctance to accept the then-dominant position that human thought is the functional result of a thinking (psycho-), embodied (physical) subject. Immanuel Kant (1998) had already in 1789 tried to investigate how human reasoning abilities are to be thought of as transcendental investigation. Such a transcendental investigation is not first and foremost interested in the way a particular thought emerges within the psychophysical subject.

Instead it aims to reveal the general conditions for the possibility for human experience. However, at the time when Husserl started to engage with these issues, Kant's transcendental philosophy was interpreted in such a way that the focus turned towards functional processes of the mind or the nervous system (Windelband, 1924). This concept was known as the 'psychologism', i.e., the belief in the existence of laws of thought that rule human intuition and thought. Husserl formulated an early and damaging critique of this position (Kusch, 2011). However, if the rules and regulations of human thought are no longer fixed by such a presupposed psychological framework, then the question invariably emerges where else one would find a starting point to research the conscious relation that a human subject has with the objects outside itself.

In an attempt to answer to this question, Husserl (1984a) developed his phenomenological approach by advocating a *going back to the things themselves*. Nevertheless, Husserl advised that going to the *things* does not focus upon the objects of the outside world; what he was interested in were the *things* as they appear consciously. However, such an approach to the consciously appearing things necessitates adherence to a number of paradigms. These are:

a) the importance of intentionality as a relation established between the object and the subject that allows the subject's consciousness to be conscious of something outside of itself;
b) the exact description of the experiences;
c) the importance of the first-person perspective.

It is important to note here that these paradigms are characteristics of all phenomenological approaches and not only limited to Husserl (Luft and Overgaard, 2014). With this general idea about phenomenology, it is time to see where phenomenology appears to promise some *surplus value* over traditional approaches to account for consciousness in an educational context.

Phenomenology: a second take on the issue

In order to maintain focus, this chapter will stay close to Husserl's phenomenology. As already mentioned, there are probably as many phenomenologies as there are phenomenologists, but staying close to Husserl should support an understanding of the underlying principles and provide a starting position to individually assess the different movements.

Husserl (1984a) is interested in the relation between a conscious mind and the objects this mind or person is conscious of. He refers to this relation as the *intentional* relation. Intentionality as a philosophical concept, and quite different from the everyday use of the word, was a concept reintroduced into philosophy by Brentano (1995). It concerns the fact that some mental states are about something, i.e., that they are directed towards the object that they are about. Husserl uses this intentional relation to conduct the first systematic investigation of human consciousness (Mayer, 2009).

It is important to realise here that Husserl's (1984a) sole focus is the experience of these conscious acts. He is not concerned with the physiological genesis of a sound in terms of sound waves hitting the eardrum and being transformed into neuronal signals to be processed by the nervous system. Husserl is interested in the individual experience of that sound, what it feels like to experience the sound. This is a remarkable difference from the neuroscientific way of explaining the mind by following the neuronal processing. However, as intentionality is always directed towards an object, every intentional act is comprised of two aspects. This is the 'act-matter', i.e., what the mental act is about (the object), and the 'act-quality', i.e., what it is like to experience this specific act (Moran, 2000). An example might be helpful here: The desk that this author sat at during her school days would be, according to the representationalist account, passively received via sense data, enabling the receiver to have a mirror image of this desk projected into her mind. This would include the elaborate working of the relevant physiological (neuronal) structures involved in such processes, i.e., what current cognitive-psychological and neuroscientific accounts aim to trace. However, in order to understand what *seeing this desk* actually means from the perspective of phenomenology, it would be necessary to focus upon the experiences that one has when looking at this table. The example case of the school desk would reveal the experiences of the onlooker. This recourse to the conscious episode of 'experiencing' the desk allows for the possibility that learner and instructor can look at the same piece of furniture but that they experience it differently, i.e., that the act-matter (the desk) is clouded in different act-qualities. The learner may perceive the desk as a token of him/her being condemned to a despised educational control-regime and as a potential medium to evade expected boredom by means of inflicting skilful (or not so skilful) engravings, while the instructor may experience this desk as a mere part of the classroom furniture.

Questions for discussion

Can you think about education-relevant situations or objects that appear in different ways to different learners or to the instructor?

Husserl thus opens a way of assessing the experiences that any consciously appearing object is always surrounded by. The teacher sees the PowerPoint slides as a means to get through a session covering unfamiliar contents, while the student experiences them as the promise of eternal boredom; the teacher sees the upcoming exam as a means to assess the learners, while the learner experiences this as an evil intervention to establish educational failure.

Husserl's phenomenology provides an explanatory account to understand the individual uniqueness of human experience. This is far beyond the explanatory reach of the representationalist account used by cognitive and cognitive-neuroscientific psychology (Feldges, 2013). Nevertheless, this is only part of the obvious advantages that phenomenology could bring. Going back to the notion of the uniqueness of human experiences, one not only finds different individual inclinations contributing to the act-quality, one also finds a unique perspective. Whatever one may see, hear or experience, it is always heard, seen or experienced from the unique location of the experiencing individual in relation to the source of this experience (Husserl, 1973).

Again, an example may aid a better understanding. Recognising the projector to show PowerPoint being mounted on the classroom's ceiling with its main switch underneath leaves this author with a clear experience of the intentional object (act-matter = the projector) but the object is, due to this author's height of 1.63 metres, experienced as 'out of reach'. Hence the perfectly working projector (once it would be switched on) is less experienced as a means to the teacher's end, but as an obstacle. Any colleague, having grown beyond 1.80 metres, will not experience this obstacle at all. Feldges (2018) has discussed the inherent blind eye that current

Educational phenomenology 123

cognitive-psychological approaches turn towards the educational experiences and Husserl's phenomenology – with this differentiation between the content and the associated feeling of mental states – appears to be able to rectify this problem. Phenomenology could possibility provide an important and new access-routes to

a) an enhanced understanding of motivational aspects of learning; but also,
b) with the embodied-ness of subjectivity, an enriched perspective upon practical and/or vocational education.

This embodied-ness of subjectivity reveals the indexicality of Husserl's phenomenology, i.e., that experience is always located at the specific spatio-temporal location of the experiencing individual. This indexical notion highlights the importance of the individual's body, as this is where the sense-information is gathered to subsequently cater for the emerging experiences (Husserl, 1952). Although Husserl is not overly concerned with the body, he nevertheless develops an account of how a 'lasting style or personal character' is formed by a 'substrate of habitualities' (Husserl, 1950a: 101). Husserl's notion of an identical pole of experiences, or a habitus, forms an 'identical lasting unity' (Husserl, 1968: 212) whereby the individual experiences its surroundings. In relation to the invariable human situated-ness this habitualisation of experiences and experiential comportment is one that is intrinsically linked with the individual's body. Merleau-Ponty (1945) expands on this with his concept of a body-schema according to which humans experience their world intentionally in relation to their body as an 'I can', or as an 'I cannot' as in the case of this author and the overhead projector. Heidegger (1962) develops this differently with his notion of affording objects that are *ready-to-hand*. Hence, utilising the hammer – Heidegger's famous example – one is not aware of the hammer itself. The hammer – within normal hammering – remains transparent, it is not made an explicit object of our concerns, but it appears as something to drive nails into something, to do the hammering. According to Heidegger, one only experiences the hammer as such when it breaks down, i.e., when it cannot fulfil its function anymore, when the hammer fails to do the hammering, when it is no longer *ready-to-hand*.

Questions for discussion

Can you think about educationally relevant instances where a habitualised 'I can'/'I cannot' become relevant in the context of learning?

Can you think about the breakdown of affordances when things all of a sudden become conscious just because they do not work anymore for us?

It appears obvious from this rather short outline of phenomenology how it can be useful to capture exact descriptions of conscious experiences from the first-person perspective via the concept of intentionality, and all that within an educational context. However, exactly the insight that phenomenology seems to promise in terms of the individual's experience leaves phenomenology open to its critics. How would it be possible to go back to the individual experiences as a foundation for a science of *that which appears* (phenomenology) by avoiding the danger of sinking into a bog of idiosyncrasies?

Husserl's phenomenology as a structural investigation

Husserl battles with mere physiological accounts of the mind, promoting his approach of assessing and describing the experiential dimensions that manifest themselves individually in relation to these physiological events. When considering the *phenomena* – i.e., that which appears to consciousness – one needs to go back to these 'things' to start a phenomenological investigation. As ordinary as that may sound, it nevertheless comes with the difficulty that one may just chase individually appearing quirks. Hence, so one could suspect, it would remain impossible to develop a scientifically sufficient description from such a first-person perspective because of an insufficient sample size of always only one participant. This aspect has attracted a lot of criticism and this section will explore some of these. However, the interested reader might want to read Titchener's (1909/10) critique of Wundt's (1913) proposal to use introspective, self-reported accounts for psychological investigations or Dennett's (1991), Searle's (1994) and Wheeler's (2014) more recent objections.

Husserl, well aware of Wundt's attempts and Titchener's critique (Husserl, 1968), nevertheless aims to develop his phenomenology as a strict science of that which appears (Husserl, 1958). With this in mind, it needs pointing out that Husserl's phenomenology does not only utilise the first-person perspective to develop descriptions of the intentional relation. Husserl's objective goes further in as much as he attempts to reveal the transcendental structures of this conscious, intentional relationship between subject and object. That is, phenomenology utilises the experiences to uncover the universal and necessary preconditions according to which consciousness must function in order to be able to be conscious of something at all. Phenomenology thus considers the necessary conditions for the possibility of consciousness.

To understand what is at stake here, it is probably best to go back to the school desk example. One can see it from where one stands, and when closing one's eyes and reopening them again, one still sees that very same desk, not two, one earlier one and one current one. Both separate experiences (then and now) are merged into one intentional object: *that desk*. Although there is an interrupted perceptual sequence, consciousness does nevertheless tie these two instances together and will still be conscious of only the one desk and not of two. Having thus looked at the desk from where one stands, one might start to wander around it. Although the available sensory information of the desk is constantly changing along with the continuous alteration of the perspective, one still only looks at that one desk. One is not looking at a multitude of desks, composed of the constantly changing sense-data in relation to the different aspects of this desk. These are everyday occurrences that everyone will have experienced already and they are so bland indeed that normally not much thought is spent on these at all. However, if one uses these phenomena (that one consciously appearing desk) in relation to these changing or interrupted experiences, one is warranted to conclude that consciousness must be structured in such a way that it is capable of stringing these series of perceptual experience together over time. And that it thus becomes possible to be conscious of one permanent object only.

This is the sort of structural investigation that Husserl envisaged, i.e., the use of exact description from a first-person perspective, to utilise these to reveal the necessary structures of consciousness. In this example case Husserl uses the so-revealed object-constancy to engage in very detailed investigation about the experience of things in space (Husserl, 1973) and about the nature of our consciousness of time (Husserl, 1966).

As mentioned earlier, if one, as Husserl (1950b) suggests, utilises the things as they appear consciously to one's own consciousness, one appears to be confined to a very small basis to sample data (i.e., one person). However, that raises the problem of how far such an endeavour could ever be conceived as sufficiently scientific. Husserl (1950b, 1958) addresses this problem in detail and his solution is to conduct a structural investigation into the necessary conditions for the possibility, i.e., a *transcendental* investigation, into how consciousness must be structured in order to experience the phenomena as we do. That is then the point at which it is imperative to go back to the things themselves, and that needs a bit more explanation.

While the teacher walks past the desks at which the learners sit, s/he can spot a coin on one of the desks. The teacher sees the round shape, immediately recognised as a coin. Something like this account would be the normal story to be told about this perceptive encounter. However, it is not strictly capturing what is going on. This account is owed to the fact that the teacher too remains in what Husserl (1950b) calls the 'natural attitude', i.e., a way of seeing, shaped by the everyday experience that coins are indeed of a circular shape and that they are thus perceived in such a way. However, when one makes the willing effort of not giving in to these pre-conceptions, if one abstains from these judgements and attends to what one really 'sees', then it turns out that the coin will always appear elliptical; unless, of course, if one views it from a 90° vertical top-view upon the coin's obverse or reverse face. Abstaining from the judgements that are normally made without even realising it (coins are circular) thus allows access to what one really experiences (I see an elliptical shape). Husserl (1950b) calls it to perform the *epoché*, which is a Greek term for this abstaining from judgement (Röd, 1996) and we do not need to develop this further. Nevertheless, when looking at the gains here, it is obvious that

a) the fact that one can experience something elliptical and perceive it nevertheless as circular tells something about how consciousness must function along the intentional relation between subject and object to allow for this to happen. Even more so,
b) the seen coin's eccentricity value does not matter, i.e., it is not crucial for this kind of investigation that the actual eccentricity value of the elliptical appearance is different from the teacher's and the learner's perspectives. Something fundamental must go on in consciousness so that an elliptic experience is turned into a circular perception, and that independently from an arbitrary position.

It is exactly here that Husserl can overcome the problem of the small sample size ($N=1$) by focusing upon the structural preconditions for conscious experiences. Husserl's phenomenology is thus not at all an exercise in navel-inspection, riddled with the snares of idiosyncrasies (Stumpf, cited in Hirschberger, 1980), laying on the lunatic fringe between psychology and philosophy (Bolton, 1979). Phenomenology is much more of a disciplined and systematic investigation of conscious experiences from the first-person perspective to reveal the necessary preconditions for those experiences to occur in the way they do.

A space for phenomenological research in education?

With such a good investigative range for phenomenological research, the question nevertheless emerges as to why phenomenology has not become the dominant paradigm for any kind of psychological and probably even educational research into the conscious reality of the respective participants. There is a major debate unfolding around the phenomenological application. Some of

126 *Sonia Pieczenko*

this discussion has begun to surface in the UK educational literature (Padilla-Diaz, 2015; Williams 2018). Nevertheless, when approaching the debate it is important to bear a number of points in mind to be able to make a realistic assessment of the current state of affairs:

1. Phenomenology, as a science of the structure of conscious appearances has the explicit and limited focus upon these phenomena. Hence, phenomenology or phenomenological approaches to psychology cannot completely replace the current psychological approaches to understanding the mind or the mind–brain interaction. This is just beyond the scope of the phenomenological project. In that respect, any 'phenomenological revolution' in psychology would always be more of a localised event, regarding its specific focus-area of consciousness.
2. The fact that phenomenological investigations have not yet fully arrived in mainstream educational research – or alternatively that there is no widespread awareness of this yet – must not to be taken as a mirror image of what is happening (or not) in psychology. As mentioned in the introduction, a number of research projects are on the way in an attempt to utilise phenomenological methods for psychological purposes and – even more so – for educational purposes.

However, it would be naïve to portray the suggested pairing of phenomenology and empirical research, be it for psychological or educational purposes, as one that is already sorted in all its aspects. Although Varela (1996) envisaged something like this in his original proposal and in numerous subsequent publications on the issue, scholars on the phenomenological side of the pairing beg to differ (e.g., Zahavi, 2008). In the light of this continuing debate, it looks as if the jury is still out on how the transcendental approach of phenomenology can be married to empirical, psychological accounts, although it appears as if there is at least a potential solution in sight (Gallagher and Zahavi, 2008). Nevertheless, the field is moving fast and, despite Titchener's (1909/10) negative verdict on Wundt's (1913) introspective methods, it becomes increasingly acceptable to have participants reporting their experiences in various phenomenological approaches to investigate the conscious mind (Petitmengin, 2009).

Conclusion

This chapter began with the question as to whether there is a place for phenomenology in educational research. To provide an answer to this question, the systematic limitations of cognitive science have been revealed in terms of what Varela (1996) had called its 'experiential poverty'. But despite these confines, it nevertheless appears intuitively compelling to include the learners' and instructors' experiences into the research agendas regarding the education-transformative relationship. Or at least not to exclude these experiences completely by a methodological choice for an approach that cannot – by its own theoretical underpinnings – account for these.

With this in mind, it became possible to cast a general view upon phenomenology and to develop its three main tenets which appeared to completely alter the investigative direction. While cognitive psychology works from the outside of the subject, phenomenology starts its investigation on the inside of the conscious being, utilising the *things* (phenomena) as they appear consciously by means of these experiences. A range of educationally relevant examples illustrated how phenomenological investigations aim to evade the danger of sinking into the bog of idiosyncrasies by using these experiences to focus upon the structures of consciousness. In relation to the difficulty of

Educational phenomenology   127

explaining the relation between mind and body especially later phenomenological developments (e.g., Merleau-Ponty and Heidegger) appear to offer interesting solutions.

Although there is a still continuing debate on how far phenomenology could be useful for empirical research in general, it appears as if it would be a massive opportunity missed if the academic discipline of education did not take advantage of this approach to forward its own agenda. It is here that one has to bear in mind that education is neither bound by the strict confines of Husserl's original phenomenological project, nor by those of psychology in the form of the current cognitive and cognitive-neuroscientific approaches. Hence, the field of educationally relevant conscious processes and a possible phenomenological investigation of these is still available for the appropriation and discipline-specific development in relation to educational purposes. In that respect, the answer to the question of this chapter is rather straightforward and unreservedly positive. Yes, there is a place for phenomenology in education and it needs to be taken up as soon as possible, and – to add a rather personal note here – it would be a shame to miss this opportunity.

Summary

- By revealing the experiential poverty of current approaches to account for the mind, the limitations of the predominant cognitive paradigm become apparent.
- An overall perspective on the field of various phenomenological approaches, and on Husserl's phenomenology specifically, appears to be able to cover for interesting aspects in educational research.
- The differentiation between act-matter (content) and act-quality (lived-experience) allows a comprehensive phenomenological description of the things as they appear to consciousness.
- These descriptions can be utilised to reveal the conditions of the possibility for consciousness to be conscious about something at all.
- This promises to offer interesting and new approaches to educational research.

Recommended reading

Moran, D. (2000) *Introduction to Phenomenology*. London: Routledge.
Zahavi, D. (2003) *Husserl's Phenomenology*. Stanford (CA): Stanford University Press

References

Anderson, J. R. (2010) *Cognitive Psychology and its Implications* (7th edition). New York: Worth Publishers.
Anderson, M. and Reid, C. (2009) Don't forget about levels of explanation. *Cortex* **45**(4): 560–561.
Bear, M. F., Connors, B. W. and Paradiso, M. A. (2001) *Neuroscience: Exploring the Brain* (2nd edition). London: Lippincott Williams and Wilkins.
Beckerman, A. (1998) *Analytische Einfuehrung in die Philosophie des Geistes*. Berlin: De Gruyter.
Bolton, N. (1979) Phenomenology and education. *British Journal of Educational Studies* **27**(3): 245–258.
Brentano, F. (1995) *Psychology from an Empirical Standpoint*. London: Routledge.
Brinkmann, M. (2019) *Phänomenologische Erziehungswissenschaft von ihren Anfängen bis heute – Eine Anthologie*. Wiesbaden: Springer VS.
Carel, H. and Meacham, D. (2013) *Phenomenology and Naturalism – Royal Institute of Philosophy Supplement: 72*. Cambridge: Cambridge University Press, pp. 1–21.
Chalmers, D. J. (1996) *The Conscious Mind: In Search of a Fundamental Theory*. Oxford: Oxford University Press.
Cuthbert, A. S. (2015) Neuroscience and education: an incompatible relationship. *Sociology Compass* **9**(1): 49–61.

128 *Sonia Pieczenko*

Dennett, D. (1991) *Consciousness Explained*. London: Black Bay Books.

Depraz, N., Varela, F. and Vermersch, P. (2003) *On Becoming Aware: A Pragmatics of Experiencing*. Amsterdam: John Benjamins Publishing.

Feldges T. (2013) Neurophenomenology: current problems and historical baggage. *Journal of Consciousness Studies* **20**(3–4): 222–229.

Feldges, T. (2018) Motivation and experience versus cognitive psychological explanation. *Humana Mente – Special Issue: The Learning Brain and the Classroom* **33**: 1–18.

Feldges, T., Elton, J. and Pieczenko, S. (2017) The art of education or the science of education? *Educational Futures* **8**(1): 50–68.

Gallagher, S. and Zahavi, D. (2008) *The Phenomenological Mind: An Introduction to Philosophy of Mind and Cognitive Science*. London: Routledge.

Hebb, D. O. (1949) *Organization of Behaviour*. London: John Wiley.

Heidegger, M. (1962) *Being and Time*. Oxford: Blackwell.

Hirschberger, J. (1980) *Geschichte der Philosophie – Band II Neuzeit und Gegenwart*. Frankfurt: Zweitausendeins.

Houssaye, J. (2005) *Penser l'Educaton*. Available at: http://shs-app.univ-rouen.fr/civiic/revue/UFR_Penser_Education17.pdf (Accessed 18 January 2019).

Humboldt Universität Berlin (2017) *4th International Symposium on Phenomenological Research in Education*. Available at: www.erziehungswissenschaften.hu-berlin.de/de/allgemeine/symposion (Accessed 18 January 2019).

Husserl, E. (1950a) *Husserliana I – Cartesianische Meditationen und Pariser Vorträge*. The Hague: Martinus Nijhoff.

Husserl, E. (1950b) *Husserliana III – Ideen zu einer reinen Phänomenologie und phänomenologischen Philosophie – Erstes Buch*. The Hague: Martinus Nijhoff.

Husserl, E. (1952) *Husserliana IV – Ideen zu einer reinen Phänomenologie und phänomenologischen Philosophie – Zweites Buch*. The Hague: Martinus Nijhoff.

Husserl, E. (1958) *Husserliana II – Die Idee der Phänomenologie*. The Hague: Martinus Nijhoff.

Husserl, E. (1966) *Husserliana X – Zur Phänomenologie des Inneren Zeitbewusstseins (1893–1917)*. The Hague: Martinus Nijhoff.

Husserl, E. (1968) *Husserliana IX – Phänomenologische Psychologie*. The Hague: Martinus Nijhoff.

Husserl, E. (1973) *Husserliana XVI – Ding und Raum – Vorlesungen 1907*. The Hague: Martinus Nijhoff.

Husserl, E. (1975) *Husserliana XVIII – Logische Untersuchungen*. Den Haag: Martinus Nijhoff.

Husserl, E. (1984a) *Husserliana XIX/1 – Logische Untersuchungen – Zweiter Band – Erster Teil*. The Hague: Martinus Nijhoff.

Husserl, E. (1984b) *Husserliana XIX/2 – Logische Untersuchungen – Zweiter Band – Zweiter Teil*. The Hague: Martinus Nijhoff.

Kant, E. (1998) *Critique of Pure Reason*. Cambridge: Cambridge University Press.

Kusch, K. (2011) Psychologism. *The Stanford Encyclopedia of Philosophy*. Available at: http://plato.stanford.edu/archives/spr2014/entries/psychologism/ (Accessed 18 January 2019).

Luft, S. and Overgaard, S. (2014) *The Routledge Companion to Phenomenology*. London: Routledge.

Luria, A. R. (1996 [1973]) *Das Gehirn in Aktion – Einführung in die Neuropsychologie*. Hamburg: Rowohlt.

Mayer, V. (2009) *Edmund Husserl*. Munich: Beck.

Merleau-Ponty, M. (1945) *Phénoménologie de la perception*. Paris: Editions Gallimard.

Moran, D. (2000) *Introduction to Phenomenology*. London: Routledge.

Oxford Cognitive Neuroscience (2011) *Westminster Institute of Education*. Available at: http://cs3.brookes.ac.uk/schools/education/rescon/ocnef/ocnef.html (Accessed 18 January 2019).

Padilla-Diaz, M. (2015) Phenomenology in educational qualitative research: philosophy as science or philosophical science? *International Journal of Educational Excellence* **1**(2): 101–110.

Petitot, J., Varela, F., Pachoud, B. and Roy, J. M. (1999) *Naturalising Phenomenology*. Stanford, CA: Stanford University Press.

Petitmengin, C. (2009) *Ten Years Viewing from Within: The Legacy of Francisco Varela*. Exeter: Academic Press.

Röd, W. (1996) *Der Weg der Philosophie – Band II, 17. bis 20. Jahrhundert*. Munich: C. H. Beck.

Rosenthal, D. M. (1995) Identity theories. In S. Guttenplan (ed.), *A Companion to the Philosophy of Mind*. Oxford: Blackwell.

Searle, J. R. (1994) *The Rediscovery of the Mind*. Cambridge, MA: MIT Press.

Smart, J. J. C. (1962) Sensations and brain processes. In V. C. Chappell (ed.), *The Philosophy of Mind*. Eaglewood Cliffs, NJ: Prentice-Hall.

Smith, B. and Smith, D. W. (1995) *The Cambridge Companion to Husserl*. Cambridge: Cambridge University Press.

Titchener, E. B. (1909/10) *A Text-Book of Psychology, I-II*. London: Macmillan.

Université de Rouen, (2017) *Equipe de Recherche Interdisciplinaire sur les Aires Culturelles*. Available at: http://eriac.univ-rouen.fr/author/natalie-depraz/ (Accessed 18 January 2019).

Varela, F. (1996) Neurophenomenology: a methodological remedy for the hard problem. *Journal of Consciousness Studies* **3**: 330–349.

Varela, F. and Shear, J. (1999) *The View from Within*. Thorverton: Imprint Academic.

Wallace, B. (2007) Introduction. In B. Wallace, R. Ross, J. Davies and T. Anderson (eds.), *The Mind, the Body and the World: Psychology after Cognitivism?* Exeter: Imprint Academic Press.

Watson, J. B. (1913) Psychology as the behaviorist views it. *Psychology Review* **20**: 158–177.

Wheeler, M. (2014) The rest is science: what does phenomenology tells us about cognition? In: T. Feldges, J. Gray and S. Burwood (eds.), *Subjectivity and the Social World: A Collection of Essays around Issues Relating to the Subject, the Body and Others*. Newcastle: Cambridge Scholars Publishing.

Williams, E. (2018) 'To catch at and let go': David Dalkhurst, phenomenology and post-phenomenology. *Journal of Philosophy of Education* **52**(1): 87–104.

Windelband, W. (1924) *Lehrbuch der Geschichte der Philosophie* (11th edition). Tübingen: Mohr.

Wundt, W. (1913) *Grundriss der Psychologie* (12th edition). Leipzig: Alfred Körner Verlag.

Zahavi, D. (2008) *Subjectivity and Selfhood: Investigating the First-Person Perspective*. London: MIT Press.

11 Making sense of it all?
A concluding attempt

Tom Feldges

Introduction

People are different and therefore reading habits are different as well. It certainly does not take a philosopher to know that much. However, personal differences in interest, attitude and aptitude make it particularly difficult for the editor of a selection of chapters from a variety of authors to provide an overall frame to make sense out of all the chapters. Of course, the chapters in the book were selected in such a way that they fit together. Nevertheless, some readers may only be interested in certain aspects of the book and thus not even read the other chapters or the overall conclusion that is here developed. So the question emerges: Why bother with a conclusion at all?

However, even to ask the question would almost 'sell philosophy down the river'. Philosophy is not at all the reciting of great ideas from famous people. Philosophy is a way of engaging with problems big and small. It is a way of thinking, and while we think, it is also a tool to sharpen our thoughts. This does not mean that it can always provide the sought-after answers, but most certainly philosophy can help to formulate the questions more precisely, to assess the starting position more clearly, or – if no solution is forthcoming – to try to ask the questions differently or to start with different questions relating to the same problem. It is exactly this very essence of the philosophical pursuit that demands a conclusion, regardless of a possible 'pick-and-chose' attitude of some readers.

As outlined earlier, there are certain topics around which all the preceding chapters were arranged and some of the thoughts developed there, some of the arguments brought forward and some of the ideas presented need to be pulled together. The good work done by each one of the authors demands that their contribution is not left 'hanging there' but is arranged in such a way that single chapters add to something beyond the concern of the individual author. They contribute to an argument that formed the underlying intention of this book.

Here the question might be asked: Why explain all this to the reader? At the end of the day, most readers are interested in the content offered by a book and not necessarily in the mechanics of writing one. As true as that may be, such a question would nevertheless miss the point, and for two reasons. Right at the beginning of this book the difference between *learning about philosophy* and *doing philosophy* or *philosophising* was argued. The revelations regarding the editor's aim are thus not to be read as an instruction of 'how to edit a book', but they are more of an encouragement to engage in a genuine philosophising enquiry. The second reason is the aim to make explicit that philosophy does not happen 'just so'. Philosophical thought unfolds as an engagement with a particular problem, and existing philosophy is used to sharpen our perspective upon this problem. But most importantly,

Making sense of it all? 131

philosophical thought worthy of being written down has a clear statement of the problem to be solved and engages in a clear assessment of the relevant aspects of this problem in an attempt to offer answers. That holds even if the answer affirms that, when it comes to a specific problem, we cannot know or cannot know yet. Philosophy is thus – as every tool – designed to 'do something'. Philosophy is not just a 'party-gag' to convince others about how much one knows about all these – mostly already dead – philosophers. As in the earlier-mentioned example-case of Dewey (see Introduction), philosophies are put to use by engaging with or against them in order to develop a point.

However, in order to reach such a point and to construct an argument towards a logically coherent conclusion, it is necessary for a philosopher to have an initial idea of where this argumentative journey is going to go. And in relation to this book, the intention of the editor, i.e., that what the editor held to be very important for any future educationalist to know, was one that covered three aspects:

- the situated-ness of knowledge;
- the interrelatedness of the mind and the body; and finally
- the difference between individual experience (*this is a beautiful red*) and scientific description (*electromagnetic waves of around 700 nanometres meet the retina of my eye*).

This concluding chapter will develop these aspects in the following sections to establish a relation to the earlier chapters and to provide for a clearer understanding of these three issues.

The situated-ness of human knowledge

This book began, after Chapter 1, with a chapter focusing upon ancient Greek philosophy by engaging with Socrates. When it comes to ancient Greek philosophy Socrates (c. 470–399 bce) is indeed so important a figure that any philosophising attempt without him in mind would not be complete. Philosophy before Socrates (pre-Socratic) concerned itself with the structure and the origin of our world and, in the philosophy of Thales, tried to account for the natural phenomena without the utilisation of mythical explanations (Russell, 1995). However, Socrates marks a significant shift in that he turned philosophical attention to moral issues and more specifically to the nature of moral values (justice, courage, piety, etc.). Nevertheless, his philosophical arguments have to be understood in relation to his opposition to the Sophists. Although also interested in moral issues, they were a group of professional educators teaching primarily rhetoric, i.e., the skill to make a persuasive speech in political assemblies and courts of law. It is here that Socrates makes his argument for the power of the better argument, one that follows clear and logical coherent reasoning. This notion of the 'power of the better argument' is one that can henceforth be traced throughout the history of philosophy, as for example in Immanuel Kant's (1781/1997) or, more recently, in Jürgen Habermas' (1986) writing. However, before reason became the widely acknowledged decisive factor according to which conflicting claims would need to be settled, as in Habermas' discourse-ethics, Western philosophy deviated from these ancient roots. In that respect it is warranted to have at least a bit of history here.

> It is not possible to even try to sketch a brief history of philosophy here, but the 'Recommended reading' makes suggestions for the interested reader.

132   Tom Feldges

The Roman emperor Justinian I closed the philosophical teaching establishments of Athens in 529 ce, and that brought the era of ancient philosophy to an end. With the wider spread of the Christian faith throughout the Roman Empire, philosophy turned into scholastic philosophy. It became more and more of a theology-dependent, authority- and text-bound endeavour, dominated by the Bible as its sacred text and the classic interpretations of this text (Honderich, 2005).

This is the background against which the unavoidable situated-ness of human knowledge – i.e., the fact that all we know and could ever know is always and invariably bound back to where, when and whom we are – gains its momentum. Such a relativist position has attracted a lot of criticism and rejection. Socrates did so in relation to the Sophists' rhetorical distortion of the truth for the sake of winning an argument and Hayes (see Chapter 2) does so in relation to modern education. Relativism is criticised because it seems – in itself – unreasonable to apply the Protagorean formula that 'man is the measure of all things' (Husserl, 1901/2008: 77). Because, if that were the case, so the argument goes, one would need to give up the notion of the 'absolute' or 'objective truth' and one would face the danger of losing the ground under one's feet to fall into the abyss of vagueness and uncertainty.

However, we have to be careful here! The force of logical arguments remains uncontested even if one remains critical about a presumed inherent, objective or even absolute, truth of these arguments. This is so – and it has to be so – because every worthwhile argument is built upon

a)   the correct construction of the argument, i.e., an argument is valid or not
      and
b)   the correctness of the premises upon which the argument is built, i.e., an argument is sound or not.

As much as the belief in the irrefutable power of reason was the major concern of the Enlightenment movement, it stands – beyond reasoning – that every expected *inherent truth* of a valid argument finds its limitation in the sound-ness that one wishes to ascribe to the premises upon which the otherwise correctly formed argument rests.

To get this issue sufficiently unpacked, it is probably best to take a slight, even more historic detour. In the sixteenth century, the astronomer Nicolaus Copernicus provided the valid argument that, based upon newly emerging, objective, empirical measurements of planetary movements, our planet Earth, as well as all the other planets of our solar system are moving around the Sun. Copernicus' revolutionary shift away from the previous understanding of a stationary planet Earth as the centre of the universe, followed from his *valid* argument to that effect. However, the actual breakthrough was down to the fact that Copernicus had new data in his hands that allowed him to formulate different premises for his valid argument to reach his irrefutable conclusion. Copernicus' thesis initiated a paradigm shift (Kuhn, 1957) that challenged the then-prevalent cosmology via newly available facts. Hence, the truth of every valid argument equally rests upon what is known or what is accepted to be known at the time. Truth claims as such can probably never have an absolute character.

However, there is another side to this example. Copernicus, along with others, did not only revolutionise astronomy, but this revolution also challenged the then-prevalent, religion-induced human self-understanding of being unique and of having a place at the centre of the universe assigned to them by their Christian God. This move towards an increasingly scientific understanding of the world made it possible to critically engage with the previous scholastic pursuit of a theology-dependent philosophy as it happened prominently during a period that is now known as the Enlightenment. We must come back to this issue of a religion-dominated pursuit of philosophy, but at the moment it is important to follow the reason-based pursuit of philosophy a bit further. Undoubtedly, this new-gained intellectual freedom, probably best epitomised by Kant's *Critique of Pure Reason* (1781/ 1997), brought massive advances to human thought and human abilities to predict and utilise their word (Cassirer, 1932/1951). However, when it comes to reason about how humans ought to behave and what sort of person one should be, reason invariably runs into difficulties. Kant tried to provide an answer to these questions that gained increased importance in his time, more importance than they had been afforded since the time of the ancient Greeks. This is so because the endorsement of reason and scientific explanations instead of faith in a divine entity to guide human behaviour makes it necessary to have a reasonable foundation to define appropriate ethical conduct. Kant (1785/ 2012: 34) tried to solve this problem with his categorical imperative, according to which human conduct ought to be based upon individual reasoning along these lines: 'Act only according to that maxim whereby you can at the same time will that it should become a universal law.'

Undoubtedly, the Kantian categorical imperative has some appeal, so much so, that Nietzsche (1891/1969), at the end of the eighteenth century, could dare to proclaim that God himself had died and that, if humankind would only be able to liberate itself from the Christian moral of slaves, humans would develop into some kind of super-human. But that vision failed horribly, as Adorno and Horkheimer (1969/1997) point out very clearly. Although the unprecedented success of reason-based human dominance over nature remains uncontested, this success equally enabled humans to utilise their mastery to engage in the mechanised and merciless killing of millions of people during two horrible wars in the first half of the twentieth century, along with the genocide of the Jewish people. The rationalised, almost industrial slaughter that followed a cold and inhumane logic during this dark time of humanity leads Adorno (1966/2007) to ask how – if at all – philosophy, as a reason-based endeavour, could still be possible in the aftermath of all that had happened in the name of reason. Günther Anders (2010) in his engagement with Kant's reasoning on the occasion of visiting the former Nazi concentration camp Mauthausen sums the problem up, and although unintended, he nevertheless establishes a direct link to education:

> In Kant's eyes, tenderness, without which it would remain impossible to be 'good' to a child and without which no child could ever become 'good-natured', would fall under the heading of 'affection', hence in the area of 'sensuality' and with that in the realm of sin.
>
> (Anders, 2010: 98, translated by the author)

Anders thus claims that cold and solemnly reason-based human conduct, without human feelings, affects and emotions, cannot suffice to bring about a truly humane society. In order to be truly human, humans have to answer to the demand that other human beings pose upon them by their mere presence, and that before reason and beyond the reach of reason (Levinas, 1991).

When philosophising it is always necessary to look for the bigger picture! When looking at the philosophy of education it is necessary to be aware that philosophy always emerges in reaction to current social problems. Socrates argued against the Sophists, while Levinas was

> a prisoner of war in Nazi Germany. While it is possible to concentrate upon specific aspects – as, for example, the decisive 'power of the better argument' – it is nevertheless important to consider the further historical developments, as for example in Habermas' (1986) discourse-ethics as an attempt to situate reason within the *life-world*, i.e., a world that we always and invariably share with others.

Truly humane behaviour, and being truly humane does not necessarily preclude a life neverthe-less guided by reason as well and which develops in relation to other humans. Others place an eth-ical demand upon us and upon each other in a way that cannot sufficiently be explained or guided by reason along. This is where a) Socrates' idea of an objective truth falls short and b) where Kizel's programme of philosophy with children gains ground. The early exposure to reason and the practice of reasoning, combined with the forming of a community of enquiry leads back to a form of social situated-ness. Such a feedback-loop binds reason back to an established group's or a society's values and practices. This, as Kizel mentions, is some way off the demanding Socratic notion of an absolute or objective truth. But if children are taught not only to reason correctly, but also to take their surrounding culture into account, then a corrective mechanism is in place to hopefully prevent the inhumane 'perversion' of reason.

When reading this, one could be left with the image that reason stands in an almost antithetical relation to religious belief. After all the Enlightenment sought liberation from theological, religious constraints. Indeed, there is a bit of a tension here, as religion demands faith and reason depends on truth to substantiate its premises to get a sound argument going. If truth is taken to be justified belief (Grayling, 1997), then it looks indeed as if there is some sort of ordering going on, leaving 'truth' at the top and faith somewhere lower down. However, it is perfectly possible for religious belief to thrive alongside a scientifically explained world and to find room for the believer to have a meaningful engagement with faith as an overall ordering and divine structure (Gadamer, 1960/2011). The hostile relation mentioned above only emerges if one of the opponents transgresses into the other's remit.

This is Nur Surayyah Madhubala Abdullah's concern in Chapter 4. Overbearing demands as exerted by a social group, characterised by a strong religious background can overemphasise cultural/religious demands, and thus neglect or even supress the correct individual development of reasoning abilities or the willingness to utilise these. Although she develops her argument in the context of her own situated experiences of religion-based limitations in the teaching of philosophy to novice teachers in Indonesia, she is not only making a claim that would hold merely in her specific environment. She is equally pointing to the fact that *any* strong religious belief-system may come with the danger of limiting reason and critical engagement by dogmatic rigidity. This danger is by no means exclusively limited to this author's Muslim environment, but one that can be traced in the debates around the status of Darwin's evolutionary theory in the US school curriculum as brought forward by the Christian Creationists (Dennett, 1996).

> Although reason alone may thus not be a sufficient to guide human behaviour, too strong a religious belief on its own may fail to achieve this as well. It seems that human reasoning needs to be 'tamed' by an overall set of values and that appears to include religiously informed values.

Making sense of it all? 135

However, there is another side to this argument. The constraints of a dogmatic background where some hold the power to control what is known or could be known is one that is not exclusively limited to religion. Lisa McNulty and Lucy Henning argue that any such imposed limitation would invariably lead to an infringement of an individuals' ability to develop. This works on a multitude of levels as both authors argue in their chapter about these limitations to knowledge acquisition (epistemic injustices). It is best to develop this in relation to the earlier considerations about the incorporation (or not) of environmental awareness into the curriculum (see Chapter 1). It is possible to provide two valid arguments for and against such an incorporation, and which option is individually favoured depends upon where one stands.

- I am living in the 'now' and take what I can from the available resources to make a good life while trusting in the ability of future humans to solve the problems that, at least partially, have been created by my own current conduct.
- I see myself as merely an individual part of Dewey's ever-continuing chain of life and I thus care about the ones that come after me, once I've had my time.

If children and adults are not taught about the different ways to think through environmental issues, they probably endorse option one; while those sensitised in these issues will probably favour the second option. But depriving children the think-through option two would constitute, following McNulty's and Henning's argument, an act of epistemic injustice. Of course, children are not able to intellectually permeate complex ecological systems in their inherent interrelatedness, but as they grow up and mature, they may. However, not being sensitised to these issues would violate their 'epistemic rights in trust'; hence, they would be left unprepared for what might gain importance as they grow older. It would probably not be fair to claim that the first of the above options is preferred by people who want to continue to exploit the resources of planet Earth in an inconsiderate way for their own and immediate benefit, although there is that. However, it is probably fair to speculate about the possibility that those who favour option one have not been sufficiently sensitised to these environmental issues. Hence, their own 'epistemic rights in trust' were violated in the past and they grew up with epistemic norms that left no space for these environmental concerns to emerge.

However, in spinning this thread a bit further, if parts of a society could form valid arguments on the basis of an educational shortcoming to sufficiently sensitise them in developing their awareness of a specific problem (e.g., gender/ethnic-inequalities or climate change), then the importance of education to bring about a better world cannot be underestimated. Nevertheless, the question of what would be a 'better' world is one that cannot be decided by reasoned argument alone. Pure reason in the form of correct arguments with an assumed *inherent truth* cannot come to the rescue here. Humans have to relate, to comport themselves towards a world and they have to be 'touched' by it somehow to become part of it. Any reasoning remains dependent upon the various ways in which humans relate to their environment (e.g., feelings, moods, emotions) and this leaves one with a *fluid truth* depending on established epistemic norms, communities of inquiry and a constant need to challenge unwarranted claims. The relevant literature in terms of the change from scientific positivism to scientific realism (Popper, 1935/2002) and the resulting changes to the concept of 'truth', as much as Habermas' (1986) concept of the *life-world* as the *sounding board* for a socially mediated establishment of a *discursive truth* have established these claims in a more elaborated form than is possible here. Nevertheless, truth, according to this changed conception, appears to be more than the crude establishment of a matter of fact (e.g., *this is water and it is composed of two parts of oxygen and one part of hydrogen*). It appears to be more of a socially mediated, and thus shared ascription, of meaning or sense to a complex matter of facts (e.g., *it is not right to violate the life-chances of future generations in a reckless manner*). Accepting such a notion leaves truth and human reasoning as – at least partially – culturally situated and bound back to our social human nature, which exceeds our cognitively mediated reasoning abilities.

> Any philosophising engagement needs to start with the text and then to move beyond this text. It needs to take into account one's own background and the text's cultural and social situated-ness. It is necessary to think with and against the text while trying to make it 'do some work' in relation to current problems. And, while doing that, one needs to remain bound back to the community of enquiry, to the society for which a problem needs to be solved.

The interrelatedness of the mind and the body

The relation between the mind and the body is the field of the philosophy of the mind. Here it is not possible to even try to provide a short overview of the various positions or their underlying assumptions, let alone attempt to outline the current debates. Instead of this it is probably better to briefly outline the problems in relation to this divide between the physical and the mental.

Eugen Fink captures the difficulty of comprehending the nature of human existence. When he wrote about humans as *fragmented beings* he explained:

> Man is nature's strange creature, familiar with himself, but nonetheless questioning himself, being self-conscious, while nevertheless remaining a stranger to himself more than he is to any other object. Being subject to knowledge of a thousand kinds but unable to comprehend himself as an object.
>
> (Fink, 1964: 121, translated by the author, gendered attribution in original)

In this passage Fink highlights the difference that leaves humans with capacities that outrun a mere animalistic existence, one that is characterised as a life constrained by a set of appropriate but fixed reflexes towards environmental stimuli. Human existence is not exclusively determined by external causes, sparking off subsequent reflexes. Humans conduct their lives according to self-defined goals that constitute individual reasons to act instead (Gilbert and Lennon, 2005). Hence, humans share a biological body with the animal kingdom, but possess mental capacities way beyond the animalistic existence, allowing them to define and pursue their own goals as well.

This apparent difference between the physical and mental side of human existence has always puzzled philosophers, prominently among them René Descartes. Descartes, one of the most widely studied philosophers, argued that humans are comprised of two different substances, the 'extended matter' and the 'thinking matter' (Cottingham, 1991). The extended matter is the physical body, existing in space and time, while the thinking matter is the soul, the spirit or – to use a more current term – the mind. However, Descartes' substance-dualism was not able to explain how a non-physical substance like the mind could causally impact upon the physical substance of the body (Burwood et al., 1999). This problem warrants a wider explanation.

Descartes' difficult heritage was left for future generations of philosophers. The problem is to try to find a solution that unites the physical nature of the human being with the fact that humans also have a mind, interacting with the body to gather information about the world and to interfere with the world. When thinking about vocational education it becomes clear that this mind–body problem has multiple implications upon human learning. Hence, the method-guided study of learning and learning processes, i.e., upon education and pedagogy, is directly related to this mind–body problem. Therefore, it is important to explore the issue a little further. The realm of the physical is widely acknowledged as being causally closed. Descartes' extended matter, that is our physical body, would belong to this physical realm. Within this physical realm things do not *happen just so*, they happen because they are caused by *something*. This causing *something*, or this cause, can be observed, quantified and accounted for by physical laws and theories as much as the ensuing results can be predicted according to these laws and theories. But, as mentioned earlier in relation to Descartes, this causal closure does not leave room for the non-physical mental realm to yield any causing effect upon the physical. Hence, taking the nature of the human life as exclusively physical leaves us with an automaton, guided by physical laws determining every aspect of human behaviour. Needless to say, that any exclusive reduction of human-ness to an underlying physical basis does not appear to leave room for free will and human agency.

Think of yourself: have you chosen to study the topic of education because you wanted to and because you were interested in it?

Or – alternatively – have you picked up the subject because some electrical and chemical exchanges in your neuronal layout condemned you to do so?

As much as this is a philosophical puzzle to be solved, it is also an important question about how we perceive ourselves as human beings, and how we describe our existence, and that of our learners – are they physically determined automatons or are they human beings?

This mind–body problem of uniting the Cartesian division of the body and mind in a meaningful way has occupied philosophers ever since Descartes. Although, during our normal lives, we might be able to simply ignore this conundrum, this should not happen when it comes to education. Especially in vocational education, it seems important to not to ignore the obvious interplay of our mind with our body. The mind–body problem is thus a serious one, which educationalists should take into account. However, this overarching mind–body problem is also an umbrella term for a set of sub-problems. There are more puzzling issues waiting in the wings, and some of them deserve further discussion here. They are:

1. How can the conscious human mind be linked with existing theories about the physical properties of the body and with that the brain?
2. Could emotions and bodily feelings provide a means to connect body and mind?

138   *Tom Feldges*

And finally:

3. Even if it would be possible to solve the problem of the mind and its interaction with the body, it would remain an insular situation, not really accounting for the social nature of human existence.

In the preceding section we discussed human reasoning abilities and linked this back to values, as – at least partially – experienced via our moods, feelings and emotions. The point was made that humans exist in time and space and that they do so via their physical existence, i.e., their body. We are in one place/time and not in another one. We experience our relation to the surrounding world with our body, as much as we experience our feelings and emotions as bodily feelings.

However, Descartes' dualist legacy makes it very difficult to think about the embodied nature of human existence. Nevertheless, it is not possible to just throw Descartes' division overboard, as even the academic division of labour, whereby psychology focus upon the mind/mental, and physics, biology, bio-chemistry and neuroscience work with the body as an object for their investigations. There is, however, a clear recognition, a move towards an embodied understanding of mind, i.e., a mind that exists within a body and is shaped according to this body (see Chapter 10 on how one's physical height fixes one's perspectives upon the world). In that respect, the first of the above questions is intrinsically linked with the second. Both questions gain currently increasing momentum in the literature (e.g., Varela *et al.*, 1991). The underlying problem could probably be reduced to the question as to whether it is justified to treat the human body as a mere physical object as any other object (Thompson, 2007). The human body is always a body for *someone* and this body cannot be parted from the person, the ego or the individual mind that is associated with – in whatever form – this *body*. Nevertheless, scientific approaches treat the body and mind as separate objects for their respective investigations. They provide scientific accounts of the relevant observable processes causing further processes or behaviours. But there is a growing consent that this objectifying view ignores an important feature of human-ness, i.e., that we experience our existence individually as one that happens within a world of obstacles and possibilities (Feldges, 2018). Humans live – at least partially – a conscious existence that allows them – at least to a certain extent – to make individual decisions and provides for an ability to act upon these decisions. But as soon as we allow consciousness to creep into the picture, then previously unanimated objects like bodies or brains or neurons become parts of a conscious being, a subject. This is the change that makes it necessary to ask the question as to whether purely objectifying, scientific descriptions could ever possess the necessary explanatory reach to account sufficiently for such a human subject.

This division between the conscious mind and the physical body is the concern of Terry Hyland's Chapter 6, in which he links this problem to the often undervalued area of vocational education. Hyland takes one of the big philosophical problems and applies it to education to offer a good example of what educational philosophising should be about. Nevertheless, a word of caution is needed here. Hyland makes reference to Marchand's argument and develops this convincingly in relation to the area of vocational education. However, Marchand draws from both Dewey and Merleau-Ponty, which is where a difficulty emerges: Dewey was a pragmatist, while Merleau-Ponty was a phenomenologist. Any attempt to pair these two philosophers up is potentially dangerous as the two different backgrounds rest upon – at least partially – opposing theoretical underpinnings:

a) Pragmatism has its basis in the reflection upon successful logical-mathematical and experimental methods to gain knowledge in relation to the practical results in the context of an individual and/or social conduct of life. Hence, pragmatism is interested in the processes that lead to observed results, while

b) phenomenology takes its origin from the phenomena as they appear to the conscious mind, or in Merleau-Ponty's case to an embodied mind (Merleau-Ponty, 1945/2008). Hence, phenomenology begins with the individual experience.

Although the question of where to start an investigation (the lived experience or scientific descriptions of observable processes) is one of enormous importance, Hyland offers a worthwhile application of attempts to bridge the gap between the mind and the body, one that will hopefully enhance the acceptance of vocational education. However, the underlying philosophical problem of how to make sense of the mind–body interaction, or how to account for this in an appropriate form and beyond mere natural-scientific descriptions, remains still to be solved.

These difficulties should by no means rule out every attempt to combine existing frameworks and make them work. While approaching the second question outlined earlier, concerning the importance of emotions and feelings we find Alexandros Tillas' suggestion to relate two independent accounts together. Merleau-Ponty (1945/2008), in developing Husserl's (1990) earlier account of embodiment further, conceptualises the mind as embodied, i.e. – and putting it rather crudely – that mind depends upon a body and that the body is mindful. Such a conception allows it to understand the body as the part where sensory impressions are felt, where bodily feelings and emotions are experienced and where the body reacts in relation to these experiences. This is not a move back to the animalistic and reactive matrix of a causing stimulus and a determined subsequent response. It is more of an acknowledgement that for a great number of daily tasks the deliberate engagement of the mind is not really needed (Heidegger, 2002). Extending the notion of such an *auto-pilot guided conduct of daily tasks* like opening a door (grabbing the handle, operating it, opening the door) to an uninterrupted sequence of a multitude of tasks is what Bergson (2002) developed already in 1888, calling this ongoing sequence the *durée* or duration. Bergson's notion of the *durée* has similarities with Csikszentmihalyi (1990) concept of *flow*. By bringing the psychologist Csikszentmihalyi in conversation with the philosopher Prinz (2004), Tillas (in Chapter 7) is able to tease out the practical necessities that must be in place within a learning environment to evoke such a *flow*. Doing so, Tillas is able to provide a suggestion of how to initiate this flow and to turn it into something that could be utilised for educational purposes to enhance learning.

> Especially the philosophy of the mind shares a lot of ground with empirical psychological attempts to understand the mind and the brain. It is a worthwhile endeavour to utilise psychological data and apply philosophical theory to it in order to gain a new perspective upon old problems and new puzzles.

Nevertheless, so far the focus has mostly been upon the mind–body/brain interaction as it is supposed to happen within the individual. But it is a well-known fact that human beings do not live as solitary entities. Human life is social life (Zahavi, 1999, 2016) and this fact is the focus of Chapter 8 by Koichiro Misawa in relation to the interrelatedness of mind and body. His concerns echo the

140   *Tom Feldges*

overall idea of this book: the importance of a philosophising engagement with the various strands of enquiry that yield an influence upon educational practice and the academic enquiry regarding education. Misawa engages with current philosophers to explore the notions of 'social constructivism' and 'realism'. Social constructivism as a sociological theory maintains that human development is essentially socially situated and that knowledge is constructed through the exchange with others (Honderich, 2005), i.e., a position that might be seen as standing in direct opposition to Socrates' claims against relativism (see Chapter 2). Realism on the other hand is a position that allows for currently unobservable facts, i.e., metaphysical assumptions such as mental states, to play a role in the development of scientific theories – as, for example, psychology. However, that is only as far as the theory's central concepts and tenets relate to actually existing objects or processes – as in our case brains and neuronal, physical states – and thus provide a good approximation. Misawa, by drawing on McDowell, highlights the division between the 'law of reason' (human agency) against the 'law of causes' (natural-scientific causality) and reveals this seemingly mutually exclusive opposition as too strict. This, along with the encultured, second nature of human beings, allows Misawa to place education at the point where social demands and influences meet the undoubtedly naturalistic character of human beings. Misawa is thus making a philosophically founded case for the importance of education as a means to pass on the cultural surroundings of a society. Hence, and to extend Dewey's (1916) notion of life continuing beyond the existence of the individual living being, Misawa's conceptualisation of education allows human culture to go on beyond the individual: while biology takes care of the prolongation of living human beings, education takes care of the prolongation of cultural achievements. This is a wonderful case made for the cultural dimension of education, way beyond the mere utilisation of an educational function within a specific society as discussed in Chapter 1. Perceived in this way, education becomes much more than the mere passing on of skills for anticipated future needs. Education, from this point of view becomes a genuine culture-preserving and culture-enhancing undertaking, and one that is well worth of any educator's effort.

The difference between individual experience and scientific description

Of the three overarching issues as defined at the start of this concluding chapter, only one is left for us to discuss in the final section. Throughout this book it became apparent that the experience of living as a human subject might just be beyond the reach of what an objectifying science could account for. Although a rich body of theories, founded upon empirical data, has been brought forward, and although all this has undoubtedly enhanced our understanding of the human brain and the mind, it has not yet succeeded in giving us a better understanding of how to incorporate our lived experiences into these theories. Nevertheless, acknowledging the fact that there is an experiential blind-spot in natural-scientific accounts of education-relevant, human conduct (Feldges, 2018) is not quite enough. The question still remains as to what, if anything at all, could provide a more comprehensive account, one that encapsulates these lived experiences, and what such an alternative could add to the picture. By drawing on the existentialist philosophy of Jean-Paul Sartre, Alison Brady develops fine-grained differences in the conception of freedom in relation to a variety of educational paradigms. Moving towards the lived experience of an *inescapable struggle* within the classroom as it unfolds between teacher and learner, Brady is able to show that this existential approach provides for a far-reaching understanding of what freedom within a classroom setting means. This insight

Making sense of it all? 141

can offer a starting point to reassess the appropriateness of managerial control regimes (Feldges et al., 2015). But it can also provide a new focus upon the student's current, and not exclusively educationally motivated, needs and wants as they have been called into question by the critics of what Ecclestone and Hayes (2008) call a therapeutic educational pursuit.

However, recognising the utility of such experience-based accounts for one thing, but that does not solve the question of how to do it. Experiential accounts are concerned with experiences. By their very nature they are the experiences of someone and thus not available to others; hence they are *private*, and access to them is *privileged* to the one having them (Wittgenstein, 1953/ 1986: 264). Wittgenstein's considerations point to the problem of how to observe, how to corroborate these individualised sensations in a manner that would cater for scientific credibility. This is where Sonia Pieczenko's chapter, following Husserl's phenomenological approach, offers a way to utilise the experiences, despite their private character. She develops an overview on Husserl's phenomenological position and shows how his aim to utilise conscious experiences could find application within an educational environment to shed light on the conditions of possibility of their emergence. In that respect, Pieczenko is almost rounding up the overarching concern of this book, i.e., with Husserl's subjective constitution of phenomena, as that what appears to one's consciousness, she is substantiating the claim for the necessary situated-ness of knowledge. However, she also draws on the embodied situated-ness of knowledge and in doing so, she highlights the fact that purely natural-scientific descriptions must fall short of accounting for the entirety of human existence.

So where are we?

While Pieczenko provides an important building block, contributing to the main concerns of this book, it nevertheless remains necessary to draw a conclusion that follows from all the chapters:

- If we are willing to accept that 'truth' is not a *given*, out there to be captured by the art of correct reasoning, but rather something that is, while being based upon *valid* and *sound* reasoning, partially fixed by culture and education, we end up with the possibility of opposing truth-claims.
- If we are sympathetic to the idea that individuality is influenced by life-trajectories and different environmental influences, we may just have gained the means to make sense out of these differences in points of view.
- Linking the mind to the body, whereby the latter shrouds every mental content (Husserl's *act-matter*) with a layer of lived experience (Husserl's *act-quality*), it is possible to make sense of the educational importance of such an embodied mind.
- Nevertheless, and especially in the UK, investigative paradigms that would aim to incorporate the 'lived experience' as emanating in a Bourdieusian (1993) 'field' of educational interaction do not make use of the phenomenological tradition which explicitly focuses upon the individual lived experience.

Based upon our philosophising engagement with the educational reality and some of the relevant texts, it appears as if there is a cause to be made for attempts to develop a more comprehensive theoretical foundation for education as an academic discipline, informing educational practice. This would need to incorporate values and social norms, individual experiences and the intrinsic

142   *Tom Feldges*

interrelatedness of social interaction in various educational settings, all of which are currently not sufficiently addressed with the available approaches as informed by the relevant 'mother-disciplines' of education (sociology, psychology, history and economics). This is where, probably with the aid of historic blueprints, philosophy can be most helpful in the development of a new educational theory. A theory that is no longer characterised by the dividing lines as drawn by the 'mother-disciplines'. A theory that should interpret existing theories to fit the specialities of an embodied human mind to be educated in the social environment as provided by educational settings. Settings that impose multiple influences upon learner and teacher, while both are also subject to wider cultural and social implications from outside the classroom. Although it remains possible to perceive education to be nothing more than a function on a social/cultural level, it certainly cannot and should not be reduced to be a mere function on the level of the teacher–learner interaction as current cognitive or neuro-cognitive psychological models tend to do. A new foundation for an education theory would need to find its own way to contextualise all the multiple factors that yield impacts upon educational effort and success. However, even trying to outline what kind of theory that would need to be is beyond the scope of this book, but recognising the fact that there are 'blind-spots' in the current, mother-discipline dependent perspective of educational theories may just prove to be the first step in trying to develop such a theory.

Recommended reading

Burwood, S., Gilbert, P. and Lennon, K. (1999) *Philosophy of Mind*. Montreal: McGill-Queen's University Press.
Copi, I. and Cohen, C. (1990) *Introduction to Logic*. London: Collier Macmillan Publishers.
Gilbert, P. and Lennon, K. (2005) *The World, the Flesh and the Subject*. Edinburgh: Edinburgh University Press.
Grayling, A. C. (1997) *An Introduction to Philosophical Logic* (3rd edition). Oxford: Blackwell Publishing.
Kenny, A. (2012) *A New History of Western Philosophy*. Oxford: Oxford University Press.
West, D. (2010) *Continental Philosophy: An Introduction*. Cambridge: Polity Press

References

Adorno, T. (1966/2007) *Negative Dialectics*. New York: Continuum.
Adorno, T. and Horkheimer, M. (1969/1997) *Dialectic of Enlightenment*. London: Verso.
Anders, G. (2010) Lager Mauthausen. In U. Wickert (ed.), *Das Buch der Tugenden*. Munich: Pieper.
Bergson, H. (2002) *Henri Bergson: Key Writings*. London: Continuum.
Bourdieu, P. (1993) *The Field of Cultural Production*. Cambridge: Polity Press.
Burwood, S., Gilbert, P. and Lennon, K. (1999) *Philosophy of Mind*. Montreal: McGill-Queen's University Press.
Cassirer, E. (1932/1951) *The Philosophy of the Enlightenment*. Princeton, NJ: Princeton University Press.
Cottingham, J. (1991) *The Cambridge Companion to Descartes*. Cambridge: Cambridge University Press.
Csikszentmihalyi, M. (1990) *Flow: The Psychology of Optimal Experience*. New York: Harper and Row.
Dennett, D. (1996) *Darwin's Dangerous Idea*. New York: Touchstone.
Dewey, J. (1916) *Democracy and Education*. New York: Macmillan.
Ecclestone, K. and Hayes, D. (2008) *The Dangerous Rise of Therapeutic Education*. London and New York: Routledge.
Feldges, T. (2018) Motivation and experience versus cognitive psychological explanation. *Humana Mente: Special Issue: The Learning Brain and the Classroom* **33**: 1–18.
Feldges, T., Male, T., Palaiologou, I. and Burwood, S. (2015) The quest to re-energise academic staff in higher education in an age of performativity. *Educational Futures* **7**(1): 3–17
Fink, E. (1964) Der Mensch als Fragment. In M. Brinkman (ed.) (2019), *Phänomenologische Erziehungswissenschaft von ihren Anfängen bis heute*. Wiesbaden: Springer.
Gadamer, H. G. (1960/2011) *Truth and Method*. New York: Continuum.
Gilbert, P. and Lennon, K. (2005) *The World, the Flesh and the Subject*. Edinburgh: Edinburgh University Press.

Grayling, A. C. (1997) *An Introduction to Philosophical Logic* (3rd edition). Oxford: Blackwell Publishing.
Habermas, J. (1986) *Theory of Communicative Action, Volume 1: Reason and the Rationalisation of Society*. Cambridge: Polity Press.
Heidegger, M. (2002) *Being and Time*. Oxford: Blackwell.
Honderich, T. (2005) *The Oxford Companion to Philosophy*. Oxford: Oxford University Press.
Husserl, E. (1901/2008) *Logical Investigations: Volume 1*. Oxon: Routledge.
Husserl, E. (1990) *Ideas Pertaining to a Pure Phenomenology and to a Phenomenological Philosophy. Second Book Studies in the Phenomenology of Constitution*. London: Kluwer Academic Publishers.
Kant, I. (1781/1997) *Critique of Pure Reason*. Cambridge: Cambridge University Press.
Kant, I. (1785/2012) *Groundwork of the Metaphysics of Morals*. Cambridge: Cambridge University Press.
Kuhn, T. (1957) *The Copernican Revolution*. Cambridge, MA: Harvard University Press.
Levinas, E. (1991) *Totality and Infinity*. Dordrecht: Kluwer Academic Publishers.
Merleau-Ponty, M. (1945/2008) *Phenomenology of Perception*. London: Routledge.
Nietzsche, F. (1891/1961) *Thus Spoke Zarathustra*. London: Penguin Books.
Prinz, J. (2004). *Gut Reactions: A Perceptual Theory of Emotions*. Oxford: Oxford University Press.
Popper, K. (1935/2002) *The Logic of Scientific Discovery*. London: Routledge.
Russell, B. (1995) *History of Western Philosophy*. London: Routledge.
Thompson, E. (2007) *Mind in Life*. London: Harvard University Press.
Varela, F., Thompson, E. and Rosch, E. (1991) *The Embodied Mind*. London: MIT Press.
Wittgenstein, L. (1953/1986) *Philosophical Investigations*. Oxford: Blackwell.
Zahavi, D. (1999) *Self-Awareness and Alterity: A Phenomenological Investigation*. Evanston, IL: Northwestern University Press.
Zahavi, D. (2016) *Self and Other: Exploring Subjectivity, Empathy and Same*. Oxford: Oxford University Press.

Index

Note: ff. means 'and the following' (pages, paragraphs, etc)

Abdullah, N.S.M. 10
abortion 15, 48
Abrahamsen, A. 83
active externalism
Adab 45
Adams, Sir, J. 68
Adorno, T. 133
Akhtar, S. 41, 42, 49, 50, 52
Allah 45, 49, 50
amour de soi 107
amour propre 107
Anders, G. 133
Anderson, C. 47
Anderson, J. 14, 26
Anderson, J.R. 118
Anderson, M. 118
aporia 19, 26
Aristotle 100
Arthur, J. 42, 44
associations 11.80
Au, W. 41
autonomy 50, 62, 63, 84, 86, 88, 108, 109
autotelic motivation 82, 85
Avis, Orr, 76

bad faith 111, 112
Bakhurst, D. 101
Baldwin, T. 74
Ball, S. 105
Banks, J.A. 46
Barad, K. 75
Barrett, W. 110
Bear, M.F. 118
Beauvoir, S. de 109
Bechtel, W. 83
Beckerman, A. 119
being-for-itself 112, 113
being-for-others 112, 113, 116
being-in-itself 110
Berger, P. 92–93

Bergson, H. 139
Bérubé, M. 42, 46, 47
Bible 132
Billett, S. 74
Blackmore, S. 65
Blaschke, L.M. 36
Bless, H. 82, 86
Bloom, B.S. 73
Boghossian, P. 19
Bolton, N. 120, 125
Bostrom, N. 75
Bourdieu, P. 8, 141
Bower, M. 75
Bower, T.G.R. 80
Bradley, W. 88
Brady, A. 11, 140
Brandt, B. 36
Brennan, J. 65, 69
Brentano, F. 121
Brighouse, H. 41
Brinkman, M. 120
Bruner, J. 29, 93
Bruya, B. 84
Burnyeat, M. 19, 20
Burwood, S. 137

Cabo, R. 82
Callaghan, N. 75
Cam, P. 30
Camus, A. 109, 115
Carel, H, 119
Carr, D. 41
Carr, W. 96
Cartesian divide 10, 66, 128, 137
Cassirer, E. 133
Castells, M. 105
Chalmers, D. 65, 66, 75
Chalmers, D.J. 119
Chappell, T.D. 19, 21
Cialdini, R.B. 85

Clark, A. 75
cognitive disadvantage 60
cognitive/affective divide 73
Cohen, C. 28
Cohen, J. 24
coherentism 95, 96, 99
commodification 106
community of inquiry 28ff., 47, 91, 93
conceptual clarification 2
conceptual scheme *see* scheme 92ff., 101
conscious experience 66
constructivism 29, 92ff. 102, 140
Copernicus, N. 132
correspondence theory of truth 96ff.
Corsaro, W. 61, 63
Cottingham, J. 136
Coughlan, S. 68
Cox, C.B. 108
craftwork 65, 69ff.
Crawford, M.B. 67, 69, 70–74, 76
Csikszentmihalyi, 80, 81, 82, 139
cultural identity 44, 46
curriculum – national 55, 56, 58, 64
Cuthbert, A.S. 118

Darwin, C. 134
Davidson, D. 11, 94, 95, 96, 97, 98
De Falco, A. 72
Dearden, R. 108
Deci, E.L. 84
Deleuze, G. 33
Delle Fave, A. 80
democracy 3ff., 10, 12ff., 24, 27, 33, 46
Dennett, D. 66, 124, 134
Depraz, N. 118
Derry, J. 92
Descartes, R. 137–138
description 2, 6ff., 42, 46, 70ff., 98, 121ff.,
    131, 138ff.
Destiny 49
Dewey, J. 3–6, 24, 65, 72, 74, 131, 135, 138, 140
DfE 55, 56
DfES 106
discourse ethics 131, 134
Dreyfus, H.L. 80
Dreyfus, S.E. 80
dualism 66ff., 73, 93ff., 101ff. 137
durée 130
Durgerian, P. 70
Dyson, C.B. 108

Eagleton, T. 46
Ecclestone, K. 14, 141
Eder, D. 61
Edmonds, D. 71
Educational Neuroscience 118, 119, 127, 128, 138
embodiment 9, 139
empathy 29, 34, 36, 85, 107, 143

empiricism 94, 95, 100, 103
employability 106, 108
enculturation 3
Engeser, S. 83, 87
enlightenment 5, 49, 72, 96, 132, 134
epistemiology 46, 74, 78, 95ff.; epistemic injustice
    10, 54ff., 63ff., 135; epistemic modesty 63, 64;
    epistemic norms 56ff. 136; epistemic rights in
    trust 57ff., 135
epoché 125
Erginaell, M.M. 19, 21
eristic 15ff., 18, 25
existentialism 104, 109, 116
explanatory reach 9, 118, 122, 138
extended materialism 66
extended mind 75, 77
eacticity 111

fake news 6
familiy resemblance 69
Fanon, F. 112
Feinberg, J. 61
Feldges, T. 118, 119, 122, 138, 140
Fink, E, 136
Flow 84, 88, 89
foregrounding 65, 72
Foucault, M. 55
Fox, A. 16
freedom 11, 13, 24, 26, 61, 63, 101ff., 133, 140
Fricker, M. 54, 55, 60, 90

Gadamer, H.G. 134
Gale, K. 33
Garcia-Moriyón, F. 30
Gergen, K.J, 93
Gerstein, J. 36
Gibson, G. 65, 74
Gilbert, P. 8, 136
Gilliat, S. 44
Gingell, G. 96
Giroux, H. 93
Glasersfeldt, E. von 93
Goldstein, N.J. 85
Goldstone, R.L. 80, 86
Gorard, S. 30
Gowlland, G. 72
Grayling, A.C. 134
Green, T. 57, 59, 63
Grek, S. 105
Griskevicius, V. 85
Guattari 33, 39
Guba, E. 93
Guttari, F. 33

Habermas, J. 131, 134, 135
habitualisation 123
Halstead, J.M. 42, 43, 44, 46, 51
Harari, Y.N. 75

146   *Index*

hard problem 65ff., 74, 81, 92, 95, 119, 129
Hart Research Associates 36
Harvey, D. 106
Hase, S. 36
Hayes, D. 9, 14, 15, 22, 132, 141
Haynes, J. 29
Hebb, D.O. 119
HEFCE, 105
Heidegger, M. 109, 111, 123, 139
Hendrick, H. 55
Henning, L, 10, 58, 135
hermeneutics 55; hermeneutical injustice 54ff. 60ff.;
    hermeneutical marginalization 10, 54ff., 60ff.
Higgins, C. 19
Hill, N. 15
Hirschbeger, J. 125
Honderich, T. 132, 140
Horkheimer, M. 133
House of Commons Education Committee 76
House of Lords Select Committee on Social
    Mobility 76
Houssaye, J. 120
humanities 41, 50, 72
Humboldt Universität Berlin 120
Hussein, A. 42, 44, 45
Husserl, E. 118, 120, 121–125, 132, 139, 141
Hyland, T. 10, 69, 73, 138, 139

imagination 46, 69, 72
indoctrination 3ff.
injustice 15, 54ff. 63ff. 135
intellectual history 2
intentionality 121, 123
Islam 10, 41ff.
Islamic education 44ff.

Kant, I. 72, 95–97, 120, 121, 131, 133
Keeling, E. 19, 21
Keep, E. 68
Keller, J. 82, 86
Kennedy, M. 115
Kenyon, C. 36
Kerdeman, D. 19
Kierkegaard, S. 109
Kizel, A, 10, 29, 30, 38, 114
Kneller, G. 114
knowledge 1, 3, 5ff., 13, 18ff., 28, 30ff., 43ff.,
    54ff., 69ff., 80ff., 93ff., 114, 131ff.; propositional
    knowledge 71, 81, 84, 87; knowledge-based
    economy 105, 108
Kohan, W.O. 28, 31
Koran 44, 49
Krathwohl, D.R. 73
Kuhn, T. 132
Kusch, K. 121

Ladson-Billings, G. 62
Larson, R. 82

Lasch, C. 24
Leader, D. 72–73, 75
Lennon, K. 8, 136
Levett, M.J. 20
Levi-Strauss, C. 93
Levinas, E. 133
liberal vocationalism 69, 78
life-world 134, 135
Lincoln, Y. 93
Lindgren, G. 105
Lipman, M. 10, 28, 29, 31–35, 37–39
logical fallacy 15
Luckman, T. 92–93
Luft, S. 121
Luria, A.R. 119
Lyotard, J.F. 106

Mannell, R.C. 88
Marcel, G. 109
Marchand, T.H.J. 65, 67, 69, 70, 71, 72, 74, 75,
    76, 138
Markie, P. 94
Martin, P. 47, 70
Martinez, C. 83
Massimioni, F. 80
materialism 66
Matthews, G. 29, 30
Mayer, V. 121
McCreery, E. 44
McCulloch, G. 91
McDowell, J. 92, 94, 95, 99–102, 140
McKinsey Report 67
McNulty, L. 10, 135
Meacham, D. 119
meaning 10, 16, 28ff., 45ff., 58, 60, 77, 111ff.,
    134, 136ff.
Meletus 14, 16–18
Memon, N. 44, 45
Merleau-Ponty, M. 65, 73, 74, 123, 127, 138, 139
Merriam, S.B 36
meta-cognition 36, 39
Mezirov, J. 36
Mieschbuehler, R. 15, 21, 22
mind 3, 8ff., 18ff., 23, 34, 36, 44, 46, 59, 65ff.,
    71ff., 80ff., 89ff., 108, 111ff., 136ff.; mind-body
    problem 66, 71, 137
Misawa, K. 11, 94, 101, 139, 140
misology 13, 24
Mohr Lane, J. 28, 29
Molesworth, M. 105
Moller, 80, 82–83, 84, 86, 88
moral dilemma 48
Moran, D. 122
Morrison-Love, D. 74
multicultural society 46, 51
Murris, K. 29, 54, 60, 63
Musgrave, P.W. 67
Muslim 10, 41ff., 134

Nagel, T. 65
Nakamura, J. 82
narrative 2, 29, 30, 39, 47
National Student Survey 116
natural attitude 125
neoliberalism 104ff., 108, 114ff.
Nietzsche, F. 133
non-dualist 67
Nussbaum, M. 42, 46, 80
Nyozov, S. 45

O'Loughlin, M. 65, 73
objectivism 29
Okui, 74
operational intelligence 71
Overgaard, S. 121
Oxford Cognitive Neuroscience 118
Ozgur, N. 45

Padilla-Diaz, M. 126
panpsychism 75, 77, 78
paradigm change 31
Parks, A.C. 83
pedagogy 26, 29ff., 40ff., 51ff., 78, 108, 137;
    pedagogy of fear 30, 38ff.; pedagogy of
    searching 37ff.
peer culture 56ff.
perception 11, 28, 36, 59, 60, 70, 78, 82, 86ff.
    102ff., 125, 128, 143; perceptual experience
    100, 103, 124
Peters, R.S. 91
Petitimengin, C. 126
Petitot, J. 119
phenomenology 11, 78, 103, 118ff., 139
phenomenon 7, 43, 67, 100
Phillips, D.C 3
philosophical laboratory 10, 33ff.;
    philosophising 1ff., 24, 130ff., 140ff.;
    philosophy for Children 29ff.; Philosophy
    of Education Society of Great Britain 91;
    transcendental philosophy 99, 100, 120ff.;
    philosophy with Children 29ff.
phonemes 55, 59
Pieczenko, S. 11, 141
Pierce, C. 29
Plato 13, 15, 18
Plowden (Report) 107)
Popper, K. 135
populism 6
post-modernism 92
post-structualism 92
practical reasoner 42, 46, 48
pragmatism 103, 139
Pring, R. 65, 69, 93
Prinz, J. 80–81, 84, 139
Pritscher, C.P. 36
Proedicus 23
progressivism, progressivist movement, 108, 114, 115

proposition 42, 46ff., 71, 81, 84, 87
propositional knowledge 81, 84, 87
Protagoras 19, 22, 23, 24
psychologism 121, 128
psychology 8ff., 90ff., 116, 119ff., 138, 140, 142;
    positive psychology 38
Pye, D. 71

Qaisar, A. 45
Quine, W.V. 96

racism 44, 62
Rathund, K. 82
ready-to-hand 123
real physicalism 66
Reid, C. 118
relativism 19ff., 47, 132, 140
religion 41ff., 132ff.
religious enlightenment 49
Rheinberg, F. 83, 87
Ricci, C. 36
RICE religious Islamic cultural environments 41ff.
Rissanen, I. 43
Rorty, R. 11, 92, 95, 96, 97, 98, 99–100
Rose, N. 93
Rosenthal, D,M. 119
Rouen, Université de 120
Rousseau, J-J. 107, 109
Rubie-Davis, C. 113
Russell, B. 131

Sartre, J-P. 11, 109, 110–112, 140
schema 92ff.
Schumpeter, A. 67
scientific descriptions 2, 42, 46, 70, 131; scientific
    management 71; scientific positivism 92, 135;
    scientific realism 135
Scott, G.A. 18
Searle, J. 65, 66
secular education 41ff.
self-determination 20, 28ff. 56, 90
Seligman, M. 38
Sellars, W. 96, 98
Sennett, R. 69–70, 71, 72, 74, 75
Shah, S. 44
Sharp, 30, 31, 32, 34, 35
Shear, J. 118
Siegel, H. 3
Silver, H. 65, 69
Simmons, R. 69
situated-ness 111, 123, 13ff. 136, 141
Smart, J.J.C. 119
Smeyers, P. 48, 50
Smith, B. 119
Smith, D.W. 119
Smith, D. 47
social constructivism 92ff., 102, 140
social continuity of life 3

148 *Index*

social reality 45, 92ff., 141
socialisation 55
Socrates 9, 12–26, 131, 132, 134
Socratic method 18ff.
Sophist 14, 23, 72, 131ff.
Strawson, G. 65, 66–67, 75
subjectivism 21
Subrahmanyam, G. 67

Tarrant, H. 25, 26
Taylor, C. 48, 50
Taylorism 71
'teleological' processes 4
Thagard, P. 80
Thatcher, M. 108
theory of the mind 119
therapeutic culture 14ff., 141
Thompson, E. 138
Thrasymachus 16
Tillas, A. 11, 88, 139
Titchener, E.B. 124, 126
transcendental investigation 120ff.
transformational learning 3, 40

UNCRC 62, 63
UNICEF 62
United Nations 62

Valentin, C.D. 75
value-judgements 8, 57, 125
Varela, 118, 119, 126, 138
Vaughan, K. 72

Victor, H.A. 83
virtue 24, 26ff. 45, 48, 52, 69
vocational education and training 65, 68, 74, 76
Vygotsky, L. 93

Waghid, Y. 42, 45, 49
Walker, M. 42, 46, 47
Wallace, B. 8, 118
Walsh, P.D. 84
Walton, G.E. 80
Warburton, N. 71
Ward, S. xiii
Wartenberg, T.E. 29
Waterfield, R. 18
Watson, J.B. 119
Weare, K. 73
Webb, S. 74
wellbeing 5, 25, 41ff., 50ff.
Wheeler, M. 124
Williams, E. 126
Williams, E.L. 101
Winch, C. 69, 96
Windelband, W. 121
Wittgenstein, L. 69, 141
Wolf Report 69
Wong, M.M. 82
Wundt, W. 124, 126

Young, M.F.D. 93

Zahavi, D. 126, 139